What others are saying about

THE MAKEOVER BOOK

This is a classic . . . a real service to the user.

—Jan V. White, designer

The Makeover Book does a good job of explaining what is good design and what isn't. But the most useful tools of this book are the before-and-after illustrations.

—*Editor's Forum*

▼

. . . Short on text, long on tips—it's a mini design course desktop publishers shouldn't be without.

—*In-House Graphics*

. . . Another great reference for desktop publishers by Roger C. Parker. It serves as a concise, practical companion to any desktop publishing system and a testament to the vast capabilities of desktop design.

—*The Desktop Publisher's Forum*

1 ▲ 0 ▲ 1
DESIGN
SOLUTIONS
FOR
DESKTOP
PUBLISHING

THE MAKEOVER BOOK

By Roger C. Parker

Art Direction by Karen Wysocki

VENTANA
PRESS

The Makeover Book: 101 Design Solutions for Desktop Publishing

Library of Congress Cataloging-in-Publication Data

Parker, Roger C.
    The makeover book.

    Bibliography: p.
    Includes index.
    1. Desktop publishing.   2. Printing, Practical—Layout—
Data processing.   I. Title.
Z286.D47P36 1989   686.2'2   89-5780
ISBN: 0-940087-20-0

Cover design and graphics by Holly Russell, Durham, NC

Desktop publishing production by Johnna Webb, Pixel Plus, Chapel Hill, NC

Linotronic output by Azalea Typography, Durham, NC

Ventana Press editorial staff: Marion Laird, Elizabeth Shoemaker, Terry Patrickis

First Edition, Fifth Printing

Printed in the United States of America

Ventana Press, Inc.
P.O. Box 2468
Chapel Hill, NC 27515
919/942-0220
919/942-1140 Fax

ABOUT THE CONTRIBUTORS

Roger C. Parker

Roger C. Parker is author of the highly acclaimed *Looking Good in Print: A Guide to Basic Design for Desktop Publishing* and *Desktop Publishing with WordPerfect*, both published by Ventana Press. He has conducted numerous seminars and workshops on desktop publishing design, makeovers and newsletters. He is president of The Write Word, Inc., an advertising and marketing consulting firm based in Dover, NH. The Write Word, 466 Central Ave., Ste. 3, Dover, NH 03820. (603)742-9673.

Karen Wysocki

Art Director Karen Wysocki manages book design and production at Ventana Press. In addition to her many other responsibilities, she adds visual style and clarity to the Ventana Press titles.

The following contributors are responsible for designing the makeovers for this book.

Southern Media Design & Production

Specializes in creating desktop publications and communications from display graphics to multi-image programs. Designers are Chris Potter, Brenda Filley and Margaret Rabb. P.O. Box 68, Chapel Hill, NC 27514. (919)929-4353. Pages 31, 35, 72, 109, 111, 113, 125, 163, 173, 211, 213, 233, 235, 245, 247, 249, 251, 253, 255, 257, 258, 259.

Cassell Design

A design studio specializing in Macintosh-based design, production and illustrations. Keith Cassell is the designer. 3325 Chapel Hill Blvd., Durham, NC 27707. (919)493-8070. Pages 33, 47, 49, 71, 81, 83, 105, 107, 117, 119, 121, 123, 139, 141, 151, 165, 167, 169, 171, 181, 223, 225, 231.

ABOUT THE CONTRIBUTORS

April Leidig-Higgins A free-lance designer and assistant production manager at the University of North Carolina Press. 716B W. Main St., Carrboro, NC 27510. (919)942-3487. Pages 37, 39, 41, 43, 57, 69, 73, 75, 77, 153, 179, 183, 193, 195, 201, 203, 205, 207, 209.

Art Farm, Inc. Offers design, graphics, typesetting and page layout services for quality print reproduction and presentation. The president and creative director is Richard Farrell. Rt. 2, Box 82F, Apex, NC 27502. (919)362-9816. Pages 53, 55, 59, 115, 221, 227, 237.

Southern Types Provides typesetting, design and consulting services. 413 E. Chapel Hill St., Durham, NC 27701. (919)683-2553. Pages 78, 93, 95, 97, 99, 133, 135, 137, 229.

Allen Marketing Provides design, production and illustration on the Macintosh system. The designer is Carolyn Allen. 6070-H Six Forks Rd., Raleigh, NC 27619. (919)848-4764. Pages 79, 101, 103, 175.

creative endeavors Specializes in design and production of direct mail catalogs, brochures, newsletters and other projects. Susan S. Worsley is the designer. Rt. 4, Box 371, Pittsboro, NC 27312. (919)542-1549. Pages 197, 199.

Nancy Frame Design A marketing communications design firm. The designer is Nancy Frame. 2208 Woodrow St., Durham, NC 27705. (919)286-3567. Pages 67, 149.

Lassiter & Co. Provides desktop publishing services that include logo and graphic design. Tom and Nancy Lassiter are the designers. 1115 Grayland St., Greensboro, NC 27404. (919)274-7323. Pages 45, 51.

Mobley Enterprises A desktop publishing company specializing in news letters, forms, overhead transparencies, technical graphics and illustrations. Louanne Mobley is the designer. Rt. 2, Box 349, Selma, NC 27576. (919)965-6542. Page 177.

ABOUT THE CONTRIBUTORS

The *Makeover Book* is dedicated to those who share
their knowledge and passions with others, especially Richard Bolles, Ken Magid, Jan White, and
William Zinsser.

CONTENTS

CONTENTS

INTRODUCTION

The Makeover Book: 101 Design Solutions for Desktop Publishing is intended to show you how the fundamentals of good design can be applied to a variety of desktop publishing projects. To a great extent, this book is the result of feedback I received from the series of seminars I teach on desktop design.

Most desktop publishers feel that the primary source of problems isn't ignorance of the fundamentals of graphic design. Rather, it's the difficulty in applying those fundamentals to their own projects.

It's one thing to appreciate the importance of design and typography; it's another matter to be comfortable putting those tools to work on your own advertisement, brochure or newsletter.

That's where *The Makeover Book* comes in—to show you, by example, how abstracts translate to specifics, to help you see how minor adjustments can result in major improvements in appearance. This isn't to say that these makeovers are the last word on good design. They're simply one of many solutions to the problems apparent in the originals. Good desktop design doesn't require creative genius—it's simply the result of consistently applying fundamental rules and tools.

How to Use This Book

The Makeover Book is divided into categories that reflect the most common applications. You'll find chapters devoted to newsletters, advertisements, brochures and flyers, business correspondence, catalogs and training materials, as well as such frequently used formats as charts and graphs.

This book isn't designed to be read from cover to cover at a single sitting. Instead, I suggest you start with Chapter One, which outlines a framework for evaluating your own desktop-publishing projects. From there, turn to those chapters that interest you the most or that address the projects you're working on.

Then, turn to the other chapters. But read them with an open mind! The solution to a particularly vexing newsletter design problem might be found in the chapter on forms, for example. The ideas discussed in Chapter Nine (Charts and Graphs) might help you prepare brochures or reports that include charts.

In the interests of informality and encouraging you to form your own conclusions, descriptive text has been kept to an absolute minimum. Instead of reading, you can observe. Each page contains space for you to write your own comments about the originals and the makeovers.

Consistency versus Contrast

Throughout the makeovers on the following pages, notice how the same basic concepts are illustrated; for example, the importance of balancing consistency with contrast. Consistency is needed to avoid a "ransom-note" effect, yet contrast is needed to add visual interest and highlight important information. Perhaps your biggest challenge is to develop ways of increasing contrast without destroying consistency!

Remember: if you're sometimes unhappy with the way one of your desktop published projects turns out, *you're not alone.* Successful desktop publishing design is a learning process. Your skills will improve to the extent that you evaluate your own work, as outlined in Chapter One, and carefully analyze the "before" and "after" examples in the following chapters.

Roger C. Parker
Dover, New Hampshire

GOOD DESIGN MADE GREAT

Great advertisements, brochures and newsletters are rarely great the first time around. Good design is usually the result of a series of refinements.

The refinements that differentiate the great from the good are often relatively small in themselves, yet their cumulative effect can be critical to a document's overall effectiveness.

The easiest way to make the transition from good to great is to analyze your projects in terms of the most frequently encountered desktop publishing design elements.

Begin by asking yourself how effectively you've handled each of the 25 major problem areas of desktop publishing design. Evaluating your projects this way focuses your attention on problems that can be tackled one at a time.

You may want to use your desktop publishing or word processing program to create an evaluation worksheet based on the questions that follow. Print several copies and use one for each of your projects.

A Second Pair of Eyes

In addition to testing yourself, you might also ask each of your coworkers to fill out a copy of the evaluation worksheet. Their perspective can be extremely important in helping you to avoid one of the occupational hazards of desktop publishing—solitary work habits. It's easy to develop "desktop myopia" and lose the ability to recognize your own mistakes.

By asking your coworkers to evaluate your projects in terms of the 25 questions that follow, you'll get a more objective reaction to your project's design.

DESIGN AND LAYOUT

1 Is your document framed with enough white space?

White space is essential to readability. White space along the edges of a document emphasizes words and visuals by isolating them from their environment. It also provides "thumb areas" that let readers hold your document comfortably without obscuring some of the words.

All too often, there's a tendency to cover every square inch of a page with print, resulting in "gray" material—newsletters and books that are intimidating and difficult to read. White space along the borders makes your publication far more accessible.

White space is particularly important along the top and bottom borders of a page

A deep sink, or block of white space along the top of a page, provides page-to-page continuity as well as a place to put headlines.

Irregular white space along the bottom of a publication adds variety and opens up the page. Look at the right-hand example. The extra white space at the top of the page and the varying column lengths add visual interest and invite readers in.

2 Have you surrounded headlines and subheads with plenty of white space?

White space around headlines, subheads and pull-quotes makes them easier to read. White space has an almost magnetic quality: readers' eyes are drawn to words or visuals surrounded by white space.

Headlines set in slightly smaller type surrounded by plenty of white space often attract more attention than headlines set in large type without enough "breathing room." The same is true for subheads, subtitles, pull-quotes and captions.

When designing your publication, always remember that your goal is to make it as easy as possible for readers to understand your message. White space isolates words, making them more readable.

3 Have you eliminated white space within headlines and subheads?

The headlines and subheads in your publication will gain impact to the extent that they appear to be cohesive visual units. You can usually accomplish this by replacing your word processing or desktop publishing program's default (automatically applied) letter spacing and line spacing with your own measurements. This becomes particularly important as type size increases.

Letter spacing, called kerning, becomes exaggerated as type size increases. Word processing and desktop publishing programs automatically add additional space between lines as the type size increases. Again, this works well for small type sizes; but automatic line spacing can produce headlines with unnaturally large gaps between the lines.

Reduced line spacing pulls the elements together. It also adds more vertical white space around the headline.

4 Did you choose the correct column format?

Often, design elements are chosen more by force of habit or convenience than by conscious decision. There's nothing wrong with two- or three-column grids; sometimes they're the best choice for your message. But grids based on varying column widths can add interest to text and graphics.

In the example to the left, notice how the narrow column of white space opens up the page and emphasizes the artwork. The grid you choose should carefully define the gutter (space between columns of type). Column spacing should be proportionate to the number and width of the columns and the type size.

Likewise, insufficient gutter space may lead the eye across columns rather than down.

5 Are your pages too balanced?

Balanced pages are boring. Visual stagnation sets in when the left- and right-hand sides of a page, or the top and bottom halves of a page, are too balanced. That's one reason to add more white space along the top of a page than at the bottom.

You can avoid overly balanced pages by using grids based on columns of unequal width. One very useful technique, for example, is to combine a wide column of body copy with a narrow "miscellaneous" column. The narrow column provides a handy spot to place subheads and illustrations without interfering with the body copy.

6 Did you design your publication with two-page spreads in mind?

In desktop publishing, it's very helpful to "see beyond the screen" when designing page layouts. All too often, there's a tendency to focus on one page at a time. The problem here is that readers seldom encounter one page at a time—they open your publication and view the left- and right-hand pages as a single visual unit.

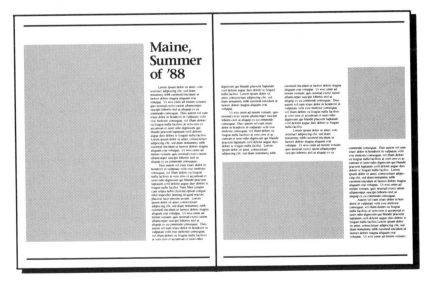

Train yourself to design in terms of two-page spreads to avoid creating pages that fight with each other. Left- and right-hand pages must work together to create a unified impression.

Two-page computer screens can help you lay out your spreads, thereby avoiding "duelling" pages.

TYPOGRAPHY

7 Are you using the right typefaces?

Literally thousands of typefaces are available. Each one "colors" a publication differently in terms of density and shape of the impression on the page. And each typeface adds its own subtle message to your words. Some are authoritative, others informal. Some communicate an old-fashioned atmosphere, some shout "contemporary!"

Type plays an important role in setting your publication apart from your competitors' products. Too often, Times Roman and Helvetica are used because those are the typefaces found on most laser printers. Relying on popular standard typefaces can limit your ability to create an outstanding visual identity for your publication.

Buy a type specimen book and try some different typefaces that will give your publication a distinctive look.

8 Have you used various type sizes to establish a hierarchy of importance?

Type size should relate to the importance of the message it communicates. For example, an important idea expressed in a headline should be visually more prominent than supporting ideas expressed in subheads.

A lack of contrast between the type sizes used in headlines, subheads, body copy and captions can confuse readers and force them to slow down to categorize and reorganize the information. In fact, the size of a publication title often isn't noticeably larger than the headlines of individual articles. This can make you look timid and indecisive.

9 Have you been consistent in your use of type?

The best-looking publications reflect consistency and restraint—only a few faces and sizes are used throughout the publication. Unless you're designing a magazine in which each article is styled as a self-contained unit, headlines, subheads and body copy should remain consistent from page to page. Issue-to-issue consistency is also important.

Each of your publications should have a distinct identity but share a common family resemblance.

10 Have you provided your reader with enough cues?

Subheads, headers, footers and other devices help readers quickly locate desired information. "Headers" refer to information such as the publication title or chapter title, placed at the top of each page. "Footers" contain such items as page numbers, at the bottom of each page.

Consider the important role key words play at the top of each page in a dictionary. Headers and footers are especially important in technical manuals, where they help readers identify each section. Headers and footers that contain the publication title and author are useful when pages are photocopied and shared with others.

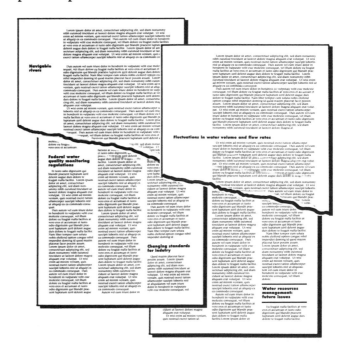

Subheads are equally important. They not only introduce white space and provide visual variety, they also help readers locate specific information.

You can place subheads in a variety of positions relative to the text they introduce. The style you choose isn't important—what's important is that you use subheads and set them in a consistent style throughout your publication.

11 Did you break up extended text with pull-quotes and initial caps?

When you're reading magazines, notice how frequently the text is broken up by pull-quotes and initial caps. Pull-quotes are short statements summarizing information on the page. Initial caps are oversized initial letters that introduce selected paragraphs.

Few things are harder to put up with than the annoyance of a good example.

Few things are harder to put up with than the annoyance of a good example.

FEW THINGS are harder to put up with than the annoyance of a good example.

Few things are harder to put up with than the annoyance of a good example.

Like subheads, initial caps can be placed in several ways. They can be incorporated in the body copy, extend above the copy, or be placed in the column next to the copy. They can be boxed or "floating" in air. The particular style is not as important as the fact that you use initial caps to mark the introduction of new ideas.

When reading periodicals, such as *Time* and *Newsweek*, which print millions of copies a week, notice how you rarely encounter more than four or five paragraphs that aren't broken up with either a pull-quote or an initial cap. Like subheads, pull-quotes introduce white space and let readers quickly decide to read or not read.

One of the best ways to draw attention to pull-quotes is to introduce them with large quotation marks. Readers are always interested in what other people have to say. Oversized quotation marks encourage readership by visually signaling "conversation" to readers.

VISUALS

12 **Did you include charts, graphs, illustrations and photographs to emphasize important ideas?**

U.S. Market Shares of Leading Personal Computer Manufacturers: Revenue (Excluding ROM-Based Personal Computers)			
	1984 $7.9 Billion*	1985 $10.7 Billion*	1986 $13.7 Billion*
Apple	18%	11%	9%
AT&T	-	4%	6%
COMPAQ	4%	4%	4%
Epson	4%	3%	3%
HP	5%	4%	4%
IBM	32%	29%	28%
Tandy	7%	4%	6%
Wang	3%	-	-
Zenith	3%	3%	3%
Other	24%	38%	37%

*Factory value
**Includes third-party peripherals

MCR601-361-03-FEB86

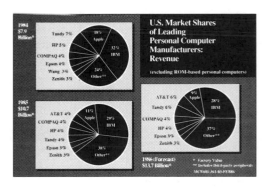

The saying, "A picture is worth a thousand words," is as true today as when it was first uttered. Visuals are particularly important when communicating numbers and the relationships between them.

Rows and columns of numbers communicate information in a straightforward, unemotional way.

The same numbers come to life when converted to a chart or graph.

13 Have you cropped and silhouetted photographs to emphasize important areas and eliminate distractions?

Just as cutting out unnecessary words is the key to effective writing, cropping can improve the communicating power of photographs by eliminating unnecessary details or distracting visual elements.

"Cropping" means changing the shape of a photograph by cutting in from the edges. "Silhouetting" means eliminating background details, retaining only important parts. Although these are traditional tools of the trade, desktop-published documents often use the photograph "as is."

14 Have you properly placed photographs and illustrations on each page?

Not only must photographs and drawings be reduced to the essence of their message, they must be properly placed on a page. A haphazard arrangement of visuals results at best in boredom; at worst, the arrangement actually impedes readership.

The starting point for placing visuals is to align them with at least one of the column grids.

Although it's usually a good idea to anchor both sides of a photograph to the column grid, there will be times—such as when you're working with photographs of short, wide objects—when you'll

want the photograph to extend into the adjoining column or the bordering white space. This will keep the photograph large enough to preserve important details.

Lorem ipsum dolor sit amet, consectetuer adipiscing elit, sed diam nonummy nibh euismod tincidunt ut laoreet dolore magna aliquam erat volutpat. Ut wisi enim ad minim veniam, quis nostrud exerci tation ullamcorper suscipit lobortis nisl ut aliquip exeacommodo consequat. Duis autemvel eum ir uredolor inme hendrerit in vulput ate velit esse molestie consequat, vel illum dolore eu feugiat nulla facilisis at vero eros et accumsan et iusto odio dignissim qui blandit praesent luptatum zzril delenit augue duis dolore te feugait nulla facilisi. Lorem ipsum dolor sit amet, consectetuer adipiscing elit, sed diam nonummy nibh euismod tincidunt ut laoreet dolore magna aliquam erat

PHOTO

volutpat. Ut wisi enim ad minim veniam, quis nostrud exerci tation ullamcorper suscipit lobortis nisl ut aliquip ex ea commodo consequat. Duis autem vel eum iriure dolor in hendrerit in vulputate velit esse molestie consequat, vel illum dolore eu feugiat nulla facilisis at vero eros et accumsan et iusto odio dignissim qui blandit praesent luptatum zzril delenit augue duis dolore te feugait nulla facilisi. Nam liber tempor cum soluta nobis eleifend option congue nihil imperdiet doming id quod mazim placerat facer possim assum. Lorem ipsum dolor sit amet, consectetuer adipiscing elit, sed diam nonummy nibh euismod tincidunt ut laoreet dolore magna aliquam erat volutpat. Ut wisi enim ad minim veniam, quis nostrud exerci tation ullamcorper

15 Have wraparounds created unsightly gaps?

Gaps of white space often occur when ragged-right type is wrapped around boxes or photographs.

Note how the irregular lines at the right edge of the left-hand column contrast with the straight left edge of the lines in the right-hand column.

16 Are captions properly located?

The caption is another important element. It summarizes the photograph and relates it to surrounding text.

The typeface and type size used for the caption should form a strong contrast to surrounding body copy. You should be consistent. The same typeface, type size and alignment (flush-left/ragged-right or justified) should be used throughout a document. Always place the caption in the same relative position for each photograph.

17 Have you chosen the right graphic enhancements?

Graphic enhancements, such as rules and borders, should be appropriate to the character of your publication. Thick rules and borders darken a page. Thin boxes around a page often create an overly formal appearance.

Often you can use different borders at the top and bottom of a page. Borders don't have to extend the full width of the page to be effective.

In the left-hand illustration, for example, the thick border at the bottom of the page unifies the two double columns of type and emphasizes the white space to the left of the columns.

You can enhance your document's appearance by using graphics that complement the typeface and type size. In the right-hand example above, the thickness of the rule under the pull-quote reinforces the effect of the initial cap that introduces it.

18 Did you overuse the tools of emphasis?

Desktop publishing makes it easy to add graphic enhancements, such as boxes and rules (lines of varying thickness), but there's a temptation to overuse them.

"Box-itis" is a frequently encountered problem characterized by "boxes within boxes." Often, boxed pages contain boxed features. So practice restraint: use boxes only when there's a definite reason to do so.

Also, use shadow boxes with discretion. They often give away the fact that a publication has been desktop-published.

Vertical rules between columns are another frequently abused graphic enhancement. Use them only when you need to separate adjacent columns. If you increase column spacing slightly, you may not need vertical rules at all.

Reverses and shaded backgrounds are other overused graphic devices. A reverse is white type placed against a black background. A shaded background ranges from light to dark shades of gray.

> **After much debate,
> the Board agreed
> to disagree.**

> **After much debate,
> the Board agreed
> to disagree.**

Always remember that type placed against shaded backgrounds is harder to read, because the graduating shades reduce the contrast between the type and the page, making it more difficult to read individual letters.

19 Have you been consistent in spacing type and graphics?

The human eye is extremely sensitive to inconsistent spacing. Tiny differences in spacing between headlines and body copy, subheads and rules, or photographs and captions that are difficult to notice on your computer screen become magnified when your project is printed. This is particularly true if you proofread your copy on standard 8 1/2- by ll-inch paper and the actual printed size of your publication is smaller.

Pay particular attention to places where horizontal rules accompany subheads or body copy. Irregular spacing there is very obvious.

Also, remember to allow more space between the end of the body copy and the subhead that follows than you use between the subhead and the body copy it introduces. White space above the subhead isolates it from the preceding material; if the space is equal above and below, it's not clear which material the subhead relates to.

REFINEMENTS

20 Have you inadvertently added too much white space to your publication?

Edit word-processed files carefully before you submit them to a desktop-publishing program. That may help you break some ingrained habits.

For example, you should break the habit of hitting the space bar twice after each period. Although this works well for typewritten manuscripts, it often adds big gaps between sentences when the files are placed in a desktop-published document.

Likewise, avoid hitting the return key twice after each paragraph. Extra space between paragraphs can be fine-tuned using your desktop publishing program's paragraph spacing command.

Often, paragraph tabs and indents must be changed. Paragraph indents that work well with wide columns of word-processed copy are exaggerated when placed in narrow columns of typeset copy—particularly if set in a smaller type size.

21 Have you eliminated widows and orphans?

A widow is a word or short phrase (less than a third of a line in length) at the end of a column creating an awkward effect. An orphan is a similar deformity at the top of a page.

They can be visually distracting. Often, you can eliminate widows and orphans by simply rewording a sentence or two in the paragraph.

22 Did you review hyphenation?

Desktop publishing and word processing programs differ in the level of sophistication of their hyphenation features. Some programs let you limit the number of consecutive lines ending in hyphenated words, while others don't. The problem of excessive hyphenation is compounded when large type is set in relatively narrow justified columns.

> There is noth-
> ing strictly im-
> mortal, but im-
> mortality. What-
> ever hath no be-
> ginning, may be
> confident of no
> end (all others
> have a depend-
> ent being and
> within the reach
> of destruction);

Too many lines ending in hyphenated words are difficult to read because hyphens draw your eyes away
from the words.

Some programs don't hyphenate capitalized
words—which can lead to irregular word spacing
within justified paragraphs.

23 Did you check for correctly spelled, misused words?

Thanks to the spell-checking programs included in
most desktop publishing and word processing
programs, misspelled words are becoming harder
and harder to find. However, spell-check programs
can't flag correctly spelled, misused words. Certain
word pairs, or triples, are frequently encountered, including:

- To, too, two
- Forward, foreword
- Hear, here
- Their, there

When using your spell-check program, be sure you
don't inadvertently execute the "add to user ...
ary" command instead of the "replace" command.

That mistake would make a misspelled word permanently accepted as correctly spelled!

The best way to avoid these embarrassing errors is to have someone else proofread your work before it goes to press.

Similarly, double-check to ensure that your spell-checker doesn't accidentally flag doubled words, as well as punctuation marks or numbers mixed in with words.

24 Did you include all necessary information?

Often, a reader's attention is derailed by small problems. How often have you been frustrated by turning to page 16 of a newspaper to continue reading an article only to have difficulty finding the continuation? Or, how often have you wanted to respond to an ad—only to find the firm's address or phone number has been omitted?

25 How practical are your reader-response forms?

Coupons and order forms should be large enough for easy use. Leave enough vertical clearance for readers to easily fill in their names and addresses. Lines should be long enough to accommodate even the longest address. Line spacing should equal typical typewriter line spacing. Nothing discourages response more than a hard-to-complete coupon or order form.

MOVING ON

These are only some of the problems that frequently crop up when evaluating desktop-published documents. As you cultivate your powers of analysis and constructive criticism, you'll be able to add your own pet irritations to the list.

Use your evaluation worksheet as the starting point for analyzing your own work, as well as the work of others. Add to the list and create new worksheets as you proceed.

As you get in the habit of evaluating and refining your projects, you'll be on your way toward making the transition from "good" to "great."

CHAPTER
2

NEWSLETTERS

Within moments of receiving your newsletter, readers will react to it in either a positive or negative way: Your page design will influence their feelings, even before they begin reading your words.

Your established following will make read vs. don't read decisions based primarily on whether the articles interest them. To catch their attention, your newsletter's visual identity must recede somewhat into the background, letting the information itself stand out. The nameplate of your newsletter, featuring the publication's name, volume number, address, etc., becomes an icon—a visual symbol easily recognized by your regular readers, allowing them to move on quickly to the contents.

New readers have different needs, however. They'll be forming their first opinion based on the credibility and the image your organization projects. The newsletter will succeed to the extent that it looks professional, "open" and easy to read. Less obvious, but no less important, is how your newsletter influences readers to identify it—and hence your firm—as contemporary, old-fashioned, dignified, down-to-earth, professional or amateurish.

The "before" and "after" examples in this chapter should help you learn the basics of good design and suggest ways to improve your newsletter.

The Front Page

The success or failure of your newsletter depends largely on how you design the front page. A good front page leads the reader easily and smoothly into the feature articles, then draws them inside.

A good front page has a strong nameplate, a table of contents and an article or two continued on the inside pages. The nameplate—or name of the publication, set in stylized type—establishes visual identity and provides the reader with cues as to what kind of material is in the copy.

The nameplate must be large enough to be noticed, yet remain proportional so that it doesn't overwhelm the page. Whenever possible, it should also communicate your purpose, as illustrated by the *Harbor Light* and *Hardwood Review* nameplates.

The "before" *Updater* illustrates two problems that occur when the title of a publication is set too small. For instance, it might give the impression that *The Updater* is a bit ashamed of its title—its small size can be interpreted as self-effacement. The revised *Updater*, with the title running across the top of the page, looks far more confident.

Notice, by the way, how eliminating empty words like "The" provides more space for the important words that follow. *Updater* is the important word—so it's made more conspicuous.

Another problem that occurs with a small nameplate is that it tends to blend in with the headline of the first article. In the "before" *Updater*, there's no division between the publication title and the first headline. As a result, both elements lose their impact and readers can become confused. In the revised issue, *Updater* is much larger. In addition, a double border encloses the positioning statement, News on Hospital Group Computer Systems, reinforcing the title and separating it from the headline that follows.

Notice that most of the newsletter samples in this chapter have a table of contents, which can capture the attention of readers who don't find anything of interest on the front page. It induces them to open the newsletter instead of discarding it.

Avoiding Grid-Lock

Grids (column widths) play a major role in determining the overall look of your newsletter. The grid you use depends on the content of your publication. All too often, newsletters are laid out on standard two- or three-column grids, which can create problems with symmetry. For one thing, they provide too much left/right balance.

Asymmetrical grids, like those used on the MIT Club newsletter, are a good alternative. The tension created by placing more weight on the right-hand side of a page than the left gives a more interesting effect.

Although many of the following examples illustrate the effect of using fewer columns of text, your publication may benefit by using more columns. A fourth column, for example, can provide a good spot for folio information—issue and date—and a statement summarizing the adjacent article.

Typography

There's a close relationship between type size and column width. In general, narrow columns of type dictate relatively small type. As column width increases, larger type and more line spacing are necessary.

Narrow columns of small type are difficult to read; wider columns of larger type are easier to read. *The Updater* is an excellent example of this. Body copy in the revised example is set larger, in wider columns. The result is a more readable newsletter, enhanced by replacing justified type (type set flush to the left and right margins) with a flush-left/ragged-right style (type set flush to left margin only, with lines of irregular length that avoid or minimize end-of-line hyphens).

Wide columns of small type are also hard to read, as the original *Service Bureau Newsletter* shows. The overall page has a monotonous "gray" look that discourages readership. In the revised example, the text is set larger in narrower columns.

The Hoof Beat also illustrates how changing from a two-column to a three-column grid can improve your newsletter's communicating power. Because the new format is tighter and more unified, an additional article can be set on the front page, creating even more interest.

In the "after" example, the headlines in screened bars directly above each article make the piece much easier to scan and read. The headlines are still surrounded by plenty of white space, as was the headline in the original; but the makeover heads clearly relate to the text. Notice the difference in type size and column width. The "before" example is difficult to read because it contains a wide column of small type. The "after" example uses a larger type size.

Several examples in this chapter illustrate the problems involved in overusing uppercase type. Readers unconsciously rely on the shapes of words to comprehend their meaning. Words set in uppercase type are harder to read, since they lack ascenders or descenders. Therefore, use uppercase type sparingly.

Type as Graphics

The hardest newsletters to redesign are those with few or no illustrations or photographs. They must rely solely on type for their effectiveness. *Practical Supervision* shows how you can use words and numbers as graphics.

In the original *Practical Supervision*, the numbers in the "Six Steps to Motivation" are set in the same type size as the copy. As a result, the numbers have little, if any, impact. Their small size also makes them hard to see. In the makeover, the numbers are set larger and in reversed boxes. As a result, they're easier to find and have more impact.

Reverses are also used effectively in the *Updater* example. The body copy is broken up with headings set in reversed boxes, which also helps to simplify the design by replacing the horizontal and vertical lines previously used. The result is a simpler, cleaner newsletter design.

Note also how reversed rectangles are used, rather than bullets, to categorize the information on each department. The rectangles (or boxes) reinforce the image created by the reverses in the nameplate and body copy.

The text in the "after" example was indented to add extra white space and to organize the copy.

The initial cap is another typographic device that adds visual interest to a page and leads the reader into the body copy. Notice how effectively this works in the first article in the MIT Club newsletter.

Background Screens

Screens (boxes printed in various shades of gray) can highlight important information. Note how the screen on the front cover of the MIT Club newsletter gives emphasis to the calendar.

A screen is also used on the inside page of the revised *Consultant* to draw attention to the individuals who have applied to join the ICCA.

Sometimes, boxes can be used to add impact, as the box around the United States map in the revised *Service Bureau Newsletter* shows.

Inside Pages

It's important that the inside pages of your newsletter continue the look established on the front page. Note how the simple horizontal screen at the top of the inside page of *The Hardwood Review* effectively reflects the style of the nameplate on the newsletter's front cover.

One easy way to maintain the identity of your newsletter is to run the nameplate in reduced size at the top of each inside page. Folio information—volume, issue number and date—can also be repeated on each two-page spread.

Moving On

Ask yourself the following questions as you re-evaluate your own newsletter in terms of the points discussed so far.

✔ Does my newsletter's nameplate accurately reflect my association's function and the newsletter's content?

✔ Are headlines easy to read or do they blend into the nameplate?

✔ Do headlines clearly relate to the copy they introduce?

✔ Are my pages so balanced that they're visually boring?

✔ Is type size properly correlated to column width?

✔ Am I overusing uppercase type?

✔ Am I using rules and background screens for emphasis?

Newsletters must be lively and well designed, or an undistinguished letter might have been better! Work closely with a graphic artist to create your nameplate and general layout.

ORIGINAL

The Hoof Beat

Applejack Riding School   Horsemanship Safety Assoc.

Number 5 · October, 1988

Fall Riding

Fall is the time to ride, when horses step a little faster, when dust settles and flies scatter, when being out-of-doors is a pleasure for both rider and animal.

Seasonal change also provides a backdrop for us to rethink our approach to horses and riding, to set new goals, improve our training procedures, ride with greater purpose and re-emphasize safety.

We are blessed with obvious advantages at Hobby Horse Stables: seventy-five acres of field, open pasture and trails twisting through the woods. We have all the facilities a good barn should have: show and dressage rings, a sturdy set of fences. Let's find ways of using what we have to the fullest.

And as we try to get more from our surroundings, we also should be using imagination to guide our riding. No matter what level — advanced or beginner — the rider ought to climb into the saddle with a plan in mind. A riding instructor teaches basic technique; the creative rider absorbs the basics, then puts them to work in a program of his or her own chosing. Riding is a free excercise, the only limitations being safety first and watching out for others.

Exploiting what we have, riding with purpose. The way to achieve these two goals is to dedicate ourselves to training, to improving our communication with the horses we ride. The fluid rider isn't just a passenger in the saddle. Hand and leg signals are communicated without wasted energy. With hard work, horse and rider can become a team, the rider giving steady direction, the horse aware of what's expected. Reaching this stage of teamwork takes time. But we can begin our training program by lunging before we ride. The lunged horse is limber, ready to receive a rider's signals.

(Please turn to p.3)

In This Issue

From Cathy / 2
Pony Club / 3
Horsemanship / 4
Horseshoeing / 5
New Ring / 6
Stable Rules / 6
Calendar / 7
Adult Meeting / 7
Did You Know That / 8

Too many visuals in a nameplate often detract from the message. In general, nameplates should be dominated by type, allowing more graphic flexibility on the rest of the page.

Ragged-right type often creates awkward white space around graphics in adjacent columns.

MAKEOVER

**Applejack
Riding School**

Horsemanship
Safety
Association

October 1988
Number 5

FALL RIDING

Fall is the time to ride, when horses step a little faster, when dust settles and flies scatter, when being out-of-doors is a pleasure for both rider and animal.

Seasonal change also provides a backdrop for us to rethink our approach to horses and riding, to set new goals, improve our training procedures, ride with greater purpose and re-emphasize safety.

We are blessed with obvious advantages at Hobby Horse Stables: seventy-five acres of field, open pasture and trails twisting through the woods. We have all the facilities a good barn should have: show and dressage rings, a sturdy set of fences. Let's find ways of using what we have to the fullest.

And as we try to get more from our surroundings, we also should be using imagination to guide our riding. No matter what level-advanced or beginner - the rider ought to climb into the saddle with a plan in mind. A riding instructor teaches basic technique; the creative rider absorbs the basics, then puts them to work in a program of his or her own choosing. Riding is a free exercise, the only limitations being safety first and watching out for others.

Exploiting what we have, riding with purpose. The way to achieve

these two goals is to dedicate ourselves to training, to improving our communication with the horses we ride. The fluid rider isn't just a passenger in the saddle. Hand and leg signals are communicated without wasted energy. With hard work, horse and rider can become a team, the rider giving steady direction, the horse aware of what's expected. Reaching this stage of teamwork takes time. But we can begin our training program by lunging before we ride. The lunged horse is limber, ready to receive a rider's signals.

Finally, continue to think about and practice safety rules. A barn can be a dangerous place: accidents happen in a moment. The Hobby Horse safety rules have been printed in the pages of "Hoof Beat" and posted in the barn. Go over them again and use them.

The months ahead offer cooling temperatures and ideal riding conditions. They also offer us a chance to learn new things and have many wonderful experiences. Let's have a great Fall.

PONY CLUB

Applejack Riding School, on behalf of its riders, will make application to join the United States Pony Club.

Among the oldest and the best

organized of equestrian organizations, Pony Club helps produce good riders by offering a battery of instructional and activity programs. These programs include riding clinics, horse management seminars and training in such areas as distance riding, dressage, show jumping and in many other aspects of horsemanship.

By affiliating with Pony Club the Applejack riders will link themselves to the largest organization of its kind in the U.S. It has fifteen chapters with 250 members in North and South Carolina. Applejack riders would become members of the Eno Triangle Chapter. The Carolinas region, in turn, makes up but a part of Pony Club's national organization that, headquartered in West Chester, PA, includes 430 chapters with *(Please turn to page 3)*

IN THE BEAT

Additional subheads help inform the reader and break up monotonous body copy.

Nearly twice as much copy now fits on the page, despite a larger nameplate!

Contents boxes should be squared off when possible.

A newsletter must at least look and feel like a newsletter—not a brochure or flyer. This is best accomplished with a well-designed nameplate and a prominent table of contents.

ORIGINAL

Information Systems Department

The Updater

News on Hospital Group Computer Systems

June 3, 1988   Volume I, Number 8

System Changes for the Month of May 1988

Attention readers: Remember that an Information Systems Bulletin number (i.e., ISB G-243) is indicated next to those changes that were originally published in bulletins. If a bulletin number is not indicated, the item was originally published through an Online Notification Message.

The following changes were implemented during the month of May 1988:

ADT

- Patient Type 4 (Recurring Outpatient) has been modified so that a patient assigned to Type 4 cannot be changed to another Patient Type.

- A free format has been added to the Embossed Card application.

- The Guarantor's Name field has been modified to clear after each admission is completed.

- The Cancel Admission function has been enhanced to accept Medical Service Codes 57 (Diagnostic Observation Patient), 58 (Medical Observation Patient), or 59 (Surgical Observation Patient).

- The "Nursing Station Census" report has been enhanced to in-

clude the patient admission time.

FUS/ICE/AML

- FUS: The "CFC Applied" adjustment codes (193-0200 and 193-9200) have been deleted.

- ICE: A new error code "A5104" has been added to the ICE edit and will appear if Occurrence Code 11 does not have a valid admission date and a Revenue Code of 410, 420, 430, 440, or 943.

MEDICAL RECORDS

- Menu Modifications: "M.P.I. List - Interim and Complete" and "Online Notification Msgs" were moved to M/R Demand Reports Menu 3. AML functions were added to the M/R Master Menu in preparation for future installation of the AML system.

- M/R Table File Inquiry from within a function has been corrected to display the table entries.

- Report Modification: The "Physician Activity Report" has

been modified to print the message "No activity found for the following Dr #'s" for Doctor Numbers that were requested but have no activity.

- The demand "Death Register" has been modified to replace the "Consulting Doctor" heading with the "Special Care" heading. The "M/R Department Code" heading has also been added.

ORDER COMMUNICATIONS

- Form Changes/Additions: The spacing on the Short Order form has been widened for improved readability and ease of alignment. The Hematology form will show all of the short form information and will repeat patient information on the portion of the form used by the analyzer. The Diagnostic Imaging form (or long form) has a patient flash card and a patient pick-up record on the upper portion. The order information prints on the lower portion using the same format as the Short Order form. The long form is used at Hollywood Medical Center only.

(Continued on Page 2)

The Pharmacy Management System--See Page 3
Reader Survey Results--See Page 3
Introducing the FLASH! System--See Page 4

June 3, 1988

Although readable, the nameplate is small and lacks character.

The contents are placed inconspicuously at the bottom of the page, where a reader's eyes aren't likely to casually wander.

The "See page" preceding the numbers on the contents isn't necessary.

MAKEOVER

The Information Systems Department   June 3, 1988   Vol. I, Number 8

UPDATER

N E W S   O N   H O S P I T A L   G R O U P   C O M P U T E R   S Y S T E M S

System Changes for the Month of May 1988

ATTENTION READERS:

Remember that an Information Systems Bulletin number (i.e.,ISB G-243) is indicated next to those changes that were originally published in bulletins. If a bulletin number is not indicated, the item was originally published through an Online Notification Message.

The following changes were implemented during the month of May 1988:

ADT

- Patient Type 4 (Recurring Outpatient) has been modified so that a patient assigned to Type 4 cannot be changed to another patient type.
- A free format has been added to the Embossed Card application.
- The Guarantor's Name field has been modified to clear after each admission is completed.
- The Cancel Admission function has been enhanced to accept Medical Service Codes 57 (Diagnostic Observation Patient), 58 (Medical Observation Patient), or 59 (Surgical Observation Patient).
- The "Nursing Station Census" report has been enhanced to include the patient admission time.

FUS/ICE/AML

- FUS: The "CFC Applied" adjustment codes (193-0200 and 193- 9200) have been deleted.
- ICE: A new error code "A5104" has been added to the ICE edit and will appear if Occurrence Code 11 does not have a valid admission date and a Revenue Code of 410, 420, 430, 440 or 943.

MEDICAL RECORDS

- Menu Modifications: "M.P.I. List - Interim and Complete" and " Online Notification Msgs" were moved to M/R Demand Reports Menu 3. AML functions were added to the M/R Master Menu in preparation for future installation of the AML system.
- M/R Table File Inquiry from within a function has been corrected to display the table entries.
- Report Modification: The "Physician Activity Report" has been modified to print the message "No activity found for the Following Dr #'s" for Doctor Numbers that were requested but have no activity.
- The demand "Death Register" has been modified to replace the "Consulting Doctor" heading with the "Special Care" heading. The "M/R Department Code" heading has also been added.

ORDER COMMUNICATIONS

- Form Changes/Additions: The spacing on the Short Order form has been widened for improved readability and ease of alignment. The Hematology form will show all of the short form information and will repeat patient information on the portion of the form used by the analyzer. The Diagnostic Imaging form (or long form) has a patient flash card and a patient pick-up record on the upper portion. The order information prints on the lower portion using the same format as the Short Order form. The long form is used at Hollywood Medical Center only.

(Continued on Page 2)

A two-column format lets you scan blocks of information easily.

It's okay to use non-journalistic motifs in a newsletter—such as reversed-type subheads.

Square bullets echo the thick rules used for the nameplate and subheads.

Desktop publishing newsletter stylesheets have given rise to a cookie-cutter look. Try to make your nameplate distinctive, even if you must break a few rules.

ORIGINAL

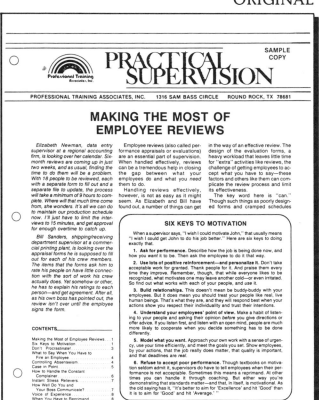

The six rules that form the nameplate confuse rather than orient the reader.

The table of contents is set in small type and cramped—hard to read at a glance.

MAKEOVER

PROFESSIONAL
TRAINING
ASSOCIATES, INC.
1316 Sam Bass Circle
Round Rock, Texas 78681

P R A C T I C A L

SAMPLE COPY

SUPER-
VISION

Making the most of
Employee Reviews

Elizabeth Newman, data entry supervisor at a regional accounting firm, is looking over her calendar. Six-month reviews are coming up in just two weeks, and as usual, finding the time to do them will be a problem. With 18 people to be reviewed, each with a separate form to fill out and a separate file to update, the process will take a minimum of 9 hours to complete. Where will that much time come from, she wonders. It's all we can do to maintain our production schedule now. I'll just have to limit the interviews to 15 minutes, and get approval for enough overtime to catch up.

Bill Sanders, shipping/receiving department supervisor at a commercial printing plant, is looking over the appraisal forms he is supposed to fill out for each of his crew members. The items that the forms ask him to rate his people on have little connection with the sort of work his crew actually does. Yet somehow or other, he has to explain his ratings to each person—and get agreement. After all, as his own boss has pointed out, the review isn't over until the employee signs the form.

Employee reviews (also called performance appraisals or evaluations) are an essential part of supervision. When handled effectively, reviews can be a tremendous help in closing the gap between what your employees do and what you need them to do.

Handling reviews effectively, however, is not as easy as it might seem. As Elizabeth and Bill have found out, a number of things can get in the way of an effective review. The design of the evaluation forms, a heavy workload that leaves little time for "extra" activities like reviews, the challenge of getting employees to accept what you have to say—these factors can complicate the review process and limit its effectiveness.

Six keys to
Motivation

*W*hen u supervisor says, *"I wish I could motivate John,"* that usually means *"I wish I could get John to do his job better."* Here are six keys to doing exactly that.

1 **Ask for performance.** Describe how the job is being done now, and how you want it to be. Then ask the employee to do it that way.

2 **Use lots of positive reinforcement—and personalize it.** Don't take acceptable work for granted. Thank people for it. And praise them every time they improve. Remember, though, that while everyone likes to be recognized, what motivates one may leave another cold—or even irritated. So find out what works with each of you people, and use it.

3 **Build relationships.** This doesn't mean be buddy-buddy with your employees. But it does mean you should treat your people like real, live human beings. That's what they are, and they will respond best when your actions show you respect their individuality and trust their intentions.

4 **Understand your employees' point of view.** Make a habit of listening to your people and asking their opinion before you give directions or offer advice. Listen first, and listen with an open mind.

5 **Model what you want.** Approach your own work with a sense of urgency, use your time efficiently, and meet the goals you set. Show employees, by your actions, that the job really does matter, that quality is important, and that deadlines are real.

6 **Refuse to accept poor performance.** Supervisors do have to tell employees when their performance is not acceptable. As the saying goes "It is better to aim for 'Excellence' and hit 'Good' than to aim for 'Good' and hit 'Average.'"

A two-tiered type treatment accents "Employee Reviews" and "Motivation," the three most important words on the page.

A pull-quote in the margin effectively draws readers into the text.

Desktop publishing makes it easy to overuse such sacred graphic arts tools as rules, screens and reverses. It's almost always better to err on the side of restraint.

ORIGINAL

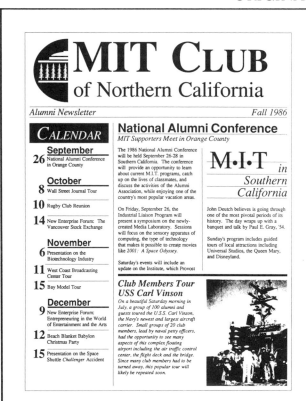

A total of 22 rules tends to confuse the reader with mixed messages.

The reverse calendar heading in the body copy fights with the otherwise attractive reverse in the nameplate.

The "logo within a logo" (MIT in Southern California) also fights with the nameplate and text.

MAKEOVER

MIT CLUB
of Northern California
Alumni Newsletter/Fall 1986

Calendar

September

26 National Alumni Conference in Orange County

October

8 *Wall Street Journal* Tour

10 Rugby Club Reunion

14 New Enterprise Forum: The Vancouver Stock Exchange

November

6 Presentation on the Biotechnology Industry

11 West Coast Broadcasting Center Tour

15 Bay Model Tour

December

9 New Enterprise Forum: Entrepreneuring in the World of Entertainment and the Arts

12 Beach Blanket Babylon Christmas Party

15 Presentation on the Space Shuttle *Challenger* Accident

National Alumni Conference
MIT Supporters Meet in Southern California

The 1986 National Alumni Conference will be held September 26-28 in Southern California. The conference will provide an opportunity to learn about current M.I.T. programs, catch up on the lives of classmates, and discuss the activities of the Alumni Association, while enjoying one of the country's most popular vacation areas.

On Friday, September 26, the Industrial Liaison Program will present a symposium on the newly created Media Laboratory. Sessions will focus on the sensory apparatus of computing, the type of technology that makes it possible to create movies like *2001: A Space Odyssey.*

Saturday's events will include an update on the Institute, which Provost John Deutch believes is going through one of the most pivotal periods of its history. The day wraps up with a banquet and talk by Paul E. Gray, '54.

Sunday's program includes guided tours of local attractions including Universal Studios, the Queen Mary and Disneyland.

Club Members Tour USS Carl Vinson

On a beautiful Saturday morning in July, a group of 100 alumni and guests toured the U.S.S. Carl Vinson, the Navy's newest and largest aircraft carrier. Small groups of 20 club members, led by naval petty officers, had the opportunity to see many aspects of this complex floating airport including the air traffic control center, the flight deck and the bridge. Since many club members had to be turned away, this popular tour will likely be repeated soon.

Quieter body copy illuminates the distinctive logo on the nameplate.

Note that only two well-positioned horizontal rules effectively lead the eyes around the page.

The reduced numbers in the calendar section are still very readable, yet don't overwhelm other important information.

Although dot-matrix output has added type and graphics capabilities, the end result still looks like dot-matrix output!

ORIGINAL

CRam Notes for Texans | **spring 1989**

Win a Cram Prize!

Really - you can win a prize but not from a lucky combination of numbers. You get this prize the old fashioned way. You work for it. (Sorry!)

Five $500.00 awards will be made to a teacher or group of teachers who are selected to make presentations at the NCGE (National Council for Geographic Education) meeting this October in Hershey. This includes teachers from grades K – 12.

For information about these prizes, contact the NCGE. Look in the April issue of "Perspectives" the journal for NCGE.

✱✱✱✱✱✱✱✱✱

We raise lots of things in Texas that were first domesticated somewhere else in the world. Have your students find these places on a world map (These are approximate.)

Using tame horses was begun in an area north of the Black Sea in Asia. Domestic cows apparently began in South Europe — Chickens began in SouthEast Asia near present day Burma — Brahma cattle originated from the Zebu in India — Soybeans first appeared in China — Cotton was first in NorthWest South America — Watermelons came from the NorthWest part of Africa near area of present day Ghana.

Who knows what evil lurks in the minds of map peddlers?

– – – – You hear all kinds of tales and claims about the merits of one world map projection and the "demerits" of some other map projection. The problems lies in the fact that you don't know whether this "advice" is good or bad. There's an old adage that says "free advice is worth just about what you pay for it". It seems to apply here!

I go way back in this argument — not clear back — but quite a way. Years ago (1921) Mr. Philip Denoyer (remember the old Denoyer Geppert map Co. ?) designed a world map projection he thought was better for young people. He wanted to show the world on a flat map with as little distortion in area and distance as he could.

Of course, he had to corrupt some other map properties but he probably did as good a job of achieving those aims as has been done — for school children.

When I worked for Denoyer Geppert we were drilled on the presentation of the world map projection. We were trained that because the map was <u>almost</u> "equal–area" (we were admonished that no school map of the world was truly equal area.) — that this was good for children.

Finally I asked the chief editor for the research that validated our claims (I was pretty dumb in those days). You guessed it, there was no educational or psychological research to support what we were saying.

Now we have people beating this same drum — — and there is still no research that proves that children benefit more from one map projection over another.

When you hear all of this rhetoric — and there's alot of it — ask the experts who are presenting it — — to prove it.

The nameplate doesn't give a clue as to the newsletter's content.

The dateline on the nameplate is unnecessarily large.

MAKEOVER

CRAM N✪TES FOR TEXANS

Ideas, suggestions, anecdotes & plain old advice for teachers of geography and more!

What evil lurks in the minds of map peddlers?

You hear all kinds of tales and claims about the merits of one world map projection and the "demerits" of some other map projection. The problem lies in the fact that you don't know whether this "advice" is good or bad. There's an old adage that says "free advice is worth just about what you pay for it." It seems to apply here!

I go way back in this argument—not clear back—but quite a way. Years ago (1921) Mr. Philip Denoyer (remember the old Denoyer Geppert Map Co.?) designed a world map projection he thought was better for young people. He wanted to show the world on a flat map with as little distortion in area and distance as he could.

Of course, he had to corrupt some other map properties but he probably did as good a job of achieving those aims as has been done—for school children.

When I worked for Denoyer Geppert we were drilled on the presentation of the world map projection. We were trained that because the map was *almost* "equal-area" (we were admonished that no school map of the world was truly equal area.)—that this was good for children.

Finally I asked the chief editor for the research that validated our claims (I was pretty dumb in those days). You guessed it, there was no educational or psychological research to support what we were saying.

Now we have people beating this same drum—and there is still no research that proves that children benefit more from one map projection over another.

When you hear all of this rhetoric—and there's a lot of it—ask the experts who are presenting it—to prove it.

We raise lots of things in Texas that were first domesticated somewhere else in the world. Have your students find these places on a world map. (These are approximate.)

Using tame horses was begun in an area north of the Black Sea in Asia. Domestic cows apparently began in South Europe. Chickens began in Southeast Asia near present-day Burma. Brahma cattle originated from the Zebu in India. Soybeans first appeared in China. Cotton was first in Northwest South America. Watermelons came from the North west part of Africa near the area of present-day Ghana.

If you would like to receive additional copies of **Cram Notes for Texans** *or need more information about our maps and globes, please write to: Cram Notes, R.R. #4 Box 91P, LaGrange, TX 78945. We also have free supplementary teaching materials and teaching aids available! Please send a SASE to the address above! Or call (409) 242-5347.*

WIN A CRAM PRIZE !!!!!!!!

Really—you can win a prize but not from a lucky combination of numbers. You get this prize the old fashioned way. You work for it. (Sorry!)

Five $500 awards will be made to a teacher or group of teachers who are selected to make presentations at the NCGE (National Council for Geographic Education) meeting this October in Hershey. This includes teachers from grades K-12.

For information about theses prizes, contact the NCGE. Look in the April issue of *Perspectives*, the journal for NCGE.

SPRING 1989

In keeping with the random content, illustrations and sidebars overlap normal column barriers.

Similarly, liberal use of type styles and faces gives the piece a deliberately thrown-together appearance.

Offsetting rules, wraparounds, type and exaggerated leading act to enhance the unorthodox contents of this piece.

ORIGINAL

TIME DIFFERENCES

Recently alot of people have been watching the "CHINA REVOLUTION" on one of the networks. That network has been showing this instead of their evening news program.

Although alot the footage was not live, the program viewed here, in the evening, was live in China – and – it was morning there! The angle of the Sun was misleading for it was low there due to the early hour. It was low here due to the late hour – so some people did not realize the time difference.

Get out your Horizon ring globe and show the time difference. Find your location and place it above the red line. Now count the hours around to Bejing. 6:PM here is 8:AM there, the next day.

23 1/2 degrees is a significant feature on a globe. This is the distance from the North Pole to the Arctic Circle; the distance between the Tropic lines and the Equator; and the distance of the South Pole to the Antarctic Circle. Do you think it has anything to do with the inclination of the Earth's axis of 23 1/2 degrees to the Sun?

Globes should be teaching tools. The mounting of the globe determines the capacity of the globe to serve as an instructional implement. Simple, unmarked globe mountings have much less capacity to instruct than those with a great deal of information on them. Globes that cannot be removed from the mounting may be safer from student molestation but are much less instructional.

How many places on the Earth have been deforested?

Spain once had many forested areas that are now – and forever barren. The Merino sheep – from North Africa, was such as valuable part of the economy that lands were deforested to provide grassy areas for them to feed.

How many places are now arid or semi–arid due the raising of certain types of animals? Goats and sheep are the principal live stock responsible for creating arid areas in the world. Even now parts of Africa are slowing becoming arid due to their feeding habits.

The prime culprit of deforestation – is MAN.

What will this do to our world environment? Find out more about this in the JRO Topic map, "The Environment in Danger: The Forests of the Earth".

Send for the detailed, 20 page catalog of these topic maps.

The nomadic, Steppe warriors ravaged Europe and China for Centuries. The great Mongol invasions brought about the development of small arms in Europe. This technical advance, in turn, provided a part of the basis for the explosion of Europeans around the globe. The inventors of gun powder, the Chinese, did not invent small arms due to their very efficient cross–bow which required little skill and was able to dismount distant horsemen

Wraparound type should fit snugly, or appropriately, around illustrations.

Excessive hyphenation, underlining and use of rules make reading even more difficult.

MAKEOVER

TIME
Differences

Recently a lot of people have been watching the "China Revolution" on one of the networks. That network has been showing this instead of its evening news program.

Although a lot of the footage was not live, the program viewed here, in the evening, was live in China—and it was morning there! The angle of the sun was misleading for it was low there due to the early hour—so some people did not realize the time difference.

Get out your Horizon ring globe and show the time difference. Find your location and place it above the red line. Now count the hours around to Beijing. 6 PM here is 8 AM there, the next day.

23 1/2°

is a significant feature on a globe. This is the distance from the North Pole to the Arctic Circle; the distance between the Tropic lines and the Equator; and the distance of the South Pole to the Antarctic Circle. Do you think it has anything to do with the inclination of the Earth's axis of 23 1/2 degrees to the sun?

How many places on the Earth have been deforested?

Spain once had many forested areas that are now—and forever barren. The Merino sheep—from North Africa—were such a valuable part of the economy that lands were deforested to provide grassy areas for them to feed.

How many places are now arid or semi-arid due to the raising of certain types of animals? Goats and sheep are the principal livestock responsible for creating arid areas in the world. Even now parts of Africa are slowly becoming arid due to their feeding habits.

The prime culprit of deforestation is MAN.

What will this do to our environment: Find out more about this in the JRO Topic map, "The Environment in Danger: The Forests of the Earth."

Send for the detailed, 20-page catalog of these topic maps.

Globes should be teaching tools. The mounting of the globe determines the capacity of the globe to serve as an instructional implement. Simple, unmarked globe mountings have much less capacity to instruct than those with a great deal of information on them. Globes that cannot be removed from the mounting may be safer from student molestation but are much less instructional.

The nomadic Steppe warriors ravaged Europe and China for centuries. The great Mongol invasions bought about the development of small arms in Europe. This technical advance, in turn, provided a part of the basis for the explosion of Europeans around the globe. The inventors of gun powder, the Chinese, did not invent small arms due to their very efficient cross-bow which required little skill and was able to dismount distant horsemen.

Woodcuts and clip art, used with caution, can inexpensively enhance a piece.

The screen plopped in the middle of the page, complete with oddball headline, furthers the "Cram Notes" motif.

The "dot-matrix nameplate" is becoming extinct as more and more businesses use laser printers and inexpensive layout software.

ORIGINAL

THE OPEN LINE

JACKSON COUNTY JUVENILE COURT

| Juvenile Division Judge
Tom Helms | **JANUARY 1988** | Administrator
Lawrence G. Myers |

YOUTH 2000

This past week, a brochure crossed my desk entitled "Youth 2000 -- A National Campaign in support of America's youths from now until the year 2000."

The brochure points out that 10 to 15% of our 16 to 19 year old youth in the United States are at risk of not successfully making the transition into productive and responsible adulthood. Some alarming facts were stated:

- One million students drop out of high school annually. One out of every four ninth graders will not graduate. In some urban areas, the drop-out rate approaches 50%.

- More than one million adolescents become pregnant annually. Half of these young mothers will never complete high school.

- One out of eight 17 year olds in this country is functionally illiterate.

- Approximately three million young people, 21% of all 14 to 17 year old youths have problems with alcohol.

- Automobile accidents, homicides and suicides are the three leading causes of death among adolescents.

- More than one million young people run away from home or are homeless each year.

The brochure goes on to talk about the year 2000, providing a window of opportunity, in that demographic shifts between now and then will provide a unique opportunity to solve the problems of youth unemployment. By the year 2000, there will be a job for every qualified youth who wants one. Some other facts about the year 2000 are:

- In contrast to the explosive growth of young people entering the labor force between 1970 and 1985, that percentage of young people entering the labor force will drop from 30 to 16% by the year 2000.

- The number of jobs expected to be created by the year 2000 will exceed the number of new entrants into the labor force.

- A growing proportion of the young labor force entrants will be minorities. By 1990, one out of five new entrants will be a minority youth.

There were also two interesting statistics regarding jobs of the future:

Jobs of the future will require higher skill levels than those of today. By 1990, three out of four jobs will require some education or technical training beyond high school.

Jobs of the future will require employees who are able to read, think,

Fully justified, non-proportional type often creates too much word spacing and excessive hyphenation.

Try to avoid "widows" and "orphans"—unsightly words isolated at the tops and bottoms of paragraphs and columns.

MAKEOVER

T H E
OPEN
L I N E

JACKSON COUNTY
JUVENILE COURT

JANUARY 1988

YOUTH 2000 REPORT PAINTS DISMAL FUTURE

This past week, a brochure crossed my desk entitled "Youth 2000—A National Campaign in support of America's youths from now until the year 2000." The brochure points out that 10% to 15% of our 16 to 19 year old youth in the United States are at risk of not successfully making the transition into productive and responsible adulthood. Some alarming facts about American teen-agers were stated:

• One million students drop out of high school annually. One out of every four ninth graders will not graduate. In some urban areas, the drop-out rate approaches 50%.

• More than one million adolescents become pregnant annually. Half of these young mothers will never complete high school.

• One out of eight 17 year olds in this country is functionally illiterate.

• Approximately three million young people, 21% of all 14 to 17 year old youths have problems with alcohol.

• Automobile accidents, homicides and suicides are the three leading causes of death among adolescents.

• More than one million young people run away from home or are homeless each year.

• By the year 2000, there will be a job for every qualified youth who wants one.

• In contrast to the explosive growth of young people entering the labor force between 1970 and 1985, that percentage of young people entering the labor force will drop from 30 to 16% by the year 2000.

• The number of jobs expected to be created by the year 2000 will exceed the number of new entrants into the labor force.

• A growing proportion of the young labor force entrants will be minorities. By 1990, one out of five new entrants will be a minority youth.

• Jobs of the future will require higher skill levels than those of today. By 1990, three out of four jobs will require some education or technical training beyond high school.

JUVENILE DIVISION JUDGE TOM HELMS • ADMINISTRATOR LAWRENCE G. MYERS

The headline (formerly "Youth 2000") has been revised to give readers some insight about the newsletter's content.

A staggered, two-column format allows a nameplate and visuals on the left, with copy on the right.

Alot of thought must be given to organizing each newsletter page, or information will be so unreadable it might look as though it came out of your computer unformatted!

ORIGINAL

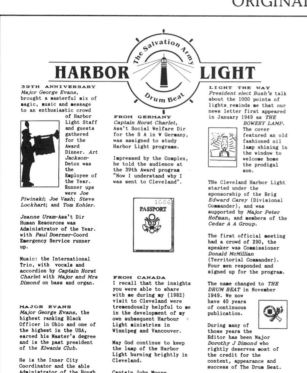

Note how difficult it is to scan a document when information isn't organized around headlines and subheads.

Avoid placing too many visuals on one page, particularly the front page, where they're likely to fight with the nameplate.

MAKEOVER

Harbor Light

The Salvation Army Drum Beat

An Equal Provider of Services and Equal Opportunity Employer

Detox Center   Harbor House   C.A.R.T. Programs   Retirement Lodge   Correctional Residence   Emergency Service

Army news from around the globe

German visitor studies our Harbor Light

Captain Horst Charlet, Assistant Social Welfare Diretor for the Salvation Army in West Germany, was assigned to study Harbor Light programs.

Impressed by the Complex, he told the audience at the 39th Award program, "Now I understand why I was sent to Cleveland."

Letter from Canada

I recall the insights you were able to share with me during my 1982 visit to Cleveland were tremendously helpful to me in the development of mu own subsequent Harbour Light ministries in Winnipeg and Vancouver. May God continue to keep the lamp of the Harbor Light burning brightly in Cleveland.

Captain John Moore
Vancouver, Canada

Service awards highlight 39th anniversary observance

Major George Evans, brought a masterful mix of magic, music and message to an enthusiastic crowd of Harbor Light Staff and guests gathered for the Award Dinner. Art Jackson, Detox, was the Employee of the Year. Runners-up were Joe Piwinski; Joe Vash; Steve Lockhart; and Tom Kohler.

Jeanne Uram, Assistant Director Human Resources, was Administrator of the Year. Paul Doerner, Coordinator Emergency Service, was runner-up.

Music: the International Trio, with vocals and accordion by Captain Horst Charlet with Major and Mrs. Dimond on bass and organ.

Newsletter marks its 40th year

President elect Bush's talk about the 1000 points of lights reminds me that our news letter first appeared in January 1949 as *The Bowery Lamp.*

The cover featured an old fashioned oil lamp shining in the window to welcome home the prodigal son. The Cleveland Harbor Light started under the sponsorship of the Brig. Edward Carey (Divisional Commander), and was supported by Major Peter Hofman, and members of the Cedar AA Group.

The first official meeting had a crowd of 290, the speaker was Commissioner Donald McMillian (Territorial Commander). Four men responded and signed up for the program.

The name changed to *The Drum Beat* in November 1949. We now have 40 years of continuous publication.

During many of those years the Editor has been Major Dorothy J. Dimond who rightly deserves most of the credit for the content, appearance and success of *The Drum Beat.*

Inner City's Major Evans wins master's degree

Major George Evans, the highest ranking Black Officer in Ohio and one of the highest in the USA, earned his Master's degree and is the past president of the Kiwanis Club. He is the Inner City Coordinator and the able Administrator of the Hough Multi-Purpose Center.

Important information about whom the newsletter serves has been moved closer to the nameplate.

Headlines and subheads have been enlarged, so that they clearly off-set the copy.

Avoid visuals that look "plopped in," one of the Seven Deadly Sins of scanner abuse! Photos and illustrations should always be an integral, well-planned part of your design.

ORIGINAL

Bold type used indiscriminately creates a screaming, "all-headline" look.

The illustration appears to address the entire newsletter, but it deals with only one of the articles, confusing readers.

MAKEOVER

The Consultant

ICCA – Northern California Chapter   May, 1986

Saying NO to Taxes!

At the May 14 dinner meeting you are invited to hear Mr. Josh Peckler of the San Francisco based accounting firm of Peckler and Evans address tax issues for 1986. Among the subjects Peckler plans to discuss are:

Peckler and Evans' perspective on what EDD is doing and how to deal with it from an accounting point of view.

Nuts and Bolts of Incorporating

Tax Shelters and Tax Reform

There will also be an extensive question and answer period as part of Peckler's presentation.

Please make your reservation by May 3rd by sending in the enclosed response card with your check.

May Vendor Presentation

by Greg Stratton

The problem: How do you speed CICS development without degrading performance? Because the demand for CICS applications far outweighs the availability of experienced programmers, most shops are looking for methods and tools to speed development. The first wave of CICS development solutions that appeared on the market helped the situation, but they have also created a new set of problems.

Fourth generation languages require an interpreter that slows response. Speeding the development of poorly designed transactions only increases maintenance workload. Applications that require a runtime monitor are slow and inefficient. And systems that lock you into too many "tools" ruin your existing software investment and limit future options.

(Vendor Presentation, Continued On Page 2)

It's okay to run nameplates sideways or at an angle, as long as they're identifiable and easy to read.

Larger type makes better use of the white space and is easier to read.

Always look for ways to preserve the character of your newsletter (nameplate, type style, column layout, etc.) throughout your document.

ORIGINAL

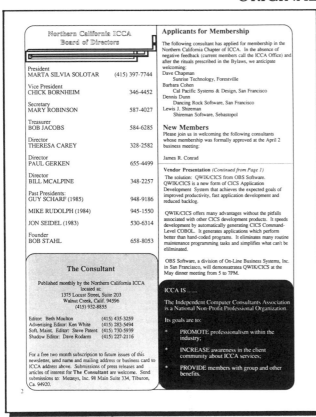

In general, adjacent screens and reverses fight each other and should be used with care.

Small outline type is hard to read and should almost never be used.

Awkward white space makes it difficult to match names and phone numbers.

MAKEOVER

Northern California ICCA Board of Directors

President
Marta Silva Solotar
(415) 397-7744

Vice President
Chick Bornheim
346-4452

Secretary
Mary Robinson
587-4027

Treasurer
Bob Jacobs
584-6285

Director
Theresa Carey
328-2582

Director
Paul Gerken
655-4499

Director
Bill McAlpine
348-2257

Past Presidents:
Guy Scharf
(1985)
948-9186

Mike Rudolph
(1984)
945-1550

Jon Seidel
(1983)
530-6314

Founder
Bob Stahl
658-8053

Vendor Presentation

(Continued from Page 1)

The solution: QWIK/CICS from OBS Software. QWIK/CICS is a new form of CICS Application Development System that achieves the expected goals of improved productivity, fast application development and reduced backlog.

QWIK/CICS offers many advantages without the pitfalls associated with other CICS development products. It speeds development by automatically generating CICS Command-Level COBOL. It generates applications which perform better than hand-coded programs. It eliminates many routine maintenance programming tasks and simplifies what can't be eliminated.

OBS Software, a division of On-Line Business Systems, Inc. in San Francisco, will demonstrate a QWIK/CICS at the May dinner meeting from 5 to 7PM.

Applicants for Membership

The following consultant has applied for membership in the Northern California Chapter of ICCA. In the absence of negative feedback (current members call the ICCA Office) and after the rituals prescribed in the Bylaws, we anticipate welcoming:

Dave Chapman — Sunrise Technology, Forestville
Barbara Cohen — Cal Pacific Systems & Design, San Francisco
Dennis Dunn — Dancing Rock Software, San Francisco
Lewis J. Shireman — Shireman Software, Sebastopol

New Members

Please join us in welcoming the following consultants whose membership was formally approved at the April 2 business meeting:

James R. Conrad

The Consultant

Published monthly by

Northern California ICCA
1375 Locust Street, Suite 203
Walnut Creek, Calif. 94596
(415) 932-8855

Editor: Beth Moulton   (415) 435-3259
Advertising Editor: Ken White   (415) 283-5494
Soft. Maint. Editor: Steve Patent (415) 730-5939
Shadow Editor: Dave Rodarm   (415) 227-2116

For a free two month subscription to future issues of this newsletter, send name and mailing address or business card to ICCA address above. Submissions of press releases and articles of interest for The Consultant are welcome. Send submissions to : Metasys, Inc., 98 Main Suite 334, Tiburon, CA 94920

The Independent Computer Consultants Association is a National Non-Profit Professional Organization.

Its goals are to :

• PROMOTE professionalism within the industry;

• INCREASE awareness in the client community about ICCA services;

• PROVIDE members with group and other benefits.

The Board of Directors information nicely fills one column of the five-column format and carries over the theme from the front page.

Screened sidebars are excellent attention-getters and help to offset copy blocks.

Newsletter design should match content—the loud, busy design of this piece accurately reflects the urgency of the subject matter.

ORIGINAL

Gadgets News-Herald

The Journal of Leading Emulation Technology

Sept. 1, 1988. Vol. 1 Issue 1

Flash! Spectre 128 orders to be accepted September 1, 1988!

Spectre 128 is to be shown at Glendale Atarifest (Sept. 16-17), Washington AtariFest (Oct. 1-2), and Comdex (Nov. 14-18). Gadgets by Small, Inc. expects to have Spectre 128 for sale at Glendale, and to ship mail orders Sept. 22.

Quotes From Chairman Dave:

"I can't see doing the 128K ROMs. It's much too difficult." -- December 1986, *GEnie*

"The 128's are possible to do, but it would be twice as much effort as the 64's, so I won't." -- April 1987, *Atari Explorer*

"Hypercard looks really neat, but I don't think you'll ever see it on the Atari ST." -- September 1987, *START magazine*

"It's extremely unlikely I'll ever do the 128's." -- January 1988, *Compuserve*

"I'm retiring." -- April, 1988, *dP newsletter*

"Do you think I should do the 128's?" -- July, 1988, *GEnie conference*

"The 128's are done, and it's for sale, starting September first." -- August, 1988, Gadgets Newsletter.
****

Gadgets By Small, Inc.

40 West Littleton Blvd.,
#210-211
Littleton, CO 80126

(303) 791-6661

Announcing Spectre 128!

- **128K ROM Support: Hypercard and Beyond!**

- **Higher Speed: 3-10 times faster**

- **Improved Compatibility**

Details start on page 2!

Inside:	Inside:
• The 64 & 128K ROMs,	• Beta Testers &
• All About Hypercard,	other good people,
• How fast is the Spectre?,	• 256K ROM questions,
• Better modem programs,	• MIDI questions,
• HFS: built in!,	• Apple LaserWriter,
• Hard Disk surprises,	• Atari LaserPrinter,
• Translator compatability,	• Accelerator Boards,
• Support,	• Full Page Displays,
• Spectre Version 2.00,	• and probably more if I can
	squeeze it into 8 pages!

"Inside" need not be repeated in the contents box.

Too many horizontal and vertical rules juxtaposed on bullets and boxes create a design hodgepodge with no distinctive appearance.

MAKEOVER

FLASH! Spectre 128 orders accepted Sept. 1

Gadgets News-Herald

The Journal of Leading Emulation Technology

September 1, 1988   Vol. 1, Issue 1

Quotes from Chairman Dave

I can't see doing the 128K ROMs. It's much too difficult.
— *December 1986, GEnie*

The 128's are possible to do, but it would be twice as much effort as the 64's, so I won't.
— *April 1987, Atari Explorer*

Hypercard looks really neat, but I don't think you'll ever see it on the Atari ST.
— *September 1987, START magazine*

It's extremely unlikely I'll ever do the 128's.
— *January 1988, Compuserve*

I'm retiring.
— *April 1988, dP newsletter*

Do you think I should do the 128's?
— *July 1988, GEnie conference*

The 128's are done, and it's for sale, starting September first.
— *August 1988, Gadgets Newsletter*

Spectre becomes reality as Atari goes 128 at last

The speculation and waiting are over — Atari will soon introduce the long-anticipated Spectre 128.

The new machine, featuring 128K ROMs, will be shown at three upcoming computer expos.

The first is Glendale AtariFest, set for Sept. 16-17. Two weeks later, Spectre 128 will star at Washington AtariFest, Oct. 1-2 . The newest Atari also will vie for attention at Comdex, Nov. 14-18. Gadgets by Small Inc.

- **128K ROM Support: Hypercard and Beyond!**
- **Higher Speed: 3-10 Times Faster**
- **Improved Compatibility**

Details start on page 2!

expects to have Spectre 128 for sale at Glendale and to ship orders Sept. 22.

Inside Gadgets News-Herald

- The 64 & 128K ROMs
- All About Hypercard
- How Fast Is The Spectre?
- Better Modem Programs
- HFS: Built-in!
- Hard Disk surprises
- Translator Compatibility
- Support
- Spectre Version 2.00

- Beta Testers & Other Good People
- 256K ROM Questions
- MIDI Questions
- Apple LaserWriter
- Atari LaserPrinter
- Accelerator Boards
- Full Page Displays
- And More — if I can squeeze it into 8 pages!

Gadgets By Small, Inc.   40 West Littleton Blvd., #210-211   Littleton, CO 80126   303 791-6661

A banner across the top makes the big news inescapable.

Exaggerated quote marks help define a monthly column.

Pull-quotes are effective ways to focus readers' attention and break up type.

A distinctive—even unorthodox—nameplate enhances even the most pedestrian material. Producing a well-designed nameplate is worth the time and money.

ORIGINAL

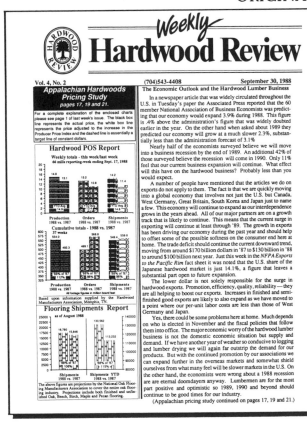

Nameplates should be clearly differentiated from the copy and graphics below.

Symbols and ideagrams aren't effective when graphic information is busy and cramped.

The all-important headline is so small that the busy reader might miss it altogether.

MAKEOVER

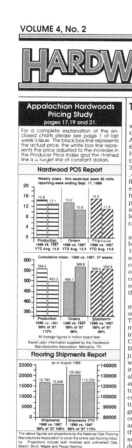

VOLUME 4, No. 2   SEPTEMBER 30. 1988

Weekly HARDWOOD REVIEW

Appalachian Hardwoods Pricing Study
pages 17,19 and 21.

For a complete explanation of the enclosed charts please see page 1 of last
week's issue. The black box line represents
the actual price, the white box line represents the price adjusted to the increase in
the Producer Price Index and the dashed
line is a target line of constant dollars.

Hardwood POS Report

Weekly totals - this week/last week 56 mills
reporting-week ending Sept. 17, 1988

Production 1988 vs. 1987 YTD Avg. 14.9 | Orders 1988 vs. 1987 YTD Avg. 13.4 | Shipments 1988 vs. 1987 YTD Avg. 14.8

Cumulative totals - 1988 vs. 1987. 37 weeks

Production 1988 vs. 1987 '88% of '87 112% | Orders 1988 vs. 1987 '88% of '87 98% | Shipments 1988 vs. 1987 '88% of '87 98%

All footage figures in million board feet

Based upon information supplied by the Hardwood
Manufacturers Association. Memphis, TN.

Flooring Shipments Report

as of August 1988

Shipments 1988 vs. 1987 '88% of '87 106% | Shipments YTD 1988 vs. 1987 '88% of '87 115%

The above figures are projections by the National Oak Flooring
Manufactures Association to cover the entire oak flooring indus-
try. Projections include both finished and unfinished Oak,
Beech, Birch, Maple and Pecan flooring.

The Economic Outlook & the Hardwood Business

In a newspaper article that was widely circulated throughout the U.S. in Tuesday's paper the Associated Press reported that the 60 member National Association of Business Economists was predicting that our economy would expand 3.9% during 1988. This figure is .4% above the administration's figure that was widely doubted earlier in the year. On the other hand when asked about 1989 they predicted our economy will grow at a much slower 2.3%, substantially less than the administration fore-cast of 3.1%

Nearly half of the economists surveyed believe we will move into a business recession by the end of 1989. An additional 42% of those surveyed believe the recession will come in 1990. Only 11% feel that our current business expansion will continue. What effect will this have on the hardwood business? Less than you would expect.

A number of people have mentioned that the articles we do on exports do not apply to them The fact is that we are quickly moving into a global economy that involves not just the U.S. but Canada, West Germany, Great Britain, South Korea and Japan just to name a few. This economy will continue to expand as our interdependence grows in the years ahead. All of our major partners are on a growth track that is likely to continue. This means that the current surge in exporting will con-tinue at least through '89. The growth in exports has been driving our economy during the past year and should help to offset some of the possible softness on the con-sumer end here at home. The trade deficit should continue the current downward trend, moving from around $170 billion dollars in '87 to $130 billion in '88 to around $100 billion next year. Just this week in the NFPA Exports to the Pacific Rim fact sheet it was noted that the U.S. share of the Japanese hardwood market is just 14.1%, a figure that leaves a substantial part open to future expansion.

The lower dollar is not solely responsible for the surge in hard-wood exports. Promotion, effi-ciency, quality, reliability—they are all helping to boost our exports. Increases in finished and semi-finished good exports are likely to also expand as we have moved to a point where our per-unit labor costs are less that those of West Germany and Japan.

Yes, there could be some prob-lems here at home. Much depends on who is elected in November and the fiscal policies that follow them into office. The major economic worry of the hardwood lumber busi-ness is not the domestic economic situation but supply and demand. If we have another year of weather so conducive to logging and lumber drying we will again far outstrip the demand for our products. But with the continued promotion by our associations we can expand further in the overseas markets and some-what shield ourselves from what many feel will be slower markets in the U.S. On the other hand, the economists were wrong about a 1988 recession, and are eternal doomsdayers anyway. Lumbermen are for the most part positive and optimistic so 1989, 1990 and beyond should continue to be good times for our industry.

(Application pricing study continued on pages 17, 19 and 21.)

Narrower columns in a three-column format are easier to read—and allow for more design flexibility.

The nameplate logo illustration has been incorporated into a design that reflects the trade.

Timely, information-crammed reports must be well organized, allowing readers to pick out pertinent information in a sea of type.

ORIGINAL

COMMENT SECTION

GENERAL: Business conditions were largely unchanged over previous weeks. Hardwood mills continued to produce large amounts of Red Oak. Some mills have continued the heavy production to rid their yards of what they see as high priced logs in a declining market. Many manufacturers are now warehousing and sticking inventory as they feel that selling into the current market is difficult. Many are confident that the market is close to firming up, but when asked to define close we got a range of answers from "Sometime in October" to "Around the first of the year" to "Early 1989 after all this inventory is used up."

A noticeable turn towards aggressive selling has been noticed in the past month. Yards are mentioning hearing from mills they have not heard from in quite some time. Salespeople are traveling, meeting new contacts and re-establishing contact with old customers. Some have mentioned that they are finding markets for their material by doing so but that you have to be in the right place at the right time with what the customer needs.

The wide ranges in the selling prices of Red Oak have many concerned. Case in point—in this week's information we had selling prices on 4/4 #1 Com. Appalachian Red Oak KD ranging from $670 to $865. The lower prices seem to be by far the exception than the norm as most prices fell in the and around the $760-$800 mark. When word begins circulating about the few lesser priced loads a number of people jump as they feel that price indicative of the market when in fact it is not. In a situation such as we have today watch for this type of thing. FAS Red Oak, FAS Cherry, #1 Com. White Oak, we all hear the rumors about who sold what to whom at what price. A note of caution, let's not let the rumor mill run rampant, all it can do is hurt the industry.

NORTHERN: The Northern producers and users continue to find good markets for their products. Furniture and flooring plants in this region remain quite busy. There is some added availability on some key kiln dried items but most are continuing to move their lumber through the pipeline. Hard Maple remains a very good species with mills extending order files and having very little available for sale. Kiln dried Sel&Btr Hard Maple is an especially good mover at this time. Soft Maple is much more available to the user with a couple of sellers noticing a softness in some thicknesses and grades. Northern Soft Grey Elm is a good export item but there are many chasing the limited production of this species. Red Oak sales are good with an improved availability making orders slightly more competitive. #1 Com. Red Oak is continuing to move both green and kiln dried at the listed prices. The limited production of Northern Ash showed movements both green and kiln dried in this week's information.

SOUTHERN: White Oak continued to move at a decent pace in the South, especially for those exporting the FAS/1F. White Oak #1 Com. was a so-so item, depending on who you talked to. Some we moving it, some were not. Kiln dried #1 Com. White Oak prices were lower and the range at the right was adjusted downward be $20. Red Oak FAS/1F, #1 Com. and #2 Com. kiln dried were softer as the heavy production continues to have its effect. The kiln dried ranges were adjusted to better reflect this week's market. Green sales were also softer in the #1&Btr Red Oak and the list price was adjusted accordingly. #2&3A Red and White Oak for the flooring plants is building in inventory at the mills. Production of the lesser desired species is heavy as mills seemed to be cutting quite a bit of Sap Gum, Hackberry, Soft Maple, etc. Some concern was shown about Ash but sale prices continued firm in both the green and the kiln dried in all thicknesses. Poplar sales in the FAS/1F continued good in 4/4 through 8/4 thicknesses. The #1 Com. Poplar moves better in the South at prices ranging from $330 to $390 but averaging around $355.

APPALACHIAN: Good movement of kiln dried Ash 4/4 through 8/4 in #2&Btr. showed in this week's information. Prices were firm on all the KD stock. Some softness was noted in green #2 Com. Ash prices for which an adjustment was made. Sel&Btr Basswood KD moved within the price range, #1 Com. prices varied widely. Cherry was slower for the majority we contacted although a few did mention that they are moving most of what they have available. 4/4 FAS KD was noticeably slower. Cherry prices overall required an adjustment in this week's issue. Hard Maple continued to move well in Sel&Btr and limited amounts of #1 Com. to the Yards. Furniture manufacturers mention ample Hard Maple inventories, the shipments to them in our information range from slightly above to slightly below our current list. Soft Maple is much the same but some mills are finding improved markets over the past few weeks. Red Oak prices in the 4/4 FAS KD in both regions were softer as Yard inventories are heavy at this time. #1 Com. Red Oak sales were just fair with the wide range of prices discussed above making selling difficult for some we talked to. Like the South, #2&3A Oak inventories are heavy at the flooring plants with some restricting receipts of incoming lumber. 8/4 FAS Red Oak KD is very available with the selling prices reported highlighting the need for a slight adjustment to the range. 6/4 and 8/4 FAS and #1 Com. White Oak sales have been heavier in our information over the past 2 weeks. 4/4 and 5/4 FAS White Oak are also moving well, again especially for those exporting this material. Poplar markets remained unchanged. Walnut movement remained steady with the price on KD stock falling within the listed ranges. A wide range of prices was received on 4/4 FAS Walnut with some above, some below but most within the published $1770-$1870 range.

page 14

The eyes have a difficult time digesting long lines of type, something to particularly avoid when designing newsletters and promotional material.

The type is too small for readers to scan the material.

MAKEOVER

COMMENT SECTION

GENERAL: Business conditions were largely unchanged over previous weeks. Hardwood mills continued to produce large amounts of *Red Oak*. Some mills have continued the heavy production to rid their yards of what they see as high priced logs in a declining market. Many manufactures are now warehousing and sticking inventory as they feel that selling into the current market is difficult. Many are confident that the market is close to firming up, but when asked to define close we got a range of answers from "Sometime in October" to "Around the first of the year" to "Early 1989 after all this inventory is used up."

A noticeable turn towards aggressive selling has been noticed in the past month. Yards are mentioning hearing from mills they have not heard from in quite some time. Salespeople are traveling, meeting new contacts and reestablishing contact with old customers. Some have mentioned that they are finding markets for their material by doing so but that you have to be in the right place at the right time with what the customer needs.

The wide ranges in the selling prices of *Red Oak* have many concerned. Case in point—in this week's information we had selling prices on 4/4#1 Com. Appalachian *Red Oak* KD ranging from $670 to $865. The lower prices seem to be by far the exception than the norm as most prices fell in and around the $760-$800 mark. When word begins circulating about the few lesser priced loads a number of people jump as they feel that price indicative of the market when in fact it is not. In a situation such as we have today watch for this type of thing. FAS *Red Oak*, FAS *Cherry*, #1Com. *White Oak*, we all hear the rumors about who sold what to whom at what price. A note of caution, let's not let the rumor mill run rampant, all it can do is hurt the industry.

NORTHERN: The Northern producers and users continue to find good markets for their prod-ucts. Furniture and flooring plants in this region remain quite busy. There is some added availability on some key kiln dried items but most are continuing to move their lumber through the pipeline. *Hard Maple* remains a very good species with mills extending order files and having very little available for sale. Kiln dried Sel&Btr *Hard Maple* is an especially good mover at this time. *Soft Maple* is much more available to the user with a couple of sellers noticing a softness in some thicknesses and grades. *Northern Soft Grey Elm* is a good export item but there are many chasing the limited production of this species. *Red Oak* sales are good with an improved availability making orders slightly more competitive. #1 Com. *Red Oak* is moving both green and kiln dried at the listed prices. The limited production of Northern *Ash* showed movements both green and kiln dried in this week's information.

SOUTHERN: *White Oak* continued to move at a decent pace in the South, especially for those exporting the FAS/1F. *White Oak* #1 Com. was a so-so item, depending on who you talked to. Some were moving it, some were not. Kiln dried #1 Com. *White Oak* prices were lower and the range at the right was adjusted downward by $20. *Red Oak* FAS/1F, #1 Com. and #2 Com. kiln dried were softer as the heavy production continues to have its effect. The kiln dried ranges were adjusted to better reflect this week's market. Green sales were also softer in the #1&Btr. *Red Oak* and the list price was adjusted accordingly. #2&3A *Red* and *White Oak* for the flooring plants is building in inventory at the mills. Production of the lesser desired species is heavy as mills seemed to be cutting quite a bit of *Sap Gum, Hackberry, Soft Maple*, etc. Some concern was shown about *Ash* but sale prices continued firm in both the green and the kiln dried in all thicknesses. *Poplar* sales in the FAS/1F continued good in 4/4 through 8/4 thicknesses. The #1 Com. *Poplar* moves better in the South at $330 to $390 but averaging around $355.

APPALACHIAN: Good movement of kiln dried *Ash* 4/4 through 8/4 in #2&Btr. showed in this week's information. Prices were firm on all the KD stock. Some softness was noted in green #2 Com. *Ash* prices for which an adjustment was made. Sel&Btr *Basswood* KD moved within the price range, #1 Com. prices varied widely. *Cherry* was slower for the majority we contacted although a few did mention that they are moving most of what they have available. 4/4 FAS KD was noticeably slower. *Cherry* prices overall required an adjustment in this week's issue. *Hard Maple* continued to move well in Sel&Btr. and limited amounts of #1 Com. to the Yards. Furniture manufacturers mention ample *Hard Maple* inventories, the shipments to them in our information range from slightly above to slightly below our current list. *Soft Maple* is much the same but some mills are finding improved markets over the past few weeks. *Red Oak* prices in the 4/4 FAS KD in both regions were softer as Yard inventories are heavy at this time. #1 Com. *Red Oak* sales were just fair with the wide range of prices discussed above making selling difficult for some we talked to. Like the South, #2&3A *Oak* inventories are heavy at the flooring plants with some restricting receipts of incoming lumber. 8/4 FAS *Red Oak* KD is very available with the selling prices reported highlighting the need for a slight adjustment to the range. 6/4 and 8/4 FAS and #1 Com. *White Oak* sales have been heavier in our information over the past 2 weeks. 4/4 and 5/4 FAS *White Oak* are also moving well, again especially for those exporting this material. *Poplar* markets remained unchanged. *Walnut* movement remained steady with the price on KD stock falling within the listed ranges. A wide range of prices was received on 4/4 FAS *Walnut* with some above, some below but most within the published $1770-$1870 range.

Italics are easier to read than underlined type.

A multi-column format helps break up type.

Explore visual aids—rules, reverses, initial caps—to make long runs of text more lively.

ORIGINAL

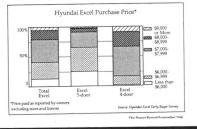

Ford Products...

through Ford's styling theme and will be executed more as a functional luxury car than a traditional luxury car.

Ford Thunderbird/Mercury Cougar — For 1987 the Ford Thunderbird and Mercury Cougar will get their first major changes since their introduction in 1983. Both cars will receive new front and rear treatments that give these cars an even more aero look. An SVO Thunderbird, offering a 2.8–liter turbo that produces 200 horsepower, may be announced shortly after the 1987 model year. In 1988, the Thunderbird/Cougar will have a complete redesign, but will retain their rear-wheel-drive configuration. The Ford Thunderbird's styling will be similar to that of a BMW 635 CSi and its execution will move the car closer to functional performance than the present model.

Ford Mustang III — The U.S. joint-venture project between Ford and Mazda will yield its first model in the spring of 1988. Tentatively named the Mustang III, the new model will be built in conjunction with a Mazda version of the same car, but offering different sheet metal.

The Mustang III will be positioned between the existing Escort EXP and Mustang and priced in the $12,000-to-$14,000 market. The new joint-venture plant producing this line of sporty cars will generate 240,000 units annually, with about 55 percent of production going to Ford and the balance of the units to Mazda.

Ford Barchetta — Ford will begin importing the Australian-built Barchetta beginning in 1989. The Barchetta will be a sporty coupe slightly smaller than the Mustang III. The Barchetta could be sold through either Ford or Lincoln-Mercury dealers; however, it is believed that L-M dealers are the more likely candidates since Ford dealers already will be selling the similarly sized Mustang III.

Merkur GN34-Cobra — Beginning the 1989 model year, Ford will begin importing a high-performance sports car from Europe. The new sports car will be designed by Chausson, the French automotive design house, and will be priced in the neighborhood of $25,000. We are assuming the GN34 will be sold as a Merkur model, as its market and price positioning are more compatible with Merkur's product line than those of Ford or Lincoln-Mercury. The GN34 is

expected to be similar to that of the Ford Cobra 230 ME concept car.

Ford GN48 — Ford and Lincoln-Mercury dealers may begin marketing a full-size, front-wheel-drive car that will

Excels Selling At or Above MSRP

Price appears to be a very strong factor in the decision to purchase a Hyundai Excel, according to J.D. Power and Associates Hyundai Excel Early Buyer Survey. The median purchase price paid by Hyundai Excel buyers shows a clear price advantage of other basic-small vehicles. The 5-door Excel has a $1,400 price advantage over the average basic-small car based on early 1985 new-car buyer data from J.D. Power and Associates New-Car Initial Quality Survey, while the 4-door Excel, not available in the base trim level, has a $500 price advantage over the same vehicles. This price advantage, coupled with shoppers' perceptions of Hyundai's quality, feature content and value, seem to make the Excel a logical choice for value-conscious new-car buyers.

The 5-door Excel, positioned by Hyundai as the price/value leader, does not appear to be marked up by dealers to the same extent as the 4-door Excels. A larger proportion of 5-door Excel buyers paid a purchase price in the $6,000 to $6,999 range than did 4-door Excel buyers.

Fewer than three in ten 5-door Excel buyers paid over the manufacturer's suggested retail price, compared with nearly 40 percent of 4-door Excel buyers. The Excel has a strong draw on potential basic-small new-car buyers

because of its attractive price advantage compared with overall basic-small cars and the Japanese basic-small cars, in particular, which were still being price inflated with dealer add-ons during the Hyundai introductory period. The results of the survey show that the MSRP on the Excel models is at or below market expectations, with one-third of the units going out the door at somewhat inflated prices and less than 10 percent of the models being discounted.

As the prices of Japanese models continue to climb as a result of unfavorable yen exchange rates, it is expected the competition for Hyundai will be centered more with domestic models such as the Horizon/Omni America Series, Ford Escort and Chevrolet Chevette, until the Japanese manufacturers readjust marketing strategies.

Since low labor and production costs are paramount in marketing low-priced cars, with the current yen situation the Japanese will have a difficult time cracking this market without moving production to a Third World nation. It is likely the Japanese manufacturers may begin incentive programs, offering low-rate financing or rebates to maintain competitiveness with low-priced Hyundai and domestic small-cars.PR

replace the aging rear-wheel-drive Ford Crown Victoria and Mercury Grand Marquis. The new front-wheel-drive replacements will be based off a stretched version of the Taurus with platform wheelbase at 110 inches.PR

Hyundai Excel Purchase Price*

100%				$9,000 or More
				$8,000-$8,999
				$7,000-$7,999
50%				
				$6,000-$6,999
0	Total Excel	Excel 5-door	Excel 4-door	Less than $6,000

*Price paid as reported by owners excluding taxes and license

Source: Hyundai Excel Early Buyer Survey

The Power Report/September 1986

Too much space between columns produces awkward white space, compounded by the use of a ragged-right format.

Data that are not presented well graphically defeat their purpose of quickly informing the reader.

MAKEOVER

Ford Products. . .

through Ford's styling theme and will be executed more a functional luxury car than a traditional luxury car.

Ford Thunderbird/Mercury Cougar

For 1987 the Ford Thunderbird and Mercury Cougar will get their first major changes since their introduction in 1983. Both cars will receive new front and rear treatments that give these cars an even more aero look. An SVO Thunderbird, offering a 2.8-liter turbo that produces 200 horsepower, may be announced shortly after the 1987 model year. In 1988, the Thunderbird/Cougar will have a complete redesign, but will retain their rear-wheel-drive configuration. The Ford Thunderbird's styling will be similar to that of a BMW 635 CSi and its execution will move the car closer to functional performance than the present model.

Ford Mustang III

The U.S. joint-venture project between Ford and mazda will yield its first model in the spring of 1988. Tentatively named the Mustang III, the new model will be built in conjunction with a mazda version of the same car, but offering different sheet metal.

The Mustang III will be positioned between the existing Escort EXP and Mustang and priced in the $12,000-to-$14,000 market. The new joint-venture plant producing this line of sporty cars will generate 240,000 units annually, with about 55 percent of production going to Ford and the balance of the units to Mazda.

Ford Barchetta

Ford will begin importing Australian-built Barchetta beginning in 1989. The Barchetta will be a sporty coupe slightly smaller than the Mustang III. The Barchetta could be sold through either Ford or Lincoln-Mercury dealers; however, it is believed that L-M dealers are the more likely candidates since Ford dealers already will be selling the similarly sized Mustang III.

Merkur GN34-Cobra

Beginning the 1989 model year, Ford will begin importing a high-performance sports car from Europe. The new sports car will be designed by Chausson, the French automotive design house, and will be priced in the neighborhood of $25,000. We are assuming the GN34 will be sold as a Merkur model, as its market and price positioning are more compatible with Merkur's product line than is expected to be similar to that of the Ford Cobra 230 ME concept car.

Ford GN48

Ford and Lincoln-Mercury dealers may begin marketing a full-size, front-wheel-drive car that will replace the aging rear-wheel-drive Ford Crown Victoria and Mercury Grand Marquis. The new front-wheel-drive replacements will be bases off a stretched version of the Taurus with platform wheelbase at 110 inches. **PR**

EXCELS SELLING AT OR ABOVE MSRP

Price appears to be a very strong factor in the decision to purchase a Hyundai Excel, according to J.D. Power and Associates Hyundai Excel Early Buyer Survey. The median purchase price paid by Hyundai Excel buyers shows a clear price advantage of other basic-small vehicles. The 5-door Excel has a $1,400 price advantage over the average basic-small car based on early 1985 new-car buyer data from J.D. Power and Associates New-Car Initial Quality Survey, while the 4-door Excel, not available in the base trim level, has a $500 price advantage over the same vehicles. THis price advantage, coupled with shoppers' perceptions of Hyundai's quality, feature content and value, seem to make the Excel a logical choice for value-conscious new-car buyers.

The 5-door Excel, positioned by Hyundai as the price/value leader, does not appear to be marked up by dealers to the same extent as the 4-door Excels. A larger proportion of 5-door Excel buyers paid a purchase price in the $6,000 to $6,999 range than did 4-door Excel buyers.

Fewer than three in ten 5-door Excel buyers paid over the manufacturer's suggested retail price, compared with nearly 40 percent of 4-door Excel buyers. The Excel has a strong draw on potential basic-small new-car buyers because of its attractive price advantage compared with overall basic-small cars and the Japanese basic-small cars, in particular, which were still being price inflated with dealer add-ons during the Hyundai introductory period. The results of the survey show that the MSRP on the Excel models, is at or below market expectations, with one-third of the units going out the door at somewhat inflated prices and less than 10 percent of the models being discounted.

As the prices of Japanese models continue to climb as a result of unfavorable yen exchange rates, it is expected the competition for Hyundai will be centered more with domestic models such as the Horizon/Omni America Series, Ford Escort and Chevrolet Chevette, until the Japanese manufacturers readjust marketing strategies.

Since low labor and production costs are paramount in marketing low-priced cars, with the current yen situation the Japanese will have a difficult time cracking this market without moving production to a Third World nation. It is likely the Japanese manufacturers may begin incentive programs, offering low-rate financing or rebates to maintain competitiveness with low-priced Hyundai and domestic small-cars. **PR**

Hyundai Excel Purchase Price*

| Less than $6,000 | $6,000-$6,999 | $7,000-$7,999 | $8,000-$8,999 | $9,000 or more |

* Price paid as reported by owners excluding taxes and license

Source: Hyundai Excel Early Buyer Survey

When used sparingly, reversed headlines can add impact.

The reversed headline complements the initial cap in the body copy.

When space allows, subheads are far more readable when off-set from body copy.

A staggered two- and three-column format helps tie copy with visuals.

F ive-column formats are popular among newsletter publishers because they allow great
flexibility in creating and laying out contents boxes,
illustrations, sidebars and house ads.

ORIGINAL

In general, illustrations placed directly below a nameplate tend to clutter the page.

The map and supporting graphics float awkwardly in the white space.

The caption is orphaned from the illustration, confusing readers.

MAKEOVER

THE NEWSLETTER FOR
MICROGRAPHIC
SERVICE BUREAUS
& DEALERS

A PUBLICATION OF
TECHNOLOGY
DATABASE
ASSOCIATES

SPECIAL FREE ISSUE

OCTOBER 1986

TOTAL SERVICE MARKET GROWS 58 PERCENT IN FIVE YEARS

Micrographic services provided by independent dealers, service bureaus and national service organizations have shown a 58% growth from 1980 to 1985 and have reached annual sales of $680 Million. Several service bureaus have predicted that 1986 should exceed a 15% increase. Supplies have grown 34% in the same period. The total market for equipment has only grown 11% in this five-year period.

Thus, the good news for independent equipment dealers is that they are capturing a larger share of the equipment market even though the total equipment market plateaued in 1985.

Bob Zagami, President of Information Technology Inc. Needham, Massachusetts stated in his February 1985 AIIM newsletter article, The Independent Dealer: The Future of Our Industry? "The dealer group that was once outcast has suddenly become the way of life in the '80s for the distribution of micrographics products and services." There are over 900 dealers and service bureaus in the United States. A few of these that were founded less than 15 years ago have exceeded $5 Million in sales. There is no doubt about the continued growth opportunities for service bureaus. ∎

These maps were computer generated by Technology Database Associates for publication in the forthcoming '86-'87 International Micrographics Source Book. All data was obtained from companies that responded to the questionnaire from Microfilm Publishing Inc., PO Box 950, Larchmont, NY 10538.

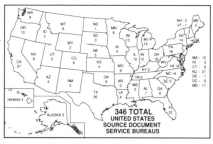

346 TOTAL
UNITED STATES
SOURCE DOCUMENT
SERVICE BUREAUS

346 SOURCE DOCUMENT SERVICE BUREAUS

In a few cases a source document service bureau is also a COM service bureau. The November issue of the SERVICE BUREAU NEWSLETTER will feature U.S. maps with locations of 246 COM service bureaus and 969 equipment dealers. ∎

With careful selection of type and layout, you can get more words on less paper—even using a bigger point size!

A box around the map, along with a supporting caption, melds the illustration with the copy and strengthens the overall message.

ADVERTISEMENTS

Your firm's or association's advertisements have a great deal of impact upon the overall success of your endeavors. Advertisements play two roles: one immediate and obvious, the other long-term and less obvious. The short-term goal is to attract attention and generate an immediate response. An effective advertisement is one that clearly stands out, making it easy for readers to separate your message from those that surround it. But short-term action isn't enough.

Effective advertisements also operate on a subliminal level. They can generate respect for your organization and thus for its message. Many readers will be predisposed to buying your service or supporting your cause, based on a positive impression created by your ad. If the ad projects a professional appearance, they'll be more apt to trust you—and reward you with their support. As the following examples show, desktop publishing and word processing software can be used to create a wide variety of advertisements, ranging from small-space ads and classifieds to large display ads.

Although sizes vary, the same basic requirements apply to all ads, large and small: simplicity, contrast, organization and identity.

Simplicity Sells

Simplicity makes it quick and easy for readers to identify and understand your message and find what they're looking for.

The "before" and "after" Fireside Distributors ads show one technique to simplify your ads: removing distractions. The "before" ad has a double-boxed border containing the brand names of Fireside Distributors' products. Not only are these names likely to be meaningless to the first-time fireplace buyer, but because of the design the names are impossible to read without rotating the page 90 degrees! By simplifying the border and placing the names in the body copy, the ad emphasizes the services that set Fireside Distributors apart from its competition.

The "Lightning Protection" example illustrates another important aspect of simplicity: editing. By eliminating "Call today"—which duplicates the immediacy implied by the word "Free"—the phone number can be made larger.

Create Contrast

Contrast goes hand in hand with simplicity—as you simplify, you can add more contrast. Important text or graphics can be made larger and surrounded with increased white space. For example, the lightning bolt in the original Lightning Protection ad looks like an afterthought. Eliminating the house and increasing the size of the lightning bolt give the makeover more impact—and the lightning doesn't look like smoke coming out of a chimney.

The partnership between simplicity and contrast is also seen in the way the Lightning Protection headline can be enlarged when the house is eliminated.

Another important way to add contrast to an ad is by varying the size of the type, as illustrated in the Carolina House

Doctor ad. In the "before" example, most of the type is set in the same size. As a result, the ad presents an overall "gray" appearance. It not only lacks white space, it's likely to blend into the background and be lost among surrounding ads. Notice how much easier it is to read the "decks, porches, gazebos," etc., copy in the "after" example.

Another example of the effectiveness of contrasting type sizes is the Seattle Design Store ad. Once again, information that's hard to read when set large and bold becomes easier to read when set in a smaller size, surrounded by white space.

You can also add contrast by using background screens, as the AccuGraphics example shows. When placed against a gray background, the copy emerges with added force.

The McCauley Agency example shows how both simplicity and contrast can be applied to an ad. Simplicity is achieved by slightly editing the headline; reversing and repeating the illustrations provide greater contrast. The same amount of space gives more visual impact and communicates the message more clearly.

The Artware Systems examples show both the strengths and the weaknesses of contrast. The body copy in the middle of the ad is difficult to read because it's surrounded by too much white space—it looks isolated from the headline and phone number at the bottom. At the same time, because it's set in the same size as the body copy, the firm's name is lost. Notice how much easier the "after" version reads: there's more contrast between the words describing the services offered, the types of projects and the name of the firm.

Organizing Information

To be useful, information has to be organized in a logical progression, from general to specific.

The "before" Power Report example is confusing: the big logo at the top of the ad overpowers the message that follows.

Notice how much easier it is to read the "after" version. The extended quote—the heart of the ad—is now boxed and placed in the center of the ad. The Power Report logo—which you'd respond to only if you were interested in the preceding message—is now logically located at the bottom of the ad.

The Peden Commercial Realty ad also illustrates the importance of organization. It's difficult to read the body copy in the original ad because your eye keeps getting drawn to the firm's name at the right. The text in the "after" version is easier to read because distracting elements have been removed. Logic and organization are also reflected by moving up the call to action—the phone number. In the "before" version, the firm's address formed a barrier between the text and phone number.

Shaping a Strong Identity

The final element of a successful ad is a strong and clear identity. The aspects that make up the identity of an ad are (l) the design, size and placement of the firm's logo, and (2) the typefaces.

All too often, ads are created from the top down. Logo, address and phone number are then crammed into whatever space is left over. Instead, assemble your ads from the bottom up by creating templates that have the logo and contact information built in. This way, readers can always get in touch with you.

Another approach, as the Fireside Distributors example shows, is to put telephone numbers in the body copy—where serious prospects will be certain to see them. Size is important, too: note the large telephone number in the revised Power Report ad—it's much easier to find than it was in the original.

Take Another Look

As you read today's newspaper, analyze your reactions to the ads you see. What did you learn about the advertisers, simply by looking at their ads?

Pay particular attention to the simplicity, contrast and organization; notice how the ads that jump out at you have these qualities. And notice how these characteristics are often lacking in hard-to-read ads, making you want to skip right over them.

The ads that give a comfortable or secure feeling will meet the criteria of simplicity, contrast and organization—while cluttered, "gray" and disorganized ads make you wonder if the firm can really do what it promises.

One of the best ways you can fine-tune your desktop publishing design skills is by continually observing the ads you see and analyzing your reaction to them.

As you evaluate your own desktop-published ads, ask yourself these questions:

✔ Do borders and white space help the ads stand out from the rest?

✔ Does the headline clearly present the offer included in the ad?

✔ Is all necessary buying information included?

✔ Is there a clear relationship between type size and the importance of the message?

✔ Do the graphics distract from the copy?

✔ Is your ad's design compatible with other print communications produced by your firm?

Visuals can make or break advertisements—use your computer's capabilities (and imagination) to experiment with a variety of treatments.

ORIGINAL

Too many typefaces in a small advertisement often produce a cluttered, unprofessional appearance.

Rules separate each line of the headline, making it difficult to read.

MAKEOVER

We insure all types
of vehicles

Hiland Shopping Center
West Kittanning

548-1521

M^cCAULEY
Agency

Premium Financing
Available

PIA

*The abbreviated head-
line adds punch to the
new graphic.*

*Most desktop publishing
software makes "step
and repeat" illustrations
easy to produce—here
the illustration of many
vehicles further enhan-
ces the headline and
main message.*

ADVERTISEMENTS

Too many typefaces or type styles on a page interrupt natural copy flow, regardless of how well a piece is designed. This is particularly true of small-space advertising.

Seven different typefaces and styles (bold and italic) plus an initial cap make this difficult to read.

Widows are particularly unsightly in brief copy blocks.

ORIGINAL

Helping Develop
The Triangle's Future

We provide commercial real estate services for the Triangle area. Whether you're buying, selling, or listing commercial property, give us a call.

Peden
Commercial
Realty

1815 North Blvd. □ P.O. Box 40489 □ Raleigh, NC 27629

919-832-2081

Jim Peden, Jr. • *Dave Zendels* • *Geff Bitler*

The address has been repositioned under the logo, where readers are used to finding it.

Remember to include your area code, even on local advertising—you never know who'll be reading your message.

MAKEOVER

Helping Develop the Triangle's Future

We provide commercial real estate services for the Triangle area. Whether you're buying, selling, or listing commercial property, give us a call.

919-832-2081

Peden Commercial Realty

1815 North Blvd., P.O. Box 40489
Raleigh, NC 27629

Jim Peden, Jr.   Dave Zendels   Geff Bitler

Sometimes an all-type treatment leaves a lot to the imagination, and can thus be more visually stimulating than if graphics are used.

Avoid wide letter spacing to fill space—it usually hurts the overall design.

A glass and a duck aren't everything—if the reader isn't interested in either, then the message is wasted.

ORIGINAL

E V E R Y T H I N G

SEMI-ANNUAL EVERYTHING SALE

Beginning Saturday, September 21, all merchandise at all of our Stores is on sale at up to 60% off of our Everyday Low Prices. Some merchandise is, however, limited to stock on hand so please shop early for the best selection.

10% - 60% OFF EVERY ITEM !!!

 SeattleDesignStore

A thousand words are sometimes worth a picture, and the horizontal product listing now accurately reflects the "Everything" headline.

Omitting exclamation marks often creates a persuasive understatement, particularly when the "Everything" theme is overstated in the first place!

MAKEOVER

EVERYTHING

Aprons, bakeware, barware, basket storage systems, bistro furniture, clocks, closet organizers, coffee mugs, cookbooks, cookware, cutlery, cutting boards, decanters, dinnerware, dish drainers, extention cords, flatware, folding chairs, food serving accessories, gadgets, kitchen towels, lighting, picture frames, pitchers placemats & napkins, rugs, salad bowls, shower accessories, space saving products, spice racks, stack baskets, storage jars, teakettles, teapots, tie racks, trays, umbrellas, wastebaskets, window shades, wine goblets, woks and much more.

Semi-Annual Everything Sale

10% to 60% OFF EVERY ITEM

Beginning Saturday, September 21, all merchandise at all of our Stores is on sale at up to 60% off of our Everyday Low Prices. Some merchandise is, however, limited to stock on hand, so please shop early for the best selection.

SeattleDesignStore

The literal image of the house might discourage potential commercial customers.

ORIGINAL

The small subhead is overwhelmed by less-important copy below.

MAKEOVER

The abstract lightning image shows how screens of different values can be used in tandem to create interesting effects.

Similar type sizes link the headline and telephone number—essential ingredients in small-space advertising.

The wrong headline can cut a small-space ad response to zero—regardless of the product.

AMERICA'S FINEST
/Carolina House Doctor
Durham, N.C.
National Award Winning Exterior Design & Construction

Decks • Porches
Gazebos • Patios
New or Reside and
Overhang in
Brick - Wood - Vinyl
Aluminum
544-7095
Free Estimates

ORIGINAL

"America's Finest" can apply to anything, causing readers to quickly move to the next ad.

Carolina House Doctor
America's Finest

National Award Winning Exterior Design and Construction

Decks / Porches
Gazebos / Patios
New or Reside and
Overhang in Brick,
Wood, Vinyl, Aluminum

Free Estimates
544-7095
Durham, NC

MAKEOVER

A simple screen can draw attention to display classifieds and small-space ads.

The use of different type styles and sizes establishes a hierarchy of important information.

Desktop publishing makes it too easy to produce graphics that scream at the customer. Sometimes a more conservative treatment makes a message more inviting and your document more effective.

ORIGINAL

The border is distracting—and readers probably aren't as interested in the names of individual brands as they are in other service features.

Avoid Helvetica overkill, especially in advertisements and other promotional pieces.

MAKEOVER

Who is Fireside Distributors?

We are best known as the largest fireplace accessory distributor in the U.S. But did you know Fireside Distributors offers one of the largest selections of sweep products anywhere?

Our products include: Merry Sweep, Webster, Dicon, Metalbestos, Flitz, Chimfex, Chamber-Aid, Adapt-A-Place, American Stove Products, Mirror, Lyemance, Air-Jet, Worcester, Homesaver, Kemstone, Dura-Vent, Versagrid, O.D. Funk, Condar, Chimline, Schaefer and Flam-X

In addition to stocking over 2,000 sweep and specialty fireplace products, Fireside Sweep Service includes:

–800 Toll-Free Information

–Extra 5% Check with Order Discount

–VISA and MasterCard welcomed

–No Minimum Order

–24-Hour Order Processing

–$3.50 U.P.S. Per Carton

–Prepaid Freight Available

–Credit for Qualified Sweeps

Our experienced staff looks forward to talking with you and welcomes the opportunity to answer your product and installation questions.

We make working with us easy! Give us a call today and we'll send your **FREE CATALOG**, "Products for the Sweep."

US 1-800-334-3210

NC 1-800-662-7025

Fireside Distributors, 4013 Winton Road, Raleigh, North Carolina 27604

A three-column news format makes readers feel that they're being informed, not pitched.

A sans-serif typeface helps set an informative tone throughout.

When advertising a newsletter or other publication, make sure the piece itself doesn't look like the product!

ORIGINAL

THE POWER REPORT
ON AUTOMOTIVE MARKETING • SEPT. 1986 • VOL. 8 NO. 9

"We are in the midst of an automotive retailing revolution."

The automotive marketplace will change more in the next 5 years than it did in the last 20 years.

Remember when GM, Ford and Chrysler owned the market? Today, 32 nameplates vie for a slice of the rich U.S. automotive pie. New manufacturers from east and west will swell that number to 40 by 1990.

These new nameplates are already changing the structure of automotive retailing. Consumer perspectives are evolving almost as fast, and the old certainties of automotive marketing are gone. What lies ahead? *The Power Report* will help you keep track of the major issues, such as...

- Will the overabundance of new cars lead to a bloodbath of price cuts and incentives? Who will be the winners, and who will be the losers?

- How fast is the trend toward retail consolidation and more multi-franchise operators? How do dealers view the changing marketplace?

- How will dealers compete for business from more demanding new-car shoppers? Are women buyers a significant force for trucks as well as cars?

- Can dealers combat declining consumer loyalty through improved customer satisfaction? Is the key better product or better service?

Automotive marketers and many of the nation's top dealers have found *The Power Report* keeps them informed about these trends ... and those of tomorrow.

You can be too, with a subscription to *The Power Report*.

Examine the enclosed sample copy. If you like what you see...

We'll take your order right away! **Call Collect (818) 889-6330** October 6, 1986 to October 20, 1986 Between 8 a.m. and 5 p.m. (PDT)

Or, simply fill out and return the subscription card on the back to receive *The Power Report*.

Bullets have little effect when used with long blocks of text.

The telephone number is too small, making it hard for readers to respond even after they've made a decision.

MAKEOVER

R emember when GM, Ford and Chrysler owned the market? Today, 32 nameplates vie for a slice of the rich U.S. automotive pie. New manufacturers from east and west will swell that number to 40 by 1990.

These new nameplates are already changing the structure of automotive retailing. Consumer perspectives are evolving almost as fast, and the old certainties of automotive marketing are gone. What lies ahead? *The Power Report* will help you keep track of the major issues, such as...

Will the overabundance of new cars lead to a bloodbath of price cuts and incentives?

Who will be the winners, and who will be the losers?

How fast is the trend toward retail consolidation and more multi-franchise operators?

How do dealers view the changing marketplace?

"W*e are in the midst of an automotive retailing revolution."* The automotive marketplace will change more in the next five years than it did in the last twenty years.

How will dealers compete for business from more demanding new-car shoppers?

Are women buyers a significant force for trucks as well as cars?

Can dealers combat declining consumer loyalty through improved customer satisfaction?

Is the key better product or better service?

Automotive marketers and many of the nation's top dealers have found *The Power Report* keeps them informed about these trends...and those of tomorrow. You can be too, with a subscription to *The Power Report*. **Examine the enclosed sample copy.** If you like what you see...We'll take your order right away!

Call Collect (818) 889-6330

October 6 to October 20, 1986. 8 a.m. to 5 p.m. (PDT). Or, return the subscription card on the back.

The entire ad is now organized around the compelling, authoritative pull-quote.

Rules at the top and bottom help balance the text and frame the screened pull-quote.

An initial cap helps tie the newsletter logo to the body copy.

The nameplate has been placed on the bottom and the dateline removed, to further indicate the piece is an advertisement.

ADVERTISEMENTS

Sometimes a layout can break all the rules, yet provide a workable solution—that's where convention and intuition often come together to produce the best results.

ORIGINAL

MAKEOVER

If you want the very best

Design & Production Services
For your

Business Publications
Technical Manuals &
Presentation Materials,

Make a smart move to

Artware Systems

Where art, publishing
and
tomorrow's technology
come together, today!

872-6511

Where
art,
publishing
and
tomorrow's
technology
come
together,
today!

Artware Systems

DESIGN & PRODUCTION SERVICES

**Business Publications
Technical Manuals
Presentation Materials**

872-6511

Uneven treatment of white space makes this ad uninviting.

Note how the lack of variety in type styles and sizes makes it difficult to read the message at a glance—the goal of all display advertising.

The company name has been enlarged and made more readable, while the key selling points in the text have been converted to a headline.

Usually screens and reverses don't work well together—use them with care!

One of the big advantages of desktop publishing over traditional typesetting and paste-up methods is that it lets you experiment with basic layout and positioning. Small-space advertising can look like agency work at no extra cost.

ORIGINAL

> **Don't Throw Out Used Laser Printer & PC Copier Toner Cartridges**
> *Recharge Cartridges For Only $54.85*
> • Up to 30% more printing
> • Free Pickup & Delivery
> • 100% Guaranteed & tested
> • Apple - HP - QMS - Canon
> *Save This Ad For $5 Off Your First Recharge*
>
> *AccuGraphics*
> 2007 Progress Ct., Raleigh. 27608
> **Call (919) 831-9984**

Short headlines are often more effective than long ones—particularly in small-space advertising.

Even the most ardent coupon-clipper would have trouble finding the tiny call to action, "Save this ad...."

MAKEOVER

> **SAVE**
> **Your Used Toner Cartridges**
>
> **Recharge Laser Printer or PC Copier cartridges for only $54.85**
>
> • Up to 30% more printing
> • Free Pickup & Delivery
> • 100% Guaranteed & tested
> • Apple - HP - QMS - Canon
>
> *AccuGraphics*
> 2007 Progress Ct., Raleigh
> **(919) 831-9984**
>
> *Save this ad for $5 off your first recharge!*

The copy and logo are better suited to a vertical layout.

A light screen helps separate headline, body copy and logo.

Always be on the lookout for time-tested ways to enhance your sales message—don't be afraid to make an offer stand out, using big type, banners and other attention-getters.

ORIGINAL

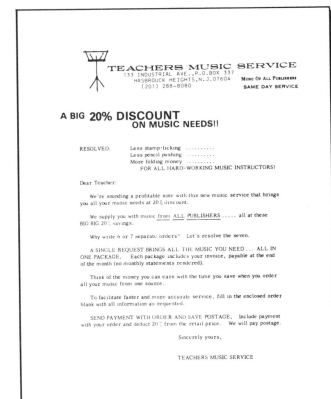

The otherwise attractive logo isn't contained on the page.

Avoid changing type sizes in mid-copy just to accent information.

MAKEOVER

TEACHERS MUSIC SERVICE

133 Industrial Ave., P.O. Box 337
Hasbrouck Heights, N.J. 07604
(201) 288-8080

Music of All Publishers
Same Day Service

A BIG
20%
DISCOUNT ON MUSIC NEEDS!!

RESOLVED. LESS stamp-licking...
LESS pencil pushing...
MORE folding money...
FOR ALL HARD WORKING MUSIC INSTRUCTORS!

Dear Teacher:

We're sounding a profitable note with this new music service that brings you all your music needs at 20% discount.

We supply you with music *from ALL PUBLISHERS*...all at these BIG BIG 20% savings.

Why write 6 or 7 separate orders? Let's resolve the seven.

A SINGLE REQUEST BRINGS ALL THE MUSIC YOU NEED... ALL IN ONE PACKAGE. Each package includes your invoice, payable at the end of the month (no monthly statements rendered).

Think of the money you can earn with the time you save when you order all your music from one source.

To facilitate faster and more accurate service, fill in the enclosed order blank with all information as requested.

SEND PAYMENT WITH ORDER AND SAVE POSTAGE. Include payment with your order and deduct 20% from the retail price. We will pay postage.

Sincerely yours,

TEACHERS MUSIC SERVICE

Reversing the logo makes it stand out against the address information and lends interest to the illustration.

The effective "Dear Teacher" copy has been boxed and a drop-shadow added to better simulate an actual letter.

Simplicity is the watchword for small-space advertising design. Use few typefaces, concise visuals and as much white space as possible.

A potpourri of typefaces, sizes and styles makes this small ad nearly impossible to read.

The thick border detracts from the message within.

ORIGINAL

Screens of various densities help promote the theme of linking Apple and IBM.

The product name and testimonial are now more prominent.

MAKEOVER

APPLE?   IBM?

Why not both!

Run & store Apple *IIe* software on a MS-DOS PC
& transfer data between Apple & IBM formats.

Trackstar E

over 15,000 units installed

"Any way you look at it, Trackstar is an amazing product!"

Compute!
Publications Inc.

Diamond Computer Systems, Inc.

470 Lakeside Drive
Sunnyvale, CA 94086
408/736-2000   FAX 408/730-5750

Apple is a registered trademard of Apple Computer, Inc.
IBM is a registered trademark of IBM Corporation

BROCHURES & FLYERS

Brochures and flyers present their own unique desktop publishing challenges. Brochures are "silent salespeople" who do their work before customers see the product or after the initial sales presentation. A brochure can range from a single one- or two-fold sheet to an elaborate publication printed on glossy paper. Since they're designed to reinforce sales, brochures must create a favorable impression of your product or service and communicate a lot of information.

Flyers are similar to brochures, but are usually more time-dependent, with less detail. They're intended for informal distribution—to be posted in public or distributed by hand. Therefore, flyers depend on their visual appeal for success; they must immediately attract the reader's attention.

BROCHURES

Brochures require visually compelling, integrated covers that attract attention and encourage readers to look inside. Successful brochures also depend on continuity. Each page—or panel—must harmonize with adjacent pages or panels, since readers see several panels at once when they open a brochure.

The Cover

Simplicity is a key to effective cover design. Brochure covers are often too complex typographically and contain too much information.

The original cover of "Understanding & Influencing Student Motivation" illustrates overuse of typographic elements. The makeover version has been simplified by using fewer typefaces and type sizes. The title gains impact by being reset in the same typeface and type size. Also, the double bar under "Student Motivation" was removed, since it competes with the title.

Organizing information in logical, sequential order also results in simplicity. Sometimes typography alone can achieve this, but visuals can enhance the type, too.

Take a look at the cover of the Howard County Showcase 1986 brochure. The original front cover didn't generate excitement. Since most of the type was set in the same size, the page had an overall "gray" look. There was also no clear hierarchy of information.

The revised cover, however, promises a fresh, contemporary approach to the issue of secondary education. The page border has been replaced by footsteps that lead the reader's eyes through the copy, now divided into easy-to-read segments.

Removing distractions and using typography to establish a hierarchy of importance is also illustrated in the D.I.N. Publications "Saying No" brochure. The original title uses a single typeface, which weakens the "How and Why" subtitle. The new cover's screened box separates "Saying No" from "How and Why," giving emphasis to the subtitle.

The importance of the cover in influencing readers is perhaps best illustrated by the InterPhase "Group Interaction and Weight Management" brochure.

The original front cover presents a less-than-dynamic appearance. It's difficult to read, lacks a dominant visual and doesn't present an upbeat, professional image.

In the makeover, organizational refinements made to the front cover include adding a line at the top that summarizes the subject and targets its audience. The key words in the title—"Group" and "Weight"—are then emphasized. The ampersand is enlarged to become the dominant visual on the page.

The cover has also been simplified by relocating the phrase "At the Bahia in beautiful San Diego" (which makes a better closing statement), and by removing the address and phone number, which aren't needed until after readers have decided to attend.

Front cover simplicity and organization are also evident in the Swimex brochure revision. In the original, all the type "shouts"—it's too large and too bold. As a result, it's hard to know where to begin reading, and the firm's motto, address and phone number get lost in the clutter.

The revised Swimex brochure illustrates another function of the front cover—to provide a transition into the inside copy. One of the most important rules direct-response marketers teach is "begin selling on the front cover." The original Swimex cover doesn't lead you to read the rest of the brochure. Because no specific products are mentioned, you can't tell what is being sold or what it costs. Moving two high-interest products to the cover clarifies the intent of the brochure and frees up space for larger product illustrations on the following pages.

The transitional role of covers is also shown by continuing the water graphic on the inside pages. This simple graphic device links the cover with the rest of the brochure.

Inside Information

Each panel of a two- or three-fold brochure must stand on its own but not compete with adjacent panels.

The Institute for Motivational Development brochure shows two ways to accomplish this. One side of the brochure is anchored by a large, single headline spanning two panels. On the other side of the brochure, one panel is screened to create a contrasting visual.

Although the panels of a brochure should relate to each other, each panel should be an entity in itself. The Inter-Phase brochure shows how simplicity, organization and panel-to-panel continuity can work together. The original panels are gray, partly because of the rounded border that unifies the panels and the monotone screen behind the copy. This screen reduces the legibility of the individual topics.

The panels of the revised brochure are easier to read because only the headings are screened, and they're set in upper- and lowercase type instead of all uppercase. The screened headings overlap the screened borders throughout, giving panel-to-panel continuity.

Using white space to provide internal organization is illustrated by the Cornell Evening Discussion Series brochure. The original inside pages use so much reversed type, they're difficult to read. Readability is enhanced by eliminating most of the reversed type, reducing its size and—most important—putting the dates and times in separate columns.

Reviewing Your Brochures

As you review your brochures, ask yourself some questions:

- ✔ Have the covers been simplified as much as possible?
- ✔ Do the covers communicate the appropriate tone?

✔ Do the covers provide a smooth transition to the inside pages?

✔ Are the inside pages and panels unified by a dominant visual?

✔ Is the material on each page or panel easy to read?

Most important, do the brochures present a logical hierarchy of information, divided into manageable parts? Is key information easier to find than subordinate information?

FLYERS

Flyers often form a large part of an organization's print communication. A flyer can be designed as a poster to hang on the wall or as a solicitation to potential customers or distributed to regular customers for later reading. Because they often are posted on the wall, most flyers are printed on one side only. The art work used in flyers can also be used for newspaper or magazine ads.

The Headline

Since flyers succeed only when they attract the attention of passers-by, headlines are more important here than in brochures. A flyer's headline must be easily read at a distance.

Many of the "before" examples in this section illustrate the dangers of "burying" headlines—by not using enough contrast between the head and the text. The Ada Expo '86 brochure is a good example. In the original, "Capture Your Share of a $20 Billion Market" doesn't stand out. The revised headline is bigger and bolder—and can be read from farther away.

The Journalism Association of Community Colleges flyer also illustrates the importance of eye-catching headlines.

Reducing the size of the logo and adding white space make room for a bigger headline.

Projecting a Strong Identity

Because flyers must make an immediate visual impression, the flyer should be designed to attract attention, and your organization's name should be prominently displayed. Look at the Monte Vista Market flyer. The original presents a somewhat low-key image—the undistinguished typeface and distracting borders don't make the market look like a place to come for Chicken Cordon Bleu! The logo and border in the revised version are definitely more contemporary and upscale, as is the new artwork.

The "Son of Heaven: Imperial Arts of China" flyer illustrates a similar problem. People are being invited to a special exhibition of China's rarest national treasures; but in the original flyer, the tone is more blunt than elegant. Adding white space enhances the exhibition title and the striking artwork. This, along with an orderly presentation of information down the left column, creates an image far more appropriate to the event and its audience.

Encouraging Response

The final requirement for a successful flyer is that it be quick and easy to read and respond to. Phone numbers must be large enough to be easily located and remembered, and coupons should be easy to find and use.

Returning to the Monte Vista Market flyer, notice how much easier it is to find the phone number in the revised version.

Price information is another important aspect of a flyer's "call to action." In the original "Son of Heaven" flyer, the price—although set in large type—is hard to find because it's surrounded by other information set in the same typeface and size. In the makeover, however, the price is surrounded by white space and set in a distinctive typeface and size. The price now logically appears after the descriptive "selling" statements that justify it. After you read about this special preview, the ticket price seems like a bargain!

The Son of Heaven flyer also shows how important it is for coupons to *look* like coupons. In the original flyer, the coupon is barely separated from the rest of the flyer by a horizontal row of bullets. In the revision, however, the coupon is neatly boxed. Notice how your eye is drawn to the "Absolute Deadline" statement at the right—this would certainly increase early registrations.

Take Another Look

Ask yourself these questions as you evaluate your flyers:

- ✔ Do they communicate all the information a reader needs to respond favorably?
- ✔ Is it clear how readers can respond to my message?
- ✔ Do my flyers accurately reflect the feeling I wish to communicate?
- ✔ Are the headlines large enough to attract attention from a distance?

Moving On

As you look at the examples that follow, notice how the revisions work on two levels. On a conscious level, the information is easier to read. On a subconscious level, the makeovers present a more appropriate image of the organization. Whether it's related to a service business, retail merchandise or a cultural exhibit, each revision presents an image more in keeping with content and potential audience.

O ften, reorganizing blocks of copy and adding emphasis to key phrases can spur reader interest.

The outside cover is awkward and uninviting, with three different type treatments on four lines.

The message is cramped in this three-panel format; an 11 x 17, four-panel format allows better design at little additional cost.

ORIGINAL

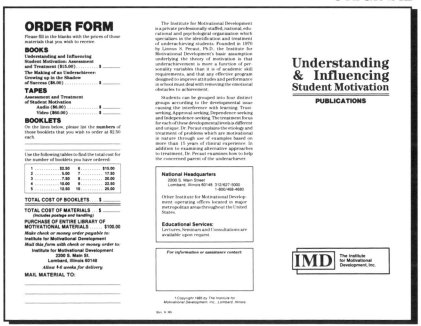

Enlarging the headline and placing it in a more prominent area set the tone and draw even a casual reader into the piece.

A simple screen gives the logo more identity.

Moving the order form to the inside of the piece (see next page) means that customers don't have to flip back and forth to place their orders.

MAKEOVER

"But you have so much potential..."

No matter how experienced the teachers, how beautiful the building, or how good the football team, a young person will not learn if he or she has chosen not to learn. The end result is that underachieving students are our nation's greatest wasted natural resource.

Now there is help for parents, teachers, administrators and counselors who have been continually frustrated in their attempts to "light a fire" under youngsters who don't seem to care about school or anything else. Since 1970, the Institute for Motivational Development in Lombard, Illinois, has had remarkable success in motivating such young people. The Institute is based on the ideas of its founder, Dr. Linnus S. Pecaut, who, through his research in clinical psychology, developed techniques for the assessment and treatment of student motivational problems.

Dr. Pecaut and his associates have counseled thousands of young people, of which the majority experienced greater success in school once they had been counseled utilizing IMD's techniques. Most also improved their relationships with families and peers.'

Through lectures, seminars, and graduate classes, Dr. Pecaut has directly presented his theories and techniques of motivation to thousands of people. He has been the subject of feature articles by *The Washington Post*, *Woman's Day*, *Better Homes and Gardens* and major newspapers

throughout the country. He has appeared on the Phil Donahue Show and other national and local radio and television programs. IMD presents Dr. Pecaut's theories and techniques of motivation in a compact book, in booklets, and on audio and video tapes. These materials fit the needs of parents, teachers, counselors, administrators, psychologists and business executives—any one who wants to motivate others to do the work they are capable of doing.

All materials are presented in a bright, understandable style. In preparing them, Dr. Pecaut has included many specific anecdotes and examples drawn from his experience. He has focused on day-to-day problems that any adult faces in working with young people—particularly unmotivated young people.

The Institute for Motivational Development is a private professionally-staffed, national, educational and psychological organization which specializes in the identification and treatment of underachieving students. Founded in 1970 by Linnus S. Pecaut, Ph.D., the Institute for Motivational Development's basic assumption underlying the theory of motivation is that underachievement is more a function of personality variables than it is of academic skill requirements, and that any effective program designed to improve attitudes and performance in school must deal with removing the emotional obstacles to achievement.

Students can be grouped into four distinct groups according to the developmental issue causing the interference with learning: Trust-seeking, Approval-seeking, Dependence-seeking and Independence-seeking. The treatment focus for each of these developmental levels is different and unique. Dr. Pecaut explains the etiology and treatment of problems which are motivational in nature through use of examples based on more that 15 years of clinical experience. In addition to examining alternative approaches to treatment, Dr. Pecaut examines how to help the concerned parent of the underachiever.

National Headquarters

2200 S. Main Street
Lombard, Illinois 60148
312/627-5000
1-800/468-4680

Other Institute for Motivational Development operating offices located in major metropolitan areas throughout the United States.

Educational Services:
Lectures, Seminars and Consultations are available upon request.

For Information or assistance contact:

©Copyright 1985 by The Institute for Motivational Development, Inc., Lombard, Illinois

Rev. 8/86

Understanding & Influencing Student Motivation

PUBLICATIONS

IMD

The Institute for Motivational Development, Inc.

R eorganizing key elements lets the reader quickly
make an informed decision.

Inconsistent type treatments in the various categories send a confusing message to the reader.

ORIGINAL

"But you have so much potential ..."

No matter how experienced the teachers, how beautiful the building, or how good the football team, a young person will not learn if he or she has chosen not to learn. The end result is that underachieving students are our nation's greatest wasted natural resource.

Now there is help for parents, teachers, administrators and counselors who have been continually frustrated in their attempts to "light a fire" under youngsters who don't seem to care about school or anything else. Since 1970, the Institute for Motivational Development in Lombard, Illinois, has had remarkable success in motivating such young people. The Institute is based on the ideas of its founder, Dr. Linnus S. Pecaut, who, through his research in clinical psychology, developed techniques for the assessment and treatment of student motivational problems.

Dr. Pecaut and his associates have counseled thousands of young people, of which the majority experienced greater success in school once they had been counseled utilizing IMD's techniques. Most also improved their relationships with families and peers.

Through lectures, seminars, and graduate classes, Dr. Pecaut has directly presented his theories and techniques of motivation to thousands of people. He has been the subject of feature articles by *The Washington Post*, *Woman's Day*, *Better Homes and Gardens* and major newspapers throughout the country. He has appeared on The Phil Donahue Show and other national and local radio and television programs. IMD presents Dr. Pecaut's theories and techniques of motivation in a compact book, in booklets, and on audio and video tapes. These materials fit the needs of parents, teachers, counselors, administrators, psychologists, and business executives — anyone who wants to motivate others to do the work they are capable of doing.

All materials are presented in a bright, understandable style. In preparing them, Dr. Pecaut has included many specific anecdotes and examples drawn from his experience. He has focused on day-to-day problems that any adult faces in working with young people — particularly unmotivated young people.

PUBLICATIONS

BOOKS

Understanding and Influencing Student Motivation: Assessment and Treatment ($15.00)

Dr. Pecaut explains why certain students lack motivation, both in school and out. Underachievers are grouped into four basic personality types: Trust-seeking, Approval-seeking, Dependence-seeking, and Independence-seeking. Typescripts and analyses of actual diagnostic interviews and treatment techniques specific to each type of underachiever are discussed in detail. Dr. Pecaut's book can and has formed the backbone of the disciplinary and counseling system for families, schools, and other organizations.

The Making of an Underachiever: Growing up in the Shadow of Success ($8.00)

Dr. Pecaut provides a poignant description of how successful fathers raise sons who manifest attributes so disdained by high achievers: uncertainty, irresponsibility, and the inability to function without constant supervision. His thesis is that the success of the father and the underachievement of the son are linked together and rooted in issues prior to the son's birth. Dr. Pecaut's book will deeply move every parent who was or has an underachieving child and will provide provocative insights for any father who wants to raise an achieving son.

CASSETTE TAPES

Assessment and Treatment of Student Motivation - Audio Tape ($6.00) - Video Tape ($60.00)

In these cassette lecture tapes (60 min.), Dr. Pecaut explains the nature of motivation and the treatment of the obstacles to motivation for children, adolescents, and adults. Included are explanations of the different personality types and techniques for treating each type. These tapes are excellent for use with individuals, parents, and groups who desire a basic knowledge of the IMD system.

The audio tape is recommended for individuals and parents; the video tape is recommended for groups; however, both tapes are beneficial for any persons who wish detailed information regarding underachievement.

BOOKLETS

The following booklets focus on specialized subjects not covered in **Understanding and Influencing Student Motivation** or in the cassette tapes. All are 16-20 pages in length and sell for $2.50 apiece. Order by number on the order blank.

1. *Failure: A Search for One's Family*
   This booklet traces the unconscious meaning of failure as an attempt to recapture unmet past and present emotional needs in one's family and how to interrupt unconscious patterns of failure.

2. *The Dynamics and Treatment of Student Indifferences*
   Nothing provokes adults more than the youngster whose only response to school is a big yawn. But you **can** light a fire under such young people, using the methods outlined here.

3. *Individual and Group Approaches to Underachievement*
   Dr. Pecaut explains which causes of underachievement are best dealt with one-on-one and which are most effectively handled in groups, and the specifics of different treatment.

4. *How to Stimulate Self-Confidence*
   There are ways to help a person develop the belief in himself that anybody needs to be successful. This booklet examines the dynamics of inferiority.

5. *Telling Someone I'm Angry*
   This booklet takes an unusual look at one of the most common problems of the frustrated, underachieving student. Namely, that his underachievement is a passive statement of anger toward others.

6. *When Bright Kids Fail to Learn*
   Bright but unmotivated kids **can** reach their potential, if you assist them in the ways outlined.

7. *How to Identify a Severe Emotional Disturbance*
   This provocative booklet knocks down several myths as it suggests signs to watch for in determining whether a youngster is severely disturbed.

8. *Interrupting Manipulative Behavior*
   Countless classes have been ruined by the student who "acts out" and turns the classroom into a stage for his performances. Listed are practical ways to help him, at the same time that you manage the class or group more effectively.

9. *Getting the Family to Cooperate When Their Children Are Having Problems*
   Every teacher, counselor, or psychologist knows that you can't motivate a young person if the family won't cooperate. Explained are ways to encourage that cooperation.

10. *Helping the Anxious Student Without Becoming Anxious*
    If you know youngsters who fear exams, other kids, their own families or failure, this booklet will give valuable assistance.

Note how even small amounts of additional white space let readers quickly browse the lists.

It's okay to have white space on the bottom of one or more columns.

The screened order form sets it apart from the body copy for easy reference.

MAKEOVER

PUBLICATIONS

BOOKS

Understanding and Influencing Student Motivation: Assessment and Treatment ($15.00)

Dr. Pecaut explains why certain students lack motivation, both in school and out. Underachievers are grouped into four basic personality types. Trust-seeking, Approval-seeking, Dependence-seeking, and Independence-seeking. Typescripts and analyses of actual diagnostic interviews and treatment techniques specific to each type are discussed in detail. Dr. Pecaut's book can and has formed the backbone of disciplinary and counseling system for families, schools, and other organizations.

The Making of an Underachiever: Growing up in the Shadow of Success ($8.00)

Dr. Pecaut provides a poignant description of how successful fathers raise sons who manifest attributes so disdained by high achievers: uncertainty, irresponsibility, and the inability to function without constant supervision. His thesis that the success of the father and the underachievement of the son are linked together and rooted in issues prior to the son's birth. Dr. Pecaut's book will deeply move every parent who was or has an underachieving child and will provide provocative insights for any father who wants to raise an achieving son.

CASSETTE TAPES

Assessment and Treatment of Student Motivation-Audio Tape ($6.00)-Video Tape ($60.00)

In these cassette lecture tapes (60 min.), Dr. Pecaut explains the nature of motivation and the treatment of the obstacles to motivation for children, adolescents, and adults. Included are explanations of the different personality types and techniques for treating each type. These tapes are excellent for use with individuals, parents, and groups who desire a basic knowledge of the IMD system.

The audio tape is recommended for individuals and parents; the video tape is recommended for groups; however, both tapes are beneficial for any persons who wish detailed information regarding underachievement.

BOOKLETS

The following booklets focus on specialized subjects not covered in the Understanding and Influencing Student Motivation or in the cassette tapes. All are 16-20 pages in length and sell for $2.50 apiece. Order by number on the order blank.

1. **Failure: A Search for One's Family**
   This booklet traces the unconscious meaning of failure as an attempt to recapture unmet past and present emotional needs in one's family and how to interrupt unconscious patterns of failure.

2. **The Dynamics and Treatment of Student Indifference**
   Nothing provokes adults more than the youngster whose only response to school is a big yawn. But you can light a fire under such young people, using the methods outlined here.

3. **Individual and Group Approaches to Underachievement**
   Dr. Pecaut explains which causes of underachievement are best dealt with one-on-one and which are most effectively handled in groups, and the specifics of different treatment.

4. **How to Stimulate Self-Confidence**
   There are ways to help a person develop the belief in himself that anybody needs to be successful. This booklet examines the dynamics of inferiority.

5. **Telling Someone I'm Angry**
   This booklet takes an unusual look at one of the most common problems of the frustrated, underachieving student. Namely, that his underachievement is a passive statement of anger toward others.

6. **When Bright Kids Fail to Learn**
   Bright but unmotivated kids can reach their potential, if you assist them in the ways outlined.

7. **How to Identify a Severe Emotional Disturbance**
   This provocative booklet knocks down several myths as it suggests signs to watch for in determining whether a youngster is severely disturbed.

8. **Interrupting Manipulative Behavior**
   Countless classes have been ruined by the student who "acts out" and turns the classroom into a stage for his performances. Listed are practical ways to help him, at the same time that you manage the class or group more effectively.

9. **Getting the Family to Cooperate When Their Children Are Having Problems**
   Every teacher, counselor, or psychologist knows that you can't motivate a young person if the family won't cooperate. Explained are ways to encourage that cooperation.

10. **Helping the Anxious Student Without Becoming Anxious**
    If you know youngsters who fear exams, other kids, their own families or failure, this booklet will give valuable assistance.

ORDER FORM

Please fill in the blanks with the prices of those materials that you wish to receive.

BOOKS

Understanding and Influencing Student Motivation: Assessment and Treatment ($15.00) .... $_____

The Making of an Underachiever: Growing up in the Shadow of Success ($8.00) .... $_____

TAPES

Assessment and Treatment of Student Motivation
Audio ($6.00) .... $_____
Video ($60.00) .... $_____

BOOKLETS

On the line below, please list the numbers of those booklets that you wish to order at $2.50 each.

_____

Use the following tables to find the total cost for the number of booklets you have ordered.

1	$2.50	6		$15.00
2	5.00	7		17.50
3	7.50	8		20.00
4	10.00	9		22.50
5	12.50	10		25.00

Total cost of booklets .... $_____

TOTAL COST OF MATERIALS $_____
(includes postage and handling)

Purchase of entire library of educational materials $100.00

Mail this form with check or money order payable to:
Institute for Motivational Development
2200 S. Main St.
Lombard, Illinois 60148   *Allow 4-6 weeks for delivery*

MAIL MATERIAL TO:

_____

_____

_____

The Makeover Book   95

Electronic clip art is becoming widely overused—much like public domain woodcuts were in the Sixties. Use clip art carefully!

ORIGINAL

Hasty desktop layout can result in a boxy effect, filled with segregated blocks and awkward white space.

Organize information in terms of what's most important to the reader. For example, is "Spring 1987" as important as "Labor Workshops"?

MAKEOVER

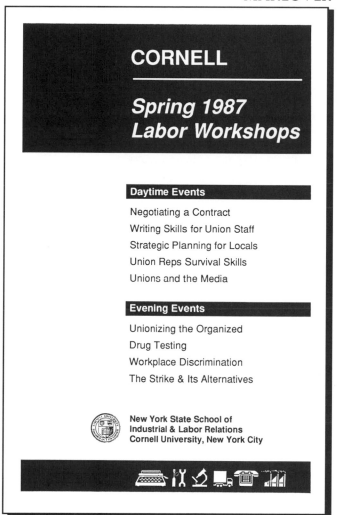

Better leading makes important course information more readable.

Seals and other insignia are sized to fit supporting type.

T ools of emphasis, such as reverses, thick rules and bullets, must be used with restraint. If everything is important, then what's unimportant?

"Reverse overkill," one of desktop publishing's seven deadly sins, screams for attention from all directions, confusing readers and diluting the message.

Ancillary information, such as "$2.50 registration fee," shouldn't appear as an integral part of a logo.

ORIGINAL

Reversed type is restricted to the headline, creating a quieter, more organized reading environment.

Note how subtle uses of bold and italic and varying type sizes can be used to organize information as effectively as bullets and other attention-getters.

MAKEOVER

Cornell ILR's Spring 1987 Evening Discussion Series...

is designed to encourage discussion and debate among unionists on important and current topics. Speakers with expertise in each topic will facilitate the discussions.

UNIONIZING THE ORGANIZED

Thursday
March 26
6:00-9:00 p.m.

This workshop will discuss overcoming worker apathy, increasing member participation—and promoting a feeling among members that it's their union.
Actual union internal organizing drives, one-to-one programs, campaigns to win contracts and other activities will be discussed and analyzed.

Discussion Leader:
Ken Margolies, Director of Labor Programs, Cornell ILR in NYC, formerly Organizing Director of the Communication Workers of America.

DRUG TESTING: WHAT EVERY WORKER SHOULD KNOW

Thursday
April 9
6:00-9:00 p.m.

The use of mandatory drug testing is spreading rapidly in the public and private sectors. This forum will explore such issues raised for workers by mandatory drug testing as:

Are the tests an invasion of privacy?
Do they violate collective bargaining agreements or laws?
How reliable is drug screening?
Union programs for dealing with drugs on the job
Negotiating contract language on drug screening

Discussion Leaders:
Robin Herbert, Resident Physician, Division of Environmental and Occupational Medicine, Mt. Sinai Hospital; Co-Chair, Health and Technology Committee, New York Committee on Occupational Safety and Health (NYCOSH).
Charles Grantham, Executive Vice President, National Basketball Association Players Association.

WORKPLACE DISCRIMINATION

Thursday
April 30
6:00-9:00 p.m.

What are the laws and regulations about workplace discrimination on the basis of:

race, sex, age, sexual preference, marital status, disabilities, national origin, religion

Are these laws being enforced fairly?
What is sexual harassment?
How is affirmative action affecting workers?

Discussion Leaders:
K.C. Wagner, Director, Working Woman's Institute
Gail Wright, Assistant Counsel, NAACP Legal Defense and Educational Fund. Ms. Wright specializes in employment discrimination cases; she formerly wrote a column for *Essence* Magazine and has lectured widely on civil rights issues.
Eddie Gonzalez, Director, Hispanic Labor Studies Program, Cornell ILR.

THE STRIKE AND ITS ALTERNATIVES

Thursday
May 7
6:00-9:00 p.m.

Throughout history, the strike has been the most visible—if not the most common—tactic workers have used to improve working conditions. In recent years several highly public strikes have been broken. This forum looks at the strike and other tactics and strategies unions are using to achieve their goals. We will discuss:

Are today's workers turned off to strikes?
Are unions supporting each others' strikes?
Where have strikes been used effectively?
What are the alternatives to strikes?

Discussion Leaders from the Labor Scholars, an Advisory Committee to the NYSSILR Extension Labor Programs. The Labor Scholars is a group of workers, students and alumni of Cornell's Labor-Liberal Arts programs who are dedicated to supporting the labor movement and organizing new workers.

Cornell Conference Center
15 East 26th Street, Fourth Floor, NYC
A $2.50 registration fee covers light refreshments and materials.

As scanning and layout techniques become even more efficient, readers won't easily forgive slapdash, unappealing advertisements.

ORIGINAL

Headline, illustrations and logo placed randomly on the page create an unappealing message.

The all-important address at the bottom of the page looks like an afterthought.

MAKEOVER

A revised headline and illustration provide a more inviting context for the message.

Screens of varying values look like layers of water.

Note how graphics juxtaposed on screens give a three-dimensional, kinetic effect.

ORIGINAL

You can improve
mediocre illustrations
by drawing attention to
surrounding type
and layout.

Avoid thick rules and
borders when informa-
tion and graphics are
dense—they usually
bury the intended
message.

MAKEOVER

The screened water motif is carried to the following pages.

Illustrations placed in a natural downward flow, rather than scattered around the page, make the piece more inviting and easier to read.

The address is repeated throughout the brochure and a telephone number has been added—you never know what page a customer will be looking at when he or she decides to act!

Readers expect a high level of credibility from brochures—so they should quietly persuade, much like a booklet or newsletter.

ORIGINAL

Type that runs in and out of screens often is difficult to read.

MAKEOVER

SAYING
NO

How and Why

Teaching kids how to say "No" to drugs and alcohol is a main topic just about everywhere these days.

And it's a good thing, too. Learning *how* to say "No" is an awfully important step in preventing substance abuse problems from getting started—or from getting out of hand, if they have already started.

Still, no less important—increasing and reinforcing real, long-lasting change—is getting the *why's* and *why not's* of drugs and alcohol across to young people.

That's where we come in.

We've worked hard and long over the past two decades to build believability with young people. Our friends tell us we succeed—where others often fail.

We present the facts (and *just* the facts) in an easy-to-read, illustrated format—one that communicates the truth about drugs and alcohol, health and sexuality, and other health topics to millions of readers every year.

Because it isn't enough to say "No." Young people today need to know why not.

But don't take our word for it. Send for our special
"Why to Say 'No'" Sampler today.
See for yourself what we do—and you'll know why it works.

d'n
PUBLICATIONS

America's best in believability. Since 1967.

Thinner rules draw more attention to the copy block.

A short, thicker rule at the bottom complements the logo and weights the piece vertically.

Be sure that inside pages are designed to reflect and complement brochure covers.

Headers and subheads are inconsistent, making it difficult to distinguish between titles and categories.

Screens juxtaposed over type make readers work to find information.

ORIGINAL

Say 'Yes' to Effective, Low-Cost D.I.N. Publications!

PAMPHLETS
25¢ each
Single titles 10/$1.95, 50/$6, 100/$11, 1000/$90

CHEMICAL AWARENESS
Information for general audiences.

102	Cocaine — *Revised!*
103	Comprehensive Drug Knowledge Test
108	Alcohol, Tobacco, Caffeine & Pregnancy
117	Smoking & Health — *New!*
119	'Ludes: New Facts about Methaqualone
124	Marijuana: Medical Uses
125	Marijuana: Personality & Behavior
126	Marijuana: Health Effects
128	Substances & Safety — *New!*
129	Pot: A Guide for Young People
134	Valium, Librium, & the Benzodiazepine Blues
137	Downers: Distressing Facts — *Revised!*
138	Aspirin: Uses & Abuses
157	Darvon/Darvocet and other Prescription Narcotics
161	Everyday Detox — *New!*

STREET SURVIVAL™
Youth-oriented street drug information.

101	Crystal, Crank, & Speedy Stuff — *Revised!*
105	Heroin: The Junk Equation
111	Barbiturates: The Oblivion Express
115	Acid: LSD Today
123	Dusted: Facts about PCP
133	Peyote & Mescaline
134	Psilocybin: 'Magic Mushrooms' De-Mystified — *New!*
135	Cleaning Yourself Up — *Revised!*
142	Amyl/Butyl Nitrite & Nitrous Oxide — *Revised!*
145	Lookalikes: The Second Generation
149	T's & Blues: Double Trouble
153	MDA/MDM: Chemical Pursuit of Ecstasy — *Revised!*
159	Designer Drugs — *Revised!*
164	Crack Attack: The New Cocaine Explosion — *New!*

ALCOHOL & ALCOHOLISM
For both problem drinkers and general audiences.

110	The *Other* Gay Plague: Gay/Lesbian Alcoholism-*New!*
120	Alcohol & Health
121	Alcohol: Combinations with Other Drugs — *New!*
130	Booze: A Guide for Young People
140	Cause & Defect: Fetal Alcohol Syndrome — *New!*
156	Hangovers: The Agony after the Ecstasy
801	Problem Drinking & Alcoholism — *Revised!*
802	Denial: The Defense that Disables
803	I'm Not that Bad, Yet — *Revised!*

804	Co-Alcoholics: The Partner Paradox — *New!*
805	The Problem Drinking Continuum — *Revised!*
806	DWI: Facts about Drunk Driving
807	Sex After Sobriety: A Woman's Guide
808	Kids of Alcoholics: Growing Up Unheard — *New!*
809	Theme Song for Recovery: A Communication Guide for Alcoholics & Families of Alcoholics — *New!*
810	The Triangle Game: Breaking Communication Triangles in Recovery— *New!*
811	Let's Make A Deal: Winning Through Family Negotiation — *New!*
812	I Love/Love You Not: Recovering Intimacy — *New!*

HEALTH & SEXUALITY
Practical information for general audiences.

H101	Not Everything Wrong Down There Is VD
H102	Male Responsibility in Birth Control — *New!*
H103	STD Blues
H104	The Herpes Perplex
H105	AIDS: Ending the 'Fear Plague' — *Revised!*

'ALL ABOUT' DRUGS & ALCOHOL
Informative, illustrated materials for 5th-8th graders.

104	Downers — *New!*	143	Sniffing — *New!*
150	Alcohol— *Revised!*	151	Marijuana— *Revised!*
152	Speed— *Revised!*	162	Smoking — *New!*
160	Comix — *New!*	163	Saying 'No' — *New!*

ELDER HEALTH™
Health information for seniors, by seniors.

181	Taking Care: A Medication Guide for Older People
182	Beating the Blues: A Guide to Overcoming Depression
183	What Senior Citizens Should Know About Drugs & Alcohol — *Revised!*

MISCELLANY

201	D.I.N. Newservice. Innovative newsletter on behavior and health. Sample $2.50, 6 issues/$15.
CT1	Alcohol, Health & Downer Drugs. Funny audiotape points out real dangers. $3.95 each.
425	Overdose, Poison, & Emergency Chart 25¢ each, 10/$1.95, 50/$6, 100/$11
426	Drug Emergency Flowchart: A Step-by-Step Schematic $1.00 each, 10/$7, 100/$50
430	'Hugs—Not Drugs' Bumpersticker $1.00 each, 10/$7.50, 100/$60, 1000/$400

BOOKLETS
$1.50 each, 10/$11, 50/$45, 100/$85, 1000/$725

203	Drugs of Abuse: Actions & Hazards (Irwin) -*Revised!*
204	Drug Abuse: A Handbook for Parents (Wittenberg)
208	Drugs: Crisis Information (Lampe)
210	Tranx: Minor Tranquilizers, Major Problems (Parker)
211	Drugs, Alcohol, & Pregnancy (Dye)
212	Drugs & Alcohol: Handbook for Young People (Parker)
215	Hallucinogens (Acton) $3.50 each, 10/$25
217	PR: A Guide to Low-Cost Use of Media (Cauble)
219	Preg-Not: A Modern Guide to the Pill & Other Contraceptives (James)
220	Health Problems & Aging (Faherty)
221	Positive Parenting: Building Character in Young People (St. Romain) $1.00 each, 10/$8, 50/$35,100/$60, 1000/$500
222	Beyond Drugs & Alcohol: A Guide to Personal Growth in Recovery (Parker) — *New!*

BOOKS
Selections from outside publishers.

904	Down-To-Earth Health Guide (Schoenfeld) $8.95
905	Drugs & Drug Abuse (Addiction Research Fdn.) $29.95
906	Cocaine: Seduction & Solution (Stone, Fromme, & Kagen) $13.95
918	Chop Wood, Carry Water: Finding Spiritual Fulfillment in Everyday Life (New Age Journal) $11.95
919	How To Get Off Drugs (Rolling Stone) $7.95

SPECIALIZED INFORMATION SERVICE
In-depth reports on current literature & research.
$3.50 each; Complete set of 12/$35.00

350	Marijuana — *Revised!*	356	Inhalants
351	T's and Blues	357	Methaqualone
352	Lookalike Drugs	358	Heroin
353	Paraquat	359	PCP— *Revised!*
354	Cocaine — *Revised!*	360	Designer Drugs— *New!*
355	LSD	361	Stimulants — *New!*

SPECIAL SAMPLERS
SAVE MONEY, SAVE TIME!

501-P	Pamphlet Sampler $12.95
501-J	Booklet Sampler $16.95
501-N	"Why To Say 'No'" Sampler $69.95 Contains everything listed, except books
501-E	Everything Sampler $129.95. Everything listed.

Reverses define major categories; 40 percent screens define sub-categories—a helpful way to organize complex lists.

MAKEOVER

Say 'YES' to Effective, Low-Cost D.I.N. Publications!

PAMPHLETS

25 cents each
Single titles: 10/$1.95, 50/$6, 100/$11, 1000/$90

Chemical Awareness

Information for general audiences.

102 Cocaine — Revised!
103 Comprehensive Drug Knowledge Test
108 Alcohol, Tobacco, Caffeine & Pregnancy
117 Smoking & Health — New!
119 'Ludes: New Facts about Methaqualone
124 Marijuana: Medical Uses
125 Marijuana: Personality & Behavior
126 Marijuana: Health Effects
128 Substances & Safety   New!
129 Pot: A Guide for Young People
134 Valium, Librium, & the Benzodiazepine Blues
137 Downers: Distressing Facts — Revised!
138 Aspirin: Uses & Abuses
157 Darvon/darvocet and other Prescription Narcotics
161 Everyday Detox — New!

Street Survival

Youth-oriented street drug information.

101 Crystal, Crank, & Speedy Stuff — Revised!
105 Heroin: The Junk Equation
111 Barbiturates: The Oblivion Express
115 Acid: LSD Today
123 Dusted: Facts about PCP
133 Peyote & Mescaline
134 Psilocybin: 'Magic Mushrooms' De-Mystified — New!
135 Cleaning Yourself Up —Revised!
142 Amyl/Butyl Nitrite & Nitrous Oxide —Revised!
145 Lookalikes: The Second Generation
149 T's & Blues: Double Trouble
153 MDA/MDM: Chemical Pursuit of Ecstasy — Revised!
159 Designer Drugs — Revised!
164 Crack attack: The New Cocaine Explosion — New!

Alcohol & Alcoholism

For both problem drinkers and general audiences.

110 The Other Gay Plague: Gay/Lesbian Alcoholism — New!
120 Alcohol & Health
121 Alcohol: Combinations with Other Drugs — New!
130 Booze: A Guide for Young People
140 Cause & Defect: Fetal Alcohol Syndrome — New!
156 Hangovers: The Agony after the Ecstasy
801 Problem Drinking & Alcoholism — Revised!
802 Denial: The Defense that Disables
803 I'm Not that Bad, Yet — Revised!

804 Co-Alcoholics: The Partner Paradox — New!
805 The Problem Drinking continuum — Revised!
806 DWI: Facts about Drunk Driving
807 Sex After Sobriety: A Woman's Guide
808 Kids of Alcoholics: Growing Up Unheard — New!
809 Theme Song for Recovery: A Communication Guide
     for Alcoholics & Families of Alcoholics — New!
810 The Triangle Game: breaking Communication Triangles
     in Recovery — New!
811 Let's Make A Deal:
     Winning Through Family Negotiation — New!
812 I Love/Love You Not: Recovering Intimacy — New!

Health & Sexuality

Practical information for general audiences.

H101 Not Everything Wrong Down There Is VD
H102 Male Responsibility in Birth Control — New!
H103 STD Blues
H104 The Herpes Perplex
H105 AIDS: Ending the 'Fear Plague' — Revised!

'All About' Drugs & Alcohol

Informative, illustrated materials for 5th-8th graders.

104 Downers — New!   143 Sniffing — New!
150 Alcohol — Revised!   151 Marijuana — Revised!
152 Speed — New!   162 Smoking — New!
160 Comix — Revised!   163 Saying 'No' — New!

Elder Health

Health Information for seniors, by seniors

181 Taking Care: A Medication Guide for Older People
182 Beating the Blues: A guide to Overcoming Depression
183 What Senior Citizens Should Know About
     Drugs & Alcohol — Revised!

MISCELLANY

201 D.I.N. Newservice. Innovative newsletter on behavior
     and health. Sample $2.50, 6 issues/$15.
CT1 Alcohol, Health & Downer Drugs.
     Funny audiotape points out real dangers. $3.95 each.
425 Overdose, Poison, & Emergency Chart
     25cents each, 10/$1.95, 50/$6, 100/$11
426 Drug Emergency Flowchart: A Step-by-Step Schematic
     $1.00 each, 10/$7, 100/$50
430 'Hugs—Not Drugs' Bumpersticker
     $1.00 each, 10/$7.50, 100/$60, 1000/$400

BOOKLETS

$1.50 each, 10/$11, 50/$45, 100/$85, 1000/$725

203 Drugs of Abuse: actions & Hazards (Irwin)— Revised!
204 Drug Abuse: A Handbook for Parents (Wittenberg)
208 Drugs: Crisis Information (Lampe)
210 Tranx: Minor Tranquilizers, Major Problems (Parker)
211 Drugs, Alcohol, & Pregnancy (Dye)
212 Drugs & Alcohol: Handbook for Young People (Parker)
215 Hallucinogens (Axton) $3.50 each, 10/$25
217 PR: Guide to Low-Cost Use of Media (Cauble)
219 Preg-Not: A Modern Guide to the Pill
     & Other Contraceptives (James)
220 Health Problems & Aging (Faherty)
221 Positive Parenting: Building Character
     in Young People (St. Romain)
     $1.00 each. 10/$8, 50/$35, 100/$60, 1000/$500
222 Beyond Drugs & Alcohol: A Guide
     to Personal Growth in Recovery (Parker) — New!

BOOKS

Selections from outside publishers.

904 Down-To-Earth Health Guide (Schoenfeld) $8.95
905 Drugs & Drug Abuse (Addiction Research Fdn.) $29.95
906 Cocaine: Seduction & Solution
     (Stone, Fromme, & Kagen) $13.95
918 Chop Wood, Carry Water: Finding Spiritual Fulfillment in
     Everyday Life (New Age Journal) $11.95
919 How To Get Off Drugs (Rolling Stone) $7.95

SPECIALIZED INFORMATION SERVICE

In-depth reports on current literature & research.
$3.50 each; Complete set of 12/$35.00

350 Marijuana — Revised!   356 Inhalants
351 T's and Blues   357 Methaqualone
352 Lookalike Drugs   358 Heroin
353 Paraquat   359 PCP — Revised!
354 Cocaine — Revised!   360 Designer Drugs — New!
355 LSD   361 Stimulants — New!

SPECIAL SAMPLERS

SAVE MONEY, SAVE TIME!

501-P Pamphlet Sampler $12.95
501-J Booklet Sampler $16.95
501-N "Why to Say 'No'" Sampler $69.95
     Contains everything listed, except books
501-E Everything Sampler $129.95. Everything listed.

O ften, the simplest visual tool creates the most compelling effect. Although no design rules govern this treatment, the footprint motif literally forces the reader to further examine the message.

ORIGINAL

Conference Program

**1986
Community
Conference
on Education**

**New Directions
in
Secondary Education**

**A Howard County
Showcase**

March 21 & 22, 1986

*Undifferentiated type
floating in a sea of white
space usually creates
an uninteresting
presentation.*

MAKEOVER

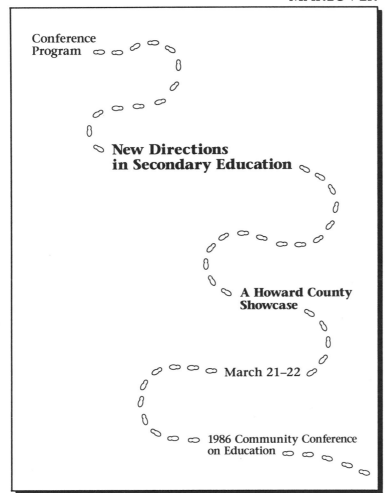

Conference
Program

**New Directions
in Secondary Education**

**A Howard County
Showcase**

March 21–22

1986 Community Conference
on Education

*The simple footprint
motif accurately reflects
subject matter and
creates continuity be-
tween blocks of type.*

*More important, the
footprints create a
whimsical, yet entirely
appropriate, visual mes-
sage. Don't be fooled
by its simplicity—in
this piece are the kernels
of great design!*

W hen presenting information about events (e.g., seminars, concerts) take care to arrange information in a way that will both inform and persuade.

Whos, whens and wheres (title, dates and location) should be featured together.

Address and telephone information has been moved to the back of the brochure, where readers are accustomed to finding it.

ORIGINAL

Comments from Past Attendees

"The IPSI helped me see myself as others see me. I'm able to help my family and co-workers understand how they can help me more."

Marilyn Rue, Client
POSITIVE CHOICE Program
Kaiser Permanente
San Diego, California

"IPSI teaching and counseling tools are excellent! They're a great addition to our new weight curriculum, and our clients enjoy taking the IPSI."

Jane Deacon, R. D., MBA
Director Weight Management Program
Santa Barbara Medical Center
Santa Barbara, California

"Research and teaching efforts with the IPSI are a major focus for us. We feel we are on the cutting edge of preventive health programs."

Dr. Vincent Felitti, M. D.
Chief - Department of Preventive Medicine
Kaiser Permanente
San Diego, California

"The IPSI model is simple yet powerful. I have incorporated it into every area of my life and work."

Ann Steinmetz-Harris
Manager, Human Resources Development
Blue Cross of Wisconsin
Milwaukee, Wisconsin

"I'm recommending the IPSI to Directors of programs I work with. It's cost effective, non-threatening to clients and based on sound theory."

Carolyn Van Housen, M.F.C.C.
Regional Program Director
Sandoz Nutrition
Minneapolis, Minnesota

THE WORKSHOP STAFF

Richard Brostrom, Ph.D.

Dick is a master teacher and an expert on human interaction. His experiences in education and international business consulting combine to bring a practical real-world perspective to any group.

Primary author of the InterPhase training materials, Dick's articles and instruments on human development and leadership have been widely published by groups like American Management Association, University Associates, and Datamation.

Dixie Lea, Ph.D.

Dixie is an internal curriculum consultant to the POSITIVE CHOICE Program at Kaiser. In addition, she conducts staff training, directs IPSI research efforts and teaches weight management classes.

Dixie is co-author/publisher of InterPhase training materials. She has consulted with business, education and medical clients for over 20 years.

Kathy Hanning, M.S. - Counseling

Kathy is an *expert* in weight management. She has successfully maintained a 150+ pound weight loss herself, and has coached hundreds of clients to overcome their weight management barriers.

A senior counselor at POSITIVE CHOICE, Kathy teaches in every program phase, coordinates volunteers and writes program materials. She is a co-author of the IPSI Facilitator Resource Guide.

At the Bahia in beautiful San Diego

Workshop
For Health Professionals

*Group Interaction
and
Weight
Management*

featuring the IPSI

November 12-14, 1986
February 11-13, 1987
June 24-26, 1987

Presented by

InterPhase
Interaction Skills Training
Post Office Box 9675
Pacific Beach, California 92109
619-270-3037

The exaggerated amper-sand forms an interest-ing visual—appropriate to the topic!

Note how effectively screens of different values can work together to produce a tailored, businesslike appearance.

Testimonials and credits off-set in bold or italic type help break up copy for a faster read.

MAKEOVER

Traditional Weight Management programs focus on diet and exercise. Both are important components in successful weight management, but they are not enough.

The newly "slim" client who re enters a world that hasn't changed is at risk! The hard work of the diet and exercise regime can soon be eroded by well-meaning family members, friends, co-workers... or by the client!

This workshop addresses the client's re-entry tasks. It explores ways to help clients change their social environment and garner support they need to maintain their healthy new lifestyle

About the IPSI

The IPSI: InterPhase Style Inventory is a systematic personal feedback source for weight management clients. Simple, yet powerful, the 48-item inventory helps clients see themselves as others do.

Trained professionals can use the IPSI as an educational feedback tool to:

- Measure client change
- Stimulate group interaction
- Re-focus clients on positive data and behavior change strategies.

The IPSI is useful in all phases of weight management:

- Screen potential clients
- Gather baseline data at program entry
- Measure progress during weight loss
- Reinforce clients during maintenance.

To learn more about the IPSI, or to order a Preview Packet please contact Dr. Dixie Lea at InterPhase.

"The IPSI helped me see myself as others see. me. I'm able to help my family and co-workers understand how they can help me more."

Marilyn Rue, Client
Positive Choice Program
Kaiser Permanente
San Diego, California

"IPSI teaching and counseling tools ar excellent! They're a great addition to our new weight curriculum, and our clients enjoy taking the IPSI."

Jane Deacon, R.D., MBA
Director
Weight Management Program
Santa Barbara Medical Center
Santa Barbara, California

"Research and teaching efforts with the IPSI are a major focus for us. We feel we are on the cutting edge of preventive health programs."

Dr. Vincent Felitti, M.D.
Chief
Department of
Preventive Medicine
Kaiser Permanente
San Diego, California

"The IPSI model is simple yet powerful. I have incorporated it into every area of my life and work."

Ann Steinmetz-Harris
Manager
Human resources Development
Blue Cross of Wisconsin
Milwaukee, Wisconsin

"I'm recommending the IPSI to Directors of programs I work with. It's cost effective, non-threatening to clients and based on sound theory."

Carolyn Van Housen, M.F.C.C.
Regional Program Director
Sandoz Nutrition
Minneapolis, Minnesota

InterPhase
Interaction Skills Training
Post Office Box 9675
Pacific Beach, California 92109
619/270-3037

Workshops for Health Professionals

GROUP
INTERACTION

WEIGHT
MANAGEMENT

November 12-14, 1986
February 11-13, 1987
June 24-26, 1987

San Diego, California

InterPhase

Brochures about seminars and other events must quickly engage—and *sell*—the reader. Copy should be concise and well organized.

Line spacing doesn't link headlines and subheads with supporting copy, blurring the distinction between categories.

Avoid open bullets, or bullets that look like letters of the alphabet. They confuse rather than clarify!

Generally, large blocks of small type shouldn't be screened. Readers have an easier time decoding black type on a white background.

ORIGINAL

WHY THIS WORKSHOP

Traditional Weight Management programs focus on diet and exercise. Both are important components in successful weight management, but they are not enough.

The newly "slim" client who re-enters a world that hasn't changed is at *risk!* The hard work of the diet and exercise regime can soon be eroded by well-meaning family members, friends, co-workers......or by the client!

This workshop addresses the client's re-entry tasks. It explores ways to help clients *change* their social environment and garner support they need to *maintain* their healthy new lifestyle.

WHO SHOULD ATTEND

Registered Dieticians
working with weight clients and programs

Medical Directors
responsible for weight programs & personnel

Weight Program Directors

Behaviorists - Counselors - Psychologists
working with struggling clients

Medical Organization Personnel
planning new weight management programs

Public Health Professionals
designing preventive health programs

Corporate Health & Wellness Directors

WORKSHOP FORMAT

A three day active learning experience in group interaction using the IPSI

Updates on state-of-the-art weight management programs & research

Opportunities to share and compare program ideas with other professionals

Practice time to use new *data-guided* techniques in counseling, teaching and screening clients

Complete set of IPSI resource materials (lesson plans, simulations, role plays, visual aids, research applications) ready to take home and use in weight programs

Small group discussion, individual consultation, mini-lectures, simulations, role plays, and use of resource center

In-depth experience with a cost effective, simple, non- threatening client feedback source....the IPSI

WORKSHOP TOPICS

o Weight Management & Social Environment: A New Perspective

o Why Clients Have Problems

o Techniques to Increase Client Success: *Maintainence* is the goal

o The IPSI and Weight Management: Client intake, counseling, teaching & research methods

o Successful Program Models

SPECIAL FEATURES

Conducted at the Bahia Resort........ overlooking San Diego Bay........... one block from the Pacific Ocean

Spectacular Graduation Dinner Cruise aboard the *Invader* sailing vessel on San Diego Harbor

Individual consultation with instructors and video-assisted feedback

CEU's (1.8) earned for participation if requested

ABOUT THE IPSI

The IPSI: InterPhase Style Inventory is a systematic personal feedback source for weight management clients. Simple, yet powerful, the 48-item inventory helps clients see themselves as others do.

Trained professionals can use the IPSI as an educational feedback tool to:
o measure client change
o stimulate group interaction
o re-focus clients on positive data and behavior change strategies

The IPSI is useful in *all* phases of weight management:
o screen potential clients
o gather baseline data at program entry
o measure progress during weight loss
o reinforce clients during maintenance

To learn more about the IPSI, or to order a Preview Packet please contact:
Dr. Dixie Lea
Post Office Box 9675
Pacific Beach, California 92109
(619) 270-3037

Information has been reorganized in sequence of importance.

Dates, times and location often are more important than long descriptive passages.

MAKEOVER

Dates

- November 12-14, 1986
- February 11-13, 1987
- June 24-26, 1987

Place

- The Bahia Resort, overlooking San Diego Bay, one block from the ocean

Format

- A three day active learning experience in group interaction using the IPSI
- Updates on state-of-the-art weight management programs and research
- Opportunities to share and compare program ideas with other professionals
- Practice time to use new data-guided techniques in counseling, teaching and screening clients
- Complete set of IPSI resource materials (lesson plans, simulations, role plays, visual aids, research applications) ready to take home and use in weight programs
- Small group discussion, individual consultation, mini-lectures, simulations, role plays, and use of resource center
- In-depth experience with a cost effective, simple, non-threatening client feedback source ... the IPSI

Topics

- Weight management and social environment: A new perspective
- Why clients have problems
- Techniques to increase client success: Maintenance is the goal
- The IPSI and weight management: Client intake, counseling, teaching and research methods
- Successful program models

Who should attend

- **Registered Dieticians** working with weight clients and programs
- **Medical Directors** responsible for weight programs and personnel
- **Weight Program Directors**
- **Behaviorists - Counselors - Psychologists** working with struggling clients
- **Medical Organization Personnel** planning new weight management programs
- **Public Health Professionals** designing preventive health programs
- **Corporate Health and Wellness Directors**

Special features

- Spectacular graduation dinner cruise aboard the Invader sailing vessel on San Diego Harbor
- Individual consultation with instructors and video-assisted feedback
- CEU's (1.8) earned for participation if requested

Workshop Staff

Richard Brostrom, Ph.D.

Dick is a master teacher and an expert on human interaction. His experiences in education and international business consulting combine to bring a practical real-world perspective to any group.

Primary author of the InterPhase training materials, Dick's article and instruments on human development and leadership have been widely published by groups like American Management Association, University Associates, and Datamation.

Dixie Lea, Ph.D.

Dixie is an internal curriculum consultant to the Positive Choice Program at Kaiser. In addition, she conducts staff training, directs IPSI research efforts and teaches weight management classes.

Dixie is co-author/publisher of InterPhase training materials. She has consulted with business, education and medical clients for over 20 years.

Kathy Hanning, M.S. Counseling

Kathy is an expert in weight management. She has successfully maintained a 150+ pound weight loss herself, and has coached hundreds of clients to overcome their weight management barriers.

A senior counselor at Positive Choice, Kathy teaches in every program phase, coordinates volunteers and writes program materials. She is a co-author of the IPSI Facilitator Resource Guide.

Border overkill is one of desktop publishing's deadly sins, often overwhelming the type and illustration, thereby discouraging readership.

ORIGINAL

THE MONTE VISTA MARKET

Have you tried
JOE'S SPECIALTIES
Made fresh daily

Stuffed Bell Peppers • Stuffed Pork Chops
Chicken Kiev
Chicken Cordon Bleu • Lemon Chicken
Chicken Rellenos • Teriyaki Chicken
Chicken Florentine
Teriyaki Beef Kabobs • Lamb Kabobs

They're Mouth Watering
Delicious
We Prepare Them
You Cook Them

372-2075

15 Soledad Drive, Monterey, California
Hours: MON. • SAT. 9am • 8pm
SUN. 10am • 7pm

Generally, borders should be seen and not heard, quietly containing copy and graphics.

The address and hours should be positioned near the logo for easy recognition—this is particularly important in Yellow Pages advertising.

MAKEOVER

Because the market specializes in take-out, the all-important phone number appears twice—and more prominently than in the original.

The large illustration shows busy chefs doing all the work that the customer presumably will avoid!

Consider oversized flyers on 8 x 14 or 11 x 17 paper—only slightly more expensive and allows larger type and graphics.

A ds for conventions and trade shows shouldn't be understated—readers expect big, bold copy and other attention-getters.

ORIGINAL

CAPTURE YOUR SHARE OF A $20 BILLION MARKET

ATTEND
Ada® Expo '86

November 19-21, 1986   Charleston, WVa, Civic Center

®Ada is a registered Trademark of the US Government (AJPO)

Held in conjunction with ACM SIGAda's and AdaJUG's 1986 fall Technical Meetings

FOUR CONFERENCE TRACKS

Ada for Managers deals with management concerns, including Ada market opportunities, compiler validation issues and responding to Ada RFP's.

Ada for Developers presents an introduction to Ada for software developers with little or no prior Ada language experience.

Software Engineering is for more experienced Ada developers and includes a tutorial on methodologies and sessions on testing and concurrency.

SIGAda/AdaJUG Sessions follow a traditional SIGAda format, including user presentations from SIGAda committees and reports from the armed services.

AN ACRE OF VENDOR EXHIBITS

Ada Expo '86 will offer the largest display of Ada vendor exhibits ever presented, including hardware, compilers, cross-compilers, development tools, environments, education and applications.

BROAD-BASED INDUSTRY SPONSORSHIP

In addition to being held in conjunction with ACM SIGAda's and AdaJUG's 1986 Fall Technical Meetings, Ada Expo '86 is co-sponsored by:

Senate Minority Leader Robert C. Byrd
The West Virginia Software Valley Corporation
The Software Engineering Institute
Defense Science and Electronics magazine

MAIL TO: Ada Expo '86 • P.O. Box 868 • Frederick, MD 21701 • Phone (301) 662-9400

Name: _____   Title: _____
Organization: _____
Street Address: _____
City: _____   St: _____   Zip: _____   Phone: _____

____ Please register me for the Exhibits and the SIGAda Sessions at **no cost** and send me more information on the Full Conference Prpgram.

____ My company may wish to Exhibit at Ada Expo '86. Please call me.

Avoid long coupon leader lines—they're usually an indication that you need to rethink the design.

Check-box information should always precede name and address data—the reader wants to take action before completing the coupon.

MAKEOVER

Capture Your Share of a $20 Billion Market

Attend Ada Expo '86

Ada® Expo '86 November 19-21, 1986
Charleston, WVa • Civic Center

Mail to: **AdaExpo '86**
P.O. Box 868
Frederick, MD 21701
(301) 662-9400

☐ Please register me for the Exhibits and
the SIGAda Sessions at no cost and
send me more information on the Full
Conference Program.

☐ My company may wish to exhibit at
Ada Expo '86. Please call me.

Name _____
Title _____
Organization _____
Address _____
City _____ St ____ Zip _____
Phone _____

Ada Expo '86

Held in conjunction with ACM SIGAda's and
AdaJUG's 1986 Fall Technical Meetings

Four Conference Tracks

Ada for Managers deals with management concerns, including Ada market
opportunities, compiler validation issues and responding to Ada RFPs.
Ada for Developers presents an introduction to Ada for software developers
with little or no prior Ada language experience.
Software Engineering is for more experienced Ada developers and includes
a tutorial on methodologies and sessions on testing and concurrency.
SIGAda/AdaJUG sessions follow a traditional SIGAda format, including user
presentations from SIGAda committees and reports from the armed services.

An Acre of Vendor Exhibits

Ada Expo '86 will offer the largest display of Ada vendor exhibits ever presented, including hardware, compilers, cross-compilers, development tools, environments, education and applications.

Broad-based Industry Sponsorship

In addition to being held in conjunction with ACM SIGAda's and AdaJUG's
1986 Fall Technical Meetings, Ada Expo '86 is cosponsored by:

Senate Minority Leader Robert C. Byrd
The West Virginia Software Valley Corporation
The Software Engineering Institute
Defense Science and Electronics magazine

© Ada is a registered Trademark of the US Government (AJPO)

A bold, perforated border framing the coupon is an often-overlooked technique in response-oriented media such as flyers and newspaper ads. Readers do cut coupons and a flyer's design should reflect that.

Note how "Ada Expo '86" now appears prominently three times—a broadcast technique that can work effectively in print.

If properly showcased, a good illustration can carry even the most mundane copy.

ORIGINAL

Avoid using horizontal rules of widely varying lengths on the same page—they tend to fight with body copy and distract the reader.

Technology
Graphics
Photography

How do we prepare for the future?

MID-WINTER FACULTY CONFERENCE
The Inn At
Morro Bay
FEBRUARY 20 - 22 1987

JACC

JOURNALISM ASSOCIATION OF COMMUNITY COLLEGES

MAKEOVER

TECHNOLOGY
GRAPHICS
PHOTOGRAPHY

How do we prepare for the future?

Mid-Winter Faculty Conference

The Inn At Morro Bay

February 20-22 1987

JACC

JOURNALISM ASSOCIATION OF COMMUNITY COLLEGES

Note how using fewer type sizes and styles augments readability.

Tighter letter spacing and a different typeface link "Journalism Association of Community Colleges" more effectively with the logo.

A lways encourage readers to complete your forms; place important information close at hand and make directions easy to read.

ORIGINAL

JOURNALISM ASSOCIATION OF COMMUNITY COLLEGES

☐ Yes ... I want to attend the JACC Mid Winter Conference at The Inn in Morro Bay.

"Old" Faculty
☐ I prefer to pay the Commuter $50 fee and find my ownlodging.

☐ I prefer a shared room and enclose my check for $100.

☐ I prefer a single room and enclose my check for $150.

☐ **New Faculty**
I am a new journalism Faculty member ... having started in the '85/'86 or '86/'87 academic year ... I am entitled to a **free** shared room at The Inn.

☐ Yes ... I want my free shared room ... a $100 value

☐ Yes ... I want my free shared room but wish to bring a guest for which I will pay an additional fee of $50.

Reservations must be received by January 10, 1986

Name _____

Address_____

Street _____

City_____ State _____ Zip_____

Phone Home (___) _____ School Phone (___) _____

School _____

Please mail your checks to: **Richard Cameron**
                                Executive Secretary
                                West Valley College
                                14000 Fruitvale Ave.

For additional Information Call: **Janek (John) Grzywacz (Gray)**
                                  Faculty Conference Chair
                                  Moorpark College
                                  7075 Campus Road

JOURNALISM ASSOCIATION OF COMMUNITY COLLEGES

The association name at the top of the page adds nothing to the piece and consumes valuable space.

For events, important information should be prominently repeated on each spread. As readers become more serious, they need vital data at their fingertips.

MAKEOVER

How do we prepare for the future?

Mid-Winter Faculty Conference

February 20-22, 1987

☐ **Yes**... *I want to attend the JACC Mid Winter Conference at The Inn At Morro Bay.*

"Old" Faculty

☐ I prefer to pay the Commuter $50 fee and find my own lodging.

☐ I prefer a shared room and enclose my check for $100.

☐ I prefer a single room and enclose my check for $150.

New Faculty

☐ I am a new journalism Faculty member ... having started in the '85/'86 or '86/'87 academic year ... I am entitled to a free shared room at the Inn.

☐ Yes...I want my free shared room...a $100 value.

☐ Yes...I want my free shared room but wish to bring a guest for which I will pay an additional fee of $50.

Reservations must be received by January 10, 1986

Name

Address

Street

City   State   Zip

Phone /Home (   )   School (   )

School

Please mail your checks to: For additional information:

Richard Cameron   **Janek (John) Grzywaca (Gray)**
Executive Secretary   Faculty Conference Chair
West Valley College   Moorpark College
14000 Fruitvale Ave.   7075 Campus Road
Saratoga, CA 95070   Moorpark, CA 93021
                                 (805) 529-2321 x254

JOURNALISM ASSOCIATION OF COMMUNITY COLLEGES

The attention-getting illustration has been reduced and carried over from the front page—a good way to repeat the theme at no extra cost!

Note how reorganizing the basic response form makes it easy for the reader to complete it.

One of the goals of good design is to organize type and graphics into the proper visual context—you don't want a flyer for an exhibit of Chinese artifacts to look too trendy and contemporary.

ORIGINAL

SESRA

* SPECIAL PRIVATE EVENING VIEWING TO EMPLOYEES OF SESRA COMPANIES *

ITS MAGNIFICENT...AWESOME...FASCINATING...A ONCE-IN-A-LIFETIME EVENT!

SON OF HEAVEN
IMPERIAL ARTS OF CHINA

* * * * * * * * * * * * * * * * * * * *

A U G U S T   1 8   (Thurs. 7 pm)
O C T O B E R   1 5   (Sat., 8 pm)

* * * * * * * * * * * * * * * * * * * *

C O S T : $ 1 1 . 0 0

Flag Pavillion (Seattle Center)

* AVOID THE CROWDS ... less than half the regular daytime capacity
* MORE CONVENIENT EVENING HOURS ... for you, the family and guests

TICKETS ARE IN EXTREMELY LIMITED SUPPLY!
(No Exchanges or Refunds)

View over 200 objects, dating from the 7th Century BC to the 18th Century AD, for the first time as China unshrouds its imperial history by sharing its rarest national treasures!

For further information contact
your company representative:_____

SESRA NIGHT.........."SON OF HEAVEN"   ABSOLUTE DEADLINE: July 29 for August viewing!
August 18 & October 15, 1988   Seattle Center

Company_____   Tickets in extremely limited supply.

Name_____   NUMBER OF _____ Thursday, Aug. 18

TICKETS: _____ Saturday, Oct. 15
Address_____
                                        AMOUNT ENCLOSED: $_____
City_____ State _____ Zip _____   (Check payable to SESRA)

Phone: DAY_____ EVENING_____

Include a STAMPED, SELF-ADDRESSED ENVELOPE with your order and return to:
        SESRA ... "Son of Heaven" Special ... P.O. Box 2806 ... Seattle, WA   98111

Because no telephone response is available, the mail-in coupon, buried in this document, is all-important.

Readers need to quickly learn the whos, whats, whens, wheres and prices of events. Be sure to make this information prominent.

MAKEOVER

Special private
evening viewings
for the employees of
Seattle Employees Services
Recreation Association
companies

August 18
Thursday, 7 pm

October 15
Saturday, 8 pm

November 26
Saturday, 7 pm

Flag Pavilion
Seattle Center

It's magnificent...
awesome...
fascinating...
a once-in-a-lifetime
event!

Avoid the crowds, less
than half the regular
daytime capacity

More convenient evening
hours for you, the family
and guests

Cost: $11

Tickets are in extremely limited
supply! (No exchanges or refunds)

For further information
contact your company
representative:

For current ticket availability,
call the SESRA Discount
Hotline (206)462-8526

SON OF HEAVEN
IMPERIAL ARTS OF CHINA

View over 200 objects, dating from the
7th century BC to the 18th Century AD,
for the first time as China unshrouds
its imperial history by sharing
its rarest national treasures.

SESRA Night — SON OF HEAVEN
Aug. 18, Oct. 15 and Nov. 26, 1988 (Seattle Center)

Company _____
Name _____
Address _____
City _____ State _____ Zip _____
Phone: Day _____ Evening _____
Include a stamped, self-addressed envelope with your order
and return to:

    SESRA...SON OF HEAVEN Special
    P.O. Box 2806
    Seattle, WA 98111

Absolute Deadline:
July 29 for August Viewing!

Tickets in extremely
limited supply.

Number of tickets:

___ Thursday, Aug. 18, 7 pm
___ Saturday, Oct. 15, 8 pm
___ Saturday, Nov. 26, 7 pm

Amount enclosed: _____

Check made payable to:
SESRA

Tickets will be mailed out two weeks prior to the performance.
If your order cannot be accommodated, you will be notified immediately.

A circular screen "pops"
the visual off the page.

A variety of typefaces is
intentionally used to
preserve the ethnic flavor.

Untold revenues have
been lost from half-
completed coupons—
be sure to make them
easy to read.

W hen you have too much copy and can't make further cuts, consider the low-cost alternative of a legal-sized page—it's no more postage and nearly the same printing cost!

ORIGINAL

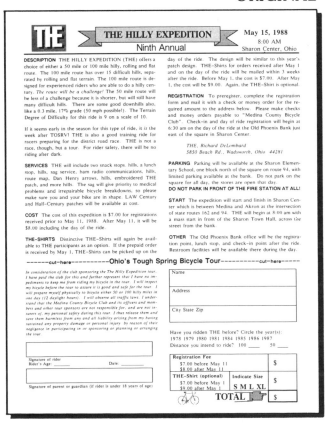

An overabundance of copy forces a cramped presentation that invariably hurts response.

Remember to feature important information prominently (times, dates, location) so that readers can easily refer to it.

MAKEOVER

A screened coupon with reverses directs readers to the section they need to complete.

DESCRIPTION

THE HILLY EXPEDITION (**THE**) offers a choice of either a 50 mile or 100 mile hilly, rolling and flat route. The 100 mile route has over 15 difficult hills, separated by rolling and flat terrain. The 100 mile rouge is designed for experienced riders who are able to do a hilly century. *The route will be a challenge!* The 50 mile route will be less of a challenge because it is shorter, but will also have many difficult hills. There are some good downhills also, like a 0.3 mile, 17% grade (50 mph possible!). The Terrain Degree of Difficulty for the ride is 9 on a scale of 10.
If it seems early in the season for this type of ride, it is the week after TOSRV! **THE** is also a good training ride for racers preparing for the district road race. **THE** is not a race, though, but a tour. For rider safety, there will be no riding after dark.

START

The expedition will start and finish in Sharon Center which is between Medina and Akron at the intersection of state routes 162 AND 94. **THE** will begin at 8:00 am with a mass start in front of the Sharon Town Hall, across the street from the bank.

SERVICES

THE will include two snack stops, hills, a lunch stop, hills, sag service, ham radio communications, hills, route map, Dan Henry arrows, hills, embroidered THE patch, and more hills. The sag will give priority to medical problems and irrepairable bicycle breakdowns, so please make sure you and your bike are in shape. LAW Century and Half-Century patches will be available at cost.

REGISTRATION

To preregister, complete the registration form and mail it with a check or money order for the required amount to the address below. Please make checks and money orders payable to "**Medina County Bicycle Club**". Check-in and day of ride registration will begin at 6:30 am on the day of the ride at the Old Phoenix Bank just east of the square in Sharon Center.

THE, Richard DeLombard
5850 Beach Rd.,
Wadsworth, Ohio 44281

COST

The cost of this expedition is $7.00 for registrations received prior to May 11, 1988. After May 11, it will be $8.00 including the day of the ride.

THE-Shirts

Distinctive THE-Shirts will again be available to **THE** participants as an option. If the prepaid order is received by May 1, THE-Shirts can be picked up on the day of the ride. The design will be similar to this year's patch design. **THE**-Shirts for orders received after May 1, and on the day of the ride will be mailed within 3 weeks after the ride. Before May 1, the cost is $7.00. After May 1, the cost will be $9.00. Again the THE-Shirt is optional.

PARKING

Parking will be available at the Sharon Elementary School, one block north of the square on route 94, with limited parking available at the bank. Do not park on the square for all day, stores are open that day.
DO NOT PARK IN FRONT OF THE FIRE STATION AT ALL!

OTHER

The Old Phoenix Bank office will be the registration point, lunch stop, and check-in point after the ride. Restroom facilities will be available there during the day.

Italic subheads lend a feeling of movement, complementing the graphics above.

— **ENTRY FORM** —

In consideration of the club sponsoring The Hilly Expedition tour, I have paid the club for this and further represent that I have no impediments to keep me from riding my bicycle in the tour. I will inspect my bicycle before the tour to assure it is good and safe for the tour. I will prepare myself physically to bicycle either 50 or 100 hilly miles in one day (12 daylight hours). I will observe all traffic laws. I understand that the Medina County Bicycle Club and its officers and members and other tour sponsors are not responsible for, and are not insurers of, my personal safety during this tour. I thus release them and save them harmless from any and all liability arising from my having sustained any property damage or personal injury by reason of their negligence in participating in or sponsoring or planning or arranging the tour.

Signature of the rider

Rider's Age: _____ Date: _____

Signature of parent or guardian (if the rider is under 18 years of age)

Name
Address
City   State   Zip
Have you ridden **THE** before? Circle the year(s):
1978 1979 1980 1981 1984 1985 1986 1987
Distance you intend to ride?   100   50

Registration Fee $
$7.00 before May 11 $8.00 after May 11
THE-Shirt (optional) $
Indicate size (S M L XL)
$7.00 before May 1 $9.00 after May 1
              TOTAL $

A three-column format creates less-imposing copy blocks, off-set by large, readable subheads.

5

REPORTS & PROPOSALS

Contrast, consistency and continuity are the critical design elements of reports and proposals. Because they're often read by busy people, reports and proposals should have a friendly appearance, yet quickly deliver important information.

A report's success depends mainly on sequencing—organizing information logically and clearly so the reader is easily led through the publication. Sequencing must begin on the front cover and continue inside.

Reports and proposals must also have clear, definitive formats throughout. A professional-looking format also plays a role in enhancing the perceived value and importance of a document. Put bluntly: Who wants to pay for a report that looks like it was typed at the last minute on a portable typewriter?

Finally, typeface, type size and type placement must correlate with the hierarchy of information. This helps readers to understand what's most important and then read through to the end.

Contrast

Too often, the information presented is designed to look as though it's all of equal importance. This destroys contrast and sequencing, and creates confusion: Which information is most important? What should be read next?

In the case of the SAE Technical Paper Series, the original cover presents information in a disorganized, zigzag fashion. Text begins at the upper right; jumps down to the publication number; moves diagonally to the left (speakers' names); only to return again to the lower right (meeting title, location and dates).

The two-column listing of names—which aren't lined up with any other visual element on the page—adds further confusion and creates another barrier for readers.

Although the front cover contains a lot of white space along the left margin, it doesn't help to organize any of the information.

A final problem is that there's little relationship between typography and precedence of information. All categories of information are presented in a similar typeface, and the type size and style aren't varied enough; everything seems equal.

In the makeover, however, the title of the publication series contrasts with the report title, and the categories of information are now clearly separated. The page looks simpler and more attractive.

Often, the changes that contribute to a makeover's success are small. For example, in the original the slogan "The Engineering Resource for Advancing Mobility" competes with the SAE logo. In the makeover, the logo and slogan complement each other with contrasting sizes. Likewise, by using two lines, in upper- and lowercase type, the address becomes more distinct from the logo.

Consistency

The rewards of consistency are also illustrated in the SAE Technical Paper Series. A strong format—or visual identity—is established on the cover and maintained inside.

The elements of this format include:

- A consistent underlying grid—or column arrangement—that organizes the text on each page.
- A strong system of borders that unifies each page.
- Repeated use of graphic accents, such as reverses and tint screens.
- Consistent placement of page numbers.

The revised cover is based on the same three-column format used inside. Two of the columns are tied together by a background screen; the text in this area is set flush-left. As a result, instead of having to zigzag through the text as in the original, you can quickly follow a straight line from the "SAE Technical Paper Series" to the series number to the title, and end with the meeting information.

Notice, again, the importance of good typography. Setting "The Users' Perspective" in italics emphasizes the subtitle and gives it a conversational tone that contrasts with the "Tomorrow's Trucks" title. Likewise, the space between the Truck & Bus Meeting and Exposition meeting title and the location and dates of the meeting add impact to both segments of information. After reading the text in the wide column, notice how easily and naturally you move to subordinate information—speakers' names and credentials—set to the left. You can pick out this information by simply scanning the column.

Continuity

Sequencing, establishing a hierarchy and a consistent page layout are also illustrated by the inside pages of the SAE makeover. Design elements introduced on the front cover continue on the inside. Notice the bold bottom border, for example, and the reverses and screens. On the second page, a full reverse separates the title from the text. And the abstract—lost in the original—becomes prominent when given plenty of white space at the beginning of the report.

The original inside pages have both too much white space and an overall "gray" look. The columns are surrounded and separated by too much white space, so they don't appear to be connected to each other. In the makeover, the columns placed closer together now clearly relate to each other.

Equally important, you can now quickly scan the revised pages and grasp their content. The subheads are easier to find because they're set larger and bolder than the text. The topic sentences summarizing each paragraph on page 3 are now set in bold italics, forming a smooth transition from the subhead into the text.

The three-column grid not only tightens up the page; it increases the word density per page, thus resulting in lower printing and mailing costs.

The three-column grid pays another substantial dividend. It's extremely hard to place illustrations, charts and graphs on two-column pages. Visuals are often too large to fit in one column, but too small to extend across both; so they "float" on the page—as in the original SAE report.

Three-column grids simplify the placement of visuals. Laying out the graph on page 3 across two columns makes it large enough to provide contrast without overwhelming the page. The revised graph makes it easy to understand, but it's not so large that the data get lost within it.

Take Another Look

As you review your reports and proposals, ask yourself these questions:

✔ Did I visually separate the series title from the report or proposal title?

✔ Does the cover invite the reader inside?

✔ Have I used a consistent format throughout?

✔ Have I used the same grid and design elements throughout?

✔ Have I used type and layout to direct the reader's eye movement throughout?

✔ Can the reader quickly grasp the information at a glance?

This piece demonstrates the need to emphasize important information so that readers can quickly scan it.

ORIGINAL

SAE *The Engineering Resource For Advancing Mobility* 400 COMMONWEALTH DRIVE WARRENDALE, PA 15096

SAE Technical Paper Series

852330

**Tomorrow's Trucks:
The Users' Perspective**

Jerry Dick
TNT-Pilot Freight Carriers
Winston-Salem, NC

Tom Harrison
Western Auto Supply Co.
Kansas City, MO

Peggy J. Fisher
Roadway Express, Inc.
Akron, OH

Blaine Johnson
Ryder Truck Rental
Miami, FL

Thomas Tahaney
JBK Truck Leasing
Marlton, NJ

John Sullivan
GELCO Truck Leasing
St. Louis, MO

Gerald Kreaden
Glengarry Transport, Ltd.
Ville St. Laurent
Quebec, Canada

William E. Tracy
The Maintenance Council
American Trucking Associations, Inc.
Alexandria, VA

Frank K. Bright
Holly Farms Industries
Wilkesboro, NC

Truck & Bus Meeting and Exposition
Chicago, Illinois
December 9–12, 1985

The title, "Tomorrow's Trucks," is overwhelmed by "SAE Technical Paper Series," of little interest to the reader.

Conversely, the theme, "Tomorrow's Trucks," is too small to capture readers' attention.

MAKEOVER

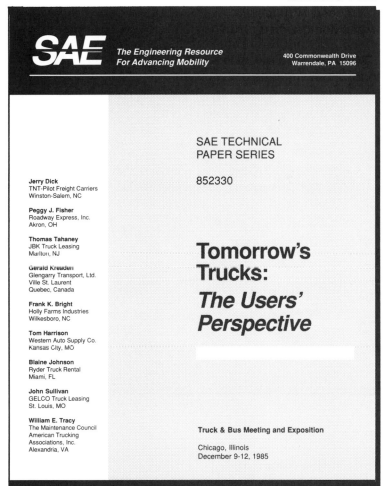

Note how your eyes immediately go to the theme on the makeover, and not the "Series" information.

Reversing the type on the nameplate effectively sets it apart from the body copy.

Information on speakers is placed away from essential information about the conference.

A thick rule at the bottom of the page helps "weight" the piece, providing vertical balance and off-setting the heavy reverse used in the nameplate.

Similar design elements are carried over to the inside pages to create a sense of continuity.

ORIGINAL

852330

Tomorrow's Trucks:
The Users' Perspective

Jerry Dick
TNT-Pilot Freight
Carriers

Peggy J. Fisher
Roadway Express, Inc.

Thomas Tahaney
JBK Truck Leasing

Gerald Kreaden
Glengarry Transport

Frank K. Bright
Holly Farms Industries

Tom Harrison
Western Auto Supply

Blaine Johnson
Ryder Truck Rental

John Sullivan
GELCO Truck Leasing

William E. Tracy
The Maintenance
Council-ATA

Abstract

Equipment users are the best source of information about the demands put upon vehicles. They know exactly how vehicles are used, and they know how well current production models perform under all operating conditions. Based on that knowledge, fleet maintenance executives have detailed some potential areas for design emphasis in future heavy-duty transport equipment.

Introduction

The Maintenance Council (TMC) of American Trucking Associations, Inc. consists of two types of members. Full Members are truck and bus fleet equipment managers. Their management responsibilities typically include all aspects of maintaining existing equipment and specifying new equipment. Associate Members are technically-oriented sales and service managers

Numbers in parentheses designate references at end of paper.

from vehicle and component manufacturer companies. For 28 years, these members have worked together, "dedicated to the improvement of equipment and its maintenance."(1)

Communication between trucking equipment suppliers and the users of their products has been fostered by TMC in several ways. Three technical meetings each year bring representatives of both segments into face-to-face contact in neutral locations. Technical problems of operating and maintaining truck fleet equipment are identified, defined, and eventually solved by working together. These solutions frequently appear as Recommended Practices or Advisories in the *TMC Recommended Maintenance Practices Manual.* These quasi-standards for equipment specifying and maintenance are the product of 28 years of suppliers and users working together.

Many equipment problems encountered by users can be solved with improved maintenance practices, changes in equipment specifications or

Because the information all looks the same, readers don't know what to read first—and often skip it altogether!

MAKEOVER

852330

Tomorrow's Trucks:
The Users' Perspective

Jerry Dick
TNT-Pilot Freight Carriers

Peggy J. Fisher
Roadway Express, Inc.

Thomas Tahaney
JBK Truck Leasing

Gerald Kreaden
Glengarry Transport, Ltd.
Quebec, Canada

Frank K. Bright
Holly Farms Industries

Tom Harrison
Western Auto Supply Co.

Blaine Johnson
Ryder Truck Rental

John Sullivan
GELCO Truck Leasing

William E. Tracy
The Maintenance Council
American Trucking
Associations, Inc.

Abstract

Equipment users are the best source of information about the demands put upon vehicles. They know exactly how vehicles are used, and they know how well current production models perform under all operating conditions. Based on that knowledge, fleet maintenance executives have detailed some potential areas for design emphasis in future heavy-duty transport equipment.

Introduction

The Maintenance Council (TMC) of American Trucking Associations, Inc. consists of two types of members. Full Members are truck and bus fleet equipment managers. Their management responsibilities typically include all aspects of maintaining existing equipment and specifying new equipment. Associate Members are technically oriented sales and service managers from vehicle and component manufacturer companies. For 20 years, these members have worked together, "dedicated to the improvement of equipment and its maintenance."(1)

Communication between trucking equipment suppliers and the users of their products has been fostered by TMC in several ways. Three technical meetings each year bring representatives of both segments into face-to-face contact in neutral locations. Technical problems of operating and maintaining truck fleet equipment are identified, defined, and eventually solved by working together. These solutions frequently appear as Recommended Practices or Advisories in the *TMC Recommended Maintenance Practices Manual*. These quasi standards for equipment specifying and maintenance are the product or 28 years of suppliers and users working together.

Many equipment problems encountered by users can be solved with improved maintenance practices, changes in

---

The title is placed in a modified nameplate, set comfortably apart from the body copy.

Again, speakers' names are placed to the left, away from more important "selling" information.

Note how the simple use of rules and columns highlights the important Abstract copy.

Poor use of white space can discourage reader interest, even when the copy is brilliantly executed!

ORIGINAL

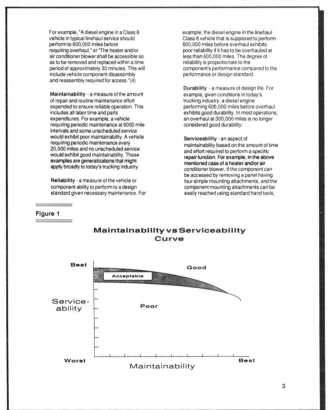

For example, "A diesel engine in a Class 8 vehicle in typical linehaul service should perform to 600,000 miles before requiring overhaul," or "The heater and/or air conditioner blower shall be accessible so as to be removed and replaced within a time period of approximately 30 minutes. This will include vehicle component disassembly and reassembly required for access."(4)

Maintainability - a measure of the amount of repair and routine maintenance effort expended to ensure reliable operation. This includes all labor time and parts expenditures. For example, a vehicle requiring periodic maintenance at 6000 mile intervals and some unscheduled service would exhibit poor maintainability. A vehicle requiring periodic maintenance every 20,000 miles and no unscheduled service would exhibit good maintainability. These examples are generalizations that might apply broadly to today's trucking industry.

Reliability - a measure of the vehicle or component ability to perform to a design standard given necessary maintenance. For example, the diesel engine in the linehaul Class 8 vehicle that is supposed to perform 600,000 miles before overhaul exhibits poor reliability if it has to be overhauled at less than 600,000 miles. The degree of reliability is proportionate to the component's performance compared to the performance or design standard.

Durability - a measure of design life. For example, given conditions in today's trucking industry, a diesel engine performing 600,000 miles before overhaul exhibits good durability. In most operations, an overhaul at 300,000 miles is no longer considered good durability.

Serviceability - an aspect of maintainability based on the amount of time and effort required to perform a specific repair function. For example, in the above mentioned case of a heater and/or air conditioner blower, if the component can be accessed by removing a panel having four simple mounting attachments, and the component mounting attachments can be easily reached using standard hand tools,

Figure 1

Maintainability vs Serviceability Curve

Note how the ragged-right Column One visually creates unsightly irregularities against the flush-left Column Two.

The chart area is so riddled with white space that the information gets lost.

MAKEOVER

For example, "A diesel engine in a Class 8 vehicle in typical linehaul service should perform to 600,000 miles before requiring overhaul," or "The heater and/or air conditioner blower shall be accessible so as to be removed and replaced within a time period of approximately 30 minutes. This will include vehicle component disassembly and reassembly required for access."(4)

Maintainability

A measure of the amount of repair and routine maintenance effort expended to ensure reliable operation. This includes all labor time and parts expenditures. For example, a vehicle requiring periodic maintenance at 6000 mile intervals and some unscheduled service would exhibit poor maintainability. A vehicle requiring periodic maintenance every 20,000 miles and no unscheduled service would exhibit good maintainability. These examples are generalizations that might apply broadly to today's trucking industry

Reliability

A measure of the vehicle or component ability to perform to a design standard given necessary maintenance. For example, the diesel engine in the linehaul Class 8 vehicle that is supposed to perform 600,000 miles before overhaul exhibits poor reliability if it has to be overhauled at less than 600,000 miles. The degree of reliability is proportionate to the component's performance compared to the performance or design standard.

Durability

A measure of design life. For example, given conditions in today's trucking industry, a diesel engine performing 600,000 miles before overhaul exhibits good durability. In most operations, an overhaul at 300,000 miles is no longer considered good durability.

Serviceability

An aspect of maintainability based on the amount of time and effort required to perform a specific repair function. For example, in the above mentioned case of a heater and/or air conditioner blower, if the component can be accessed by removing a panel having four simple mounting attachments, and the component mounting attachments can be easily reached using standard hand tools, and the component can be removed from the vehicle easily and quickly, that is good serviceability. If, on the other hand, the dashboard or parts of it, instruments and wiring and mechanical linkages have to be displaced to gain access to the component, that will require substantial time and labor effort and will exhibit poor serviceability. Maintainability and serviceability are ironically intertwined. If this blower is buried in the bowels of the vehicle and requires 20 labor-hours to remove and replace, it would exhibit poor serviceability. From a maintainability standpoint, if the blower had to be replaced every 1000,000 miles, that

would constitute poor maintainability, and if it never had to be replaced for the life of the vehicle, it would exhibit good maintainability. *(Figure 1)*

Planned Periodic Maintenance

This is scheduled, structured servicing operations designed to: maximize reliability and maintainability; preclude unscheduled repairs and vehicle downtime. Fleets typically use a three-segment inspection procedure. In linehaul applications, "A" service is most frequent, occurring each 10,000 to 15,000 miles. The "A" service usually includes oil and filter changes, chassis lube, minor adjustments and routine inspection items. The "B" service is scheduled about every 50,000 miles. It usually includes all of "A," replacement of longer life filters and components, more thorough inspections and tune-up type operations. The "C" service is the most extensive scheduled maintenance, occurring about every 100,000 miles.

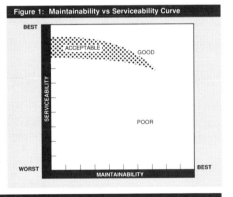

Figure 1: Maintainability vs Serviceability Curve

Full-justified type and a three-column format help tighten the report and make white space more manageable.

Bold rules at the top and bottom carry the nameplate theme from the previous pages.

The chart has been contained by the simple use of a screen.

M ost layout software programs let you access, import and format spreadsheet and database information into tables, charts and graphs.

ORIGINAL

Two At Work 1987

Evaluation Meeting

A conference for full-time employed parents held at Holman Auditorium on Saturday, March 8, 1987. Sponsored by the Holman Department of Social Services and the Tots-to-Teens Center.

	1987	1988	Status.(+ –)
EXPENSES			
Coordinator	$700.00	$2167.15	+1467.15
Conference site	0.00	$120.00	+120.00
Brochure mailing	255.46	40.38	–215.08
Brochure printing	0.00	227.80	+227.80
Brochure design/paste–up	155.00	28.49	–126.51
Purchase mailing lists	9.38	0.00	–9.38
Presenters	520.37	550.00	+29.63
Food (at $6 each, paid by W2)	426.00	480.00	+54.00
Child Care	0.00	133.00	+133.00
refunds	111.00	31.00	–80.00
Photos	30.00	0.00	–30.00
Misc expense	87.65	8.41	–79.24
TOTAL	**$2294.86**	**3786.31**	**+1491.45**
INCOME			
Balance forward	0.00	16.71	+16.71
Dollar Donations	655.00	2530.00	+1875.00
Income from participant fees	1659.00	990.00	–669.00
Exhibitors	0.00	67.50	+67.50
W C payment for brochures	0.00	36.98	+36.98
TOTAL	**2314.00**	**3641.19**	**+1327.19**
BALANCE (DEFICIT)	**+19.14**	**–145.12**	**–164.26**
INKIND DONATIONS WE CAN QUANTIFY			
Postage, copying, long distance (CCN)	165.00	128.88	–36.12
Brochure Printing donation	444.77	200.00	–244.77
Women's Center brochure mailing	0.00	215.00	+215.00
Orange Co. DSS Mailing	0.00	40.00	+40.00
Coordinator time donation	800.00	0.00	–800.00
TOTAL	**1409.77**	**583.88**	**–825.89**

Long rows of unadorned numbers can detract from a document's effectiveness.

MAKEOVER

Evaluation Meeting

Two At Work 1987

A conference for full-time employed parents
Holman Auditorium
Saturday, March 8, 1987
Sponsored by the Holman Department of Social Services and the Tots-to-Teens Center

Budget Review

EXPENSES	1986	1987	Status(+-)
Coordinator	$700.00	$2167.15	+1467.15
Conference site	0.00	120.00	+120.00
Brochure mailing	225.46	40.38	-215.08
Brochure printing	0.00	227.80	+227.80
Brochure design/paste-up	155.00	28.49	-126.51
Purchase mailing lists	9.38	0.00	9.38
Presenters	520.37	550.00	+29.63
Food (at $6 each, paid by W2)	426.00	480.00	+54.00
Child Care	0.00	133.00	+133.00
Refunds	111.00	31.00	-80.00
Photos	30.00	0.00	-30.00
Misc expense	87.65	8.41	-79.24
TOTAL	**$2204.86**	**3700.31**	**+1491.45**

INCOME			
Balance forward	0.00	16.71	+16.71
Dollar Donations	655.00	2530.00	+1875.00
Income from participant fees	1659.00	990.00	-669.00
Exhibitors	0.00	67.50	+67.50
W C payment for brochures	0.00	36.98	+36.98
TOTAL	**2314.00**	**3641.19**	**+1327.19**
BALANCE (DEFICIT)	**+19.14**	**-145.12**	**-164.26**

INKIND DONATIONS WE CAN QUANTIFY			
Postage, copying, long distance (CCN)	165.00	128.88	-36.12
Brochure Printing donation	444.77	200.00	-244.77
Women's Center brochure mailing	0.00	215.00	+215.00
Orange Co. DSS Mailing	0.00	40.00	+40.00
Coordinator time donation	800.00	0.00	-800.00
TOTAL	**1409.77**	**583.88**	**-825.89**

Single, double and bold rules help make tables and charts meaningful.

Always provide dates and times first so readers can make important decisions without having to wade through the document.

Multiple columns, rules and simple tables can be used to make numbers and lists far more appealing.

ORIGINAL

g. Demographics (optional on evaluation form)

1 aged 20-24	20 married	35 female
5 aged 25-29	21 single	8 male
14 aged 30-34		
14 aged 35-39	38 white	
6 aged 40-44	4 minority	
2 aged 45-49		
1 aged 50-54		

Education	Ages of children	Earnings
High School 3	23 aged 0-4	2 $5-9M
High School+ 7	19 aged 5-9	13 $10-19M
Some College 10	7 aged 10-14	13 $20-29M
Tech 3	5 aged 15-19	5 $30-39M
Bachelors 10		3 $40-49M
Masters 11		
PhD 1		

List of occupations:

homemaker in transition,	attorney,	clerk,
graduate student,	library assistant,	RN,
typist,	seamstress,	research analyst,
elementary teacher,	scientist,	biologist,
engineer,	nurse,	secretary,
home day care provider,	assistant controller,	professor,
state government,	real estate manager,	supervisor,
analyst,	library,	patient relations
representative,	library assistant,	baker,
librarian,	technical writer,	administrator,
chemist,	waitress,	court administrator,
housewife,	computer operator,	accountant,
elementary education,	agency director,	research technician

Recommendations – post-conference

1. If we decide to do Working Double again with the same format:
   a. Require all registrants to pay some amount out of their own pockets.
   b. Don't announce a conference fee. Announce that it is sliding-scale and give an income range, i.e. individual income under $10,000 - $2.00;
   under $14,000 - $6.00;
   under $18,000- $10.00;
   under $22,000- $15.00;
   under $26,000 - $20.00;
   under $30,000 - $25.00;
   $30.00 for everyone else.
   c. Child Care request should also have a fee attached, e.g. $.50; $1.00; $2.00 and up.
   d. Have registrants give clear employment or student information (SS# maybe).
   e. Parking for the Carolina Union was not adequate for those arriving late (presenters mostly). Try to get an area roped off or some other solution.
   f. Announce that workshops will be held with minimum of 8 and maximum of 20.
   g. Have Riddle do a full day. Have participants sign up for 2 or 4 sessions.
   h. Foster-Burgess should be identified for two-parent households.
   i. Consider a "When children won't mind" program for those with 5-9 year olds.
   j. Do program on March 4, 1989. Flu season about over, but not into heavy spring yet.

Numbers of conflicting values are nearly indecipherable.

Commas and other punctuation aren't necessary when constructing lists.

MAKEOVER

Two At Work • EVALUATION MEETING • March 8, 1987

Demographics (optional on evaluation form)

Ages of participants	Marital Status	Sex	Racial Mix
1 20-24 years	20 married	35 female	38 white
5 25-29	21 single	8 male	4 minority
14 30-34			
14 35-39			
6 40-44			
2 45-49			
1 50-54			

Education	Ages of children	Earnings
3 High School	23 0 - 4 years	2 $5- 9 M
7 High School+	19 5 - 9	13 $10-19 M
10 Some College	7 10 - 14	13 $20-29 M
3 Tech	5 15 - 19	5 $30-39 M
10 Bachelors		
11 Masters		
1 PhD		

List of occupations:

homemaker in transition	attorney	clerk	graduate student
library assistant	RN	typist	seamstress
research analyst	elementary teacher	scientist	biologist
engineer	nurse	secretary	home day care provider
assistant controller	professor	state government	real estate manager
supervisor	analyst	library	patient relations
representative	library assistant	bake	librarian
technical writer	administrator	chemist	waitress
court administrator	housewife	computer operato	accountant
elementary education	agency director	research technician	

Recommendations—post-conference

1. If we decide to do Two at Work again with the same format:
   a. Require all registrants to pay some amount out of their own pockets.
   b. Don't announce a conference fee. Announce that it is sliding-scale and give an income range, i.e. individual income

under $10,000	$2.00	under $26,000	$20.00
under $14,000	$6.00	under $30,000	$25.00
under $18,000	$10.00	everyone else	$30.00
under $22,000	$15.00		

   c. Child Care request should also have a fee attached, e.g. $.50; $1.00, $2.00 and up.
   d. Have registrants give clear employment or student information (SS# maybe).
   e. Parking for the Holman Auditorium was not adequate for those arriving late (presenters mostly). Try to get an area roped off or some other solution.
   f. Announced that workshops will be held with minimum of 8 and maximum of 20.
   g. Have Riddle do a full day. Have participants sign up for 2 or 4 sessions.
   h. Foster-Burgess should be identified for two-parent households.
   i. Consider a "When children won't mind" program for those with 5-9 year olds.
   j. Do program on March 4, 1988. Flu season about over, but not into heavy spring yet.

Lists have been broken into multiple columns to reduce excessive white space.

A simple table, organized with horizontal and vertical rules, lends credence to the numbers.

CHAPTER
6

BUSINESS CORRESPONDENCE

What sort of impression do you make with your business cards and letterhead? Do they present you as caring and competent? Or do they communicate an impersonal, take-it-or-leave-it attitude?

Remember that people's initial response is usually subconscious and emotional. Details and "atmosphere" count for more than is generally acknowledged, especially for products and services, such as insurance and transportation, that are often purchased sight unseen. As a result, prospective clients make "buy/don't buy" decisions based on questions like these:

- ✔ Does this business look like it offers the professionalism and attention to detail I expect?
- ✔ Do the owners seem to take pride in their work?
- ✔ Will I enjoy working with this business?

Readers will form answers to these questions based on how your business correspondence deals with tone, organization and attention to detail.

Setting an Appropriate Tone

The Don's Masonry makeover shows an effective use of visual imagery. The simple graphic not only identifies the business, it also creates atmosphere—humor and a sense of professionalism.

Don's letterhead, envelopes and business cards are unified by a stylized drawing of a brick wall. This drawing performs three functions. First, it immediately identifies Don's Masonry: even before you read the words, you know what type of business Don is in. Second, the illustration organizes the business correspondence graphically, weighting the bottom of the business card and letterhead.

Third, the artwork presents Don's Masonry as an up-to-date, professional operation, distinguishing this establishment from its competitors, who probably don't use such strong visual imagery.

Compare Don's original business correspondence to the makeovers. Which do you find more effective?

Illustrations should be used with restraint, however. As shown in the Lafferty Trucking Company letterhead, envelopes and business cards, a strong visual can actually make your correspondence less effective. Notice how the visual in the original letterhead competes with the firm's name next to it.

Notice, also, how the letterhead improves when the visual is simplified—in this case by removing the tree, which does little to strengthen the trucking image.

Illustrations should always be appropriate to the message. Notice how the old-fashioned truck reinforces Lafferty's

"Since 1912" slogan. This illustration would be completely inappropriate if Lafferty's was a new business competing with older, more established firms.

Sometimes, when space is limited, visuals should be omitted entirely—as in the Lafferty's business card and envelope.

Organization

Typeface, type size and graphic accents play a major role in organizing the information you're trying to communicate. The McCauley Agency correspondence provides a good example of this.

Notice how the elements in the original business card compete for your attention. You don't know whether to look at the phone number, Edward's Insurance Agency, Inc., T/A, McCauley Agency or the information at the bottom. It's hard to tell what the business is called. Is it McCauley Agency or Edward's Insurance Agency, Inc.? It's a challenge to find the president's name, and when you do, it's hard to read it when it's set in uppercase type.

The revised business card is much more effective. It's obvious now that Edward's Insurance Agency is the most important name, and its relationship to the McCauley Agency parent company is made clear. The president's name is also easier to find and to read, since it's now located at the bottom left of the card, set in upper- and lowercase type, surrounded by plenty of white space.

Notice how the new type helps to define the relationship of "Edward's" to "McCauley." "McCauley" is set in a compressed, uppercase, sans-serif type that contrasts with the relatively unimportant "Agency," which is set in much smaller upper- and lowercase italics. "McCauley" is also balanced by a wide horizontal rule the same length as the word. The rule gives the card a pleasing diagonal balance, too.

Look at the Lafferty Trucking Company makeover again, and notice how white space organizes the text. White space adds emphasis to essential information by separating it. Notice how "Since 1912" becomes a significant part of the letterhead when the address and phone number are moved to the bottom of the page.

Attention to Detail

Attention to detail makes the difference between good and great design. Note how the brick wall on the Don's Masonry correspondence bleeds to the edges. This technique contributes a great deal to the success of the drawing. If the drawing didn't extend to the bottom and side borders, it would look awkward and incomplete. If it were defined by white space, the illustration would be a separate element, not an integral part of the letterhead, business card and envelope.

Typography is a critical element in design detail. Compare the sans-serif type of the original Lafferty Trucking Company communications with the unobtrusive serif type used in the makeover. The careful choice of typeface results in an effect that's both contemporary and established.

Take Another Look

Evaluate your letterhead, envelopes, business cards and other business forms in terms of tone, organization and attention to detail. In particular, ask yourself these questions:

✔ Does my business correspondence visually reflect the type of business I'm in?

✔ Do my communications appropriately project the marketing image I'm trying to gain—e.g., conservative, established, contemporary, etc?

✔ Is all necessary information included?

✔ Is information presented in a simple and straight-forward manner?

✔ Does my letterhead reinforce the message it contains or compete with it?

Techniques such as compressed type and mixed typefaces are important in creating distinctive logos. Desktop publishing lets you experiment with endless combinations without huge typesetting costs.

Using the same typefaces or sizes throughout the logo often lessens visual effect. It's often best to off-set names and addresses with different type styles.

Logos should be uniform on all correspondence and advertising, creating a consistent corporate image.

ORIGINAL

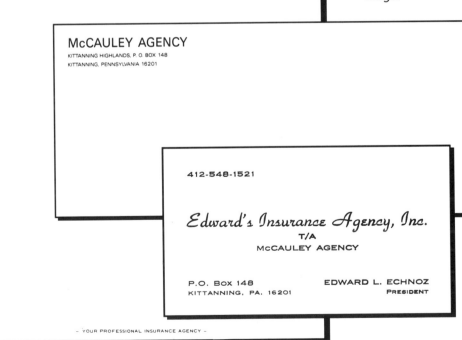

The big, bold "Mc-Cauley," off-set by the smaller, less-important "agency," adds strength to the name.

A thick bar at the top adds weight and importance to the most important word—"McCauley."

MAKEOVER

MᶜCAULEY
Agency

Insurance – Bonds
Kittanning Highlands
P.O. Box 148
Kittanning, PA 16201
412/ 548-1521

MᶜCAULEY
Agency

Kittanning Highlands
P.O. Box 148
Kittanning, PA 16201

Kittanning Highlands
P.O. Box 148, Kittanning, PA 16201
412/ 548-1521

Edward's Insurance Agency

MᶜCAULEY
Agency

Edward L. Echnoz
President

L ess is often more when working with visuals in
small spaces; keep logos clean and uncluttered.

ORIGINAL

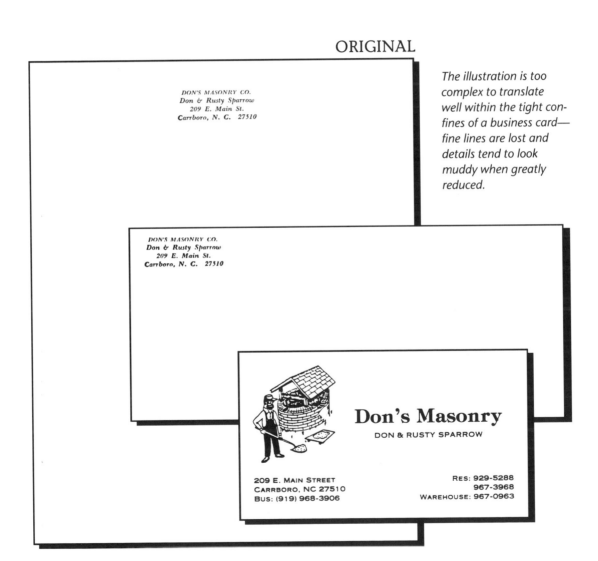

The illustration is too
complex to translate
well within the tight confines of a business card—
fine lines are lost and
details tend to look
muddy when greatly
reduced.

DON'S MASONRY CO.
Don & Rusty Sparrow
209 E. Main St.
Carrboro, N. C. 27510

DON'S MASONRY CO.
Don & Rusty Sparrow
209 E. Main St.
Carrboro, N. C. 27510

Don's Masonry
DON & RUSTY SPARROW

209 E. MAIN STREET
CARRBORO, NC 27510
BUS: (919) 968-3906

RES: 929-5288
967-3968
WAREHOUSE: 967-0963

MAKEOVER

The simple "brick" motif accurately reflects the line of business and weights the letterhead. It's flexible enough to work well above and below the logo.

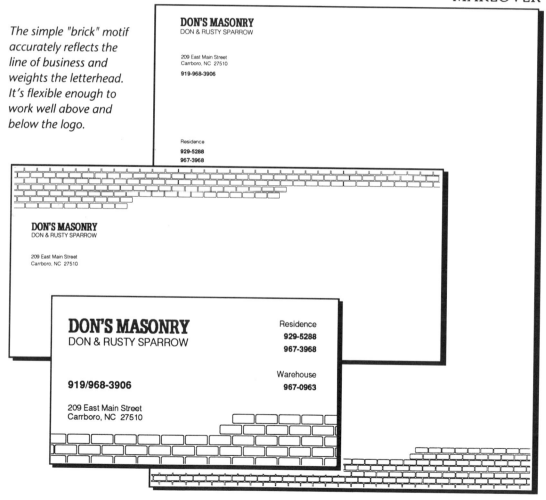

DON'S MASONRY
DON & RUSTY SPARROW

209 East Main Street
Carrboro, NC 27510
919-968-3906

Residence
929-5288
967-3968

DON'S MASONRY
DON & RUSTY SPARROW

209 East Main Street
Carrboro, NC 27510

DON'S MASONRY
DON & RUSTY SPARROW

919/968-3906

209 East Main Street
Carrboro, NC 27510

Residence
929-5288
967-3968

Warehouse
967-0963

E xperiment with logos to make certain they work well in a variety of settings. A logo might look perfect on stationery, but appear awkward on your company newsletter.

ORIGINAL

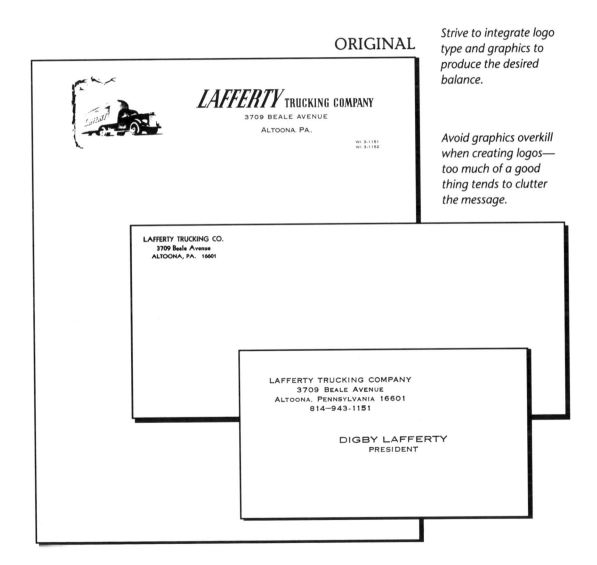

Strive to integrate logo type and graphics to produce the desired balance.

Avoid graphics overkill when creating logos— too much of a good thing tends to clutter the message.

This typeface (Cheltenham Book) adds a contemporary touch to an illustration that was done in the Forties!

Always include area codes on the telephone number, even if your business is local.

A simple repeating hairline rule lends balance and distinction to the logo and type below.

MAKEOVER

LAFFERTY
TRUCKING COMPANY
Since 1912

LAFFERTY
TRUCKING COMPANY

Digby Lafferty
President

*3709 Beale Avenue
Altoona, Pennsylvania 16601
(814) 943-1151*

LAFFERTY
TRUCKING COMPANY

*3709 Beale Avenue
Altoona, Pennsylvania 16601*

3709 Beale Avenue, Altoona, Pennsylvania 16601   (814) 943-1151

CHAPTER

7

MISCELLANEOUS DOCUMENTS

Miscellaneous documents include a wide variety of projects, from business tools—price sheets, specification sheets and purchase orders—to more formal documents such as resumes, evaluation forms and surveys.

In all cases, the goals are the same—to present information in a way that's easy to understand and easy to use. At the same time, these documents must present a professional image of your firm.

Since miscellaneous documents play such an important role in helping clients, as well as employees, form their impression of your firm, you should consider their "advertising" capacity as being equal to that of print advertisements or direct-mail newsletters. Indeed, as the original and makeover examples show, even surveys can be advertisements: effective design will increase reader response, making your results more valid.

Desktop publishing can help you produce miscellaneous communications in a cost-effective way. Projects that don't warrant the expense of conventional typesetting and layout can now be prepared quickly and cost-effectively.

Remember that specification and price sheets are usually the last print communications prospective buyers will read before opening their wallets or signing on the dotted line!

Organization

To succeed, price and specification sheets must be carefully organized. Readers must be able to clearly identify the source and quickly find the information they're looking for. Information must be categorized. Equally important, a "call to action" must be present so readers will know how to respond to the information presented.

The California Valley Homes example illustrates the advertising role of a well-designed specification sheet.

The original is homogeneous and hard to read. The large bullets introducing each listing distract you from the information they introduce. Categories of information are not clearly separated. The subheads aren't anchored and seem to "float." The relatively large, open type makes it difficult to read each line.

Most important, the original lacks identity. The California Valley Homes logo is static and small. The page lacks a dominant visual that would establish a strong identity and create a starting point for the reader.

The makeover offers a far more organized and readable presentation of the same information. Many of the improvements are based on type change.

In the makeover, the logo is reversed and set larger, spanning two columns, to tie the page together. California Valley Homes is now a logo, not just more type on the page. Notice how the tight kerning (reduced spacing between letters) creates a strong visual unit out of the individual letters.

The sans-serif type used throughout the original has been replaced with an easier-to-read serif type. There's more contrast between the subheads and the text they introduce. The subheads are also enhanced by bold horizontal rules.

Two-level indents are used to organize product information within each category, as illustrated in the "Doors and Trim" section.

George Tchobanoglous's resume illustrates many of the same techniques. Again, horizontal rules are used to organize categories and give an overall structure to the page. Flush-left alignment also organizes information. Name, address and phone number are set at the top of the page, distinguishing them from the background information that follows.

Typeface changes have also been made. Instead of the sans-serif Helvetica used in the original, the use of Helvetica in the makeovers is restricted to category headings. The related text is set in serif typeface that enhances readability.

Useless information has been omitted. The "Address" heading has been omitted, since "662 Diego Place" is self-explanatory.

Attention to detail also influences the effectiveness of business communications, as illustrated in the Don's Masonry invoice. The original design, with its dominant parallel lines, totally obscures the text. For example, try to find the "Total."

Replacing the lines with boxes helps to separate the columns and rows and makes it easier to find the labels.

The invoice illustrates again how attention to detail relates to easy use. In the original invoice, "Job Name" and "Date" are on one line; this doesn't leave much room for the job name. The makeover offers more space—likely to be appreciated by an employee who's writing while standing and holding a clipboard.

Notice another detail: the makeover's vertical rule in the "Amount" column separates dollars and cents, thereby eliminating confusion.

Surveys as Advertisements

Many of the techniques that contribute to successful advertisements can be applied to surveys. Look at the readership survey makeover for Technology Database Associates. A simple survey turns out to be a direct-response advertisement in disguise!

The original example not only looks like a survey, it's unappealing and doesn't present a professional image. The problem begins with the heading, Readership Survey.

Whenever you write a heading, ask yourself, Why should I read on? If you can't answer, chances are your reader won't be able to, either. "Readership Survey" doesn't involve the reader. It just sits there on the page without giving us any reason to find out what comes next.

The uppercase outline type for "Readership Survey" also lacks punch. It's hard to read the words because your eyes keep jumping from the white space within the letters to the outlines of the letters. The long, introductory paragraph, set in uppercase type, is equally uninviting.

The revised example presents a vivid contrast. It begins with a direct question, "Do you read us?" set in a large, bold typeface that provides impact and anchors the top of the page.

The editor's statement follows in an easy-to-read, upper- and lowercase type. The unity of the statement is reinforced by justified type, which creates a strong right-hand border leading the reader to the coupon at the bottom of the page. The publication's mission statement is personalized by setting the editor's name in "conversational" italics.

Most important, whereas the original is based on a two-column grid—with too much space between the columns—the revised survey is based on a four-column grid. The headline and introductory statement span three columns and are accented by the white space of the left column.

Enhancing Reader Response

Reader response is simplified in the Technology Database Associates survey by categorizing the response items in the second column. Whereas the original looks like a lot of work, filling out the makeover appears to be easy since you answer the questions by simply moving down the column to the category you want. The category subheads are set flush-right, which links them to the questions they introduce.

Notice how smoothly readers are invited to suggest new topics. The subtle flattery of the ...And Especially... subhead makes the reader's comments seem more important than the categories listed above.

Simple, direct headlines, introduced by an action verb, always generate the most response. Thus, the cliche, "Special Offer," which introduces the sales pitch in the original, is replaced by a strong "Read us for less!" which promises a strong benefit.

Finally, note how the gray screen makes the coupon stand out as a strong visual element. And notice how much stronger the address is when set small and flush-left in the makeover, compared to the larger, centered, uppercase boxed type of the original. Again, we see that less is more.

Avoiding Boxitis

"Boxitis"—the overuse of a desktop publishing or word processing program's box-drawing features—is a major cause of cluttering forms and surveys. Today's programs make it particularly easy to create boxes; and their parallel lines often compete with other lines.

The trainee evaluation report and speaker evaluation form originals illustrate this. In both cases, the resulting visual clutter presents a poor image of the firm or association issuing the survey. It also inhibits reader response.

The box at the top of the trainee evaluation report doesn't serve any function. Eliminating it opens up the makeover and makes it easier to move down to the evaluation sections.

Boxes often present an old-fashioned image. Pages that are boxed in by borders of equal width present a somewhat claustrophobic image, at odds with corporate and association goals. You can see this by comparing the original Howard County seminar evaluation form to the makeover. The makeover presents a far more contemporary image. The thick horizontal rules separate reader-response categories from the statements that explain them. The smaller, lighter type and the lack of additional page borders result in a far more open and reader-friendly survey.

Applying Common Sense

Remember to use common sense when you design a form. Make it easy for readers—even busy readers with messy handwriting—to complete them.

One of the best ways to do this is to provide enough space for reader response and to give clear directions. Take a look at the purchase order makeover—note how boxes and screens logically group the spaces for vendor numbers. The revised heading clearly identifies the form.

Logic and common sense also help you avoid unnecessary repetition. Note how much clearer the Howard County seminar evaluation form is when "Strongly agree—Strongly disagree" is listed only once.

Take Another Look

As you evaluate specification sheets, price lists, resumes and forms, ask yourself these questions:

✔ Is information clearly presented and sensibly organized?

✔ How clear is the call to action?

✔ Does the form or survey encourage response?

✔ Are there any unnecessary oversized graphics that detract from response?

✔ Are there enough instructions for readers to fill out the forms?

✔ Do these documents clearly reflect the tone of the firm they represent?

A dvertising that poses as surveys has become prevalent and sometimes annoying. However, readers may respond well to a survey-like, response-oriented solicitation.

ORIGINAL

READERSHIP SURVEY

THE SERVICE BUREAU NEWSLETTER IS DEDICATED TO PUBLISHING INFORMATION THAT IS OF PRACTICAL VALUE TO MICROGRAPHIC EXECUTIVES IN THE OPERATION OF THEIR BUSINESS. SO THAT WE CAN BE SURE THAT WE INCLUDE TOPICS THAT YOU WANT TO READ ABOUT PLEASE CHECKMARK THOSE TOPICS YOU ARE MOST INTERESTED IN.

MARKET PLANNING

Local market survey.

Market testing.

Market strategy

PRODUCT PLANNING

Building a profitable product mix.

Maximizing vendor relationships

SALES PROMOTION

Direct Mail

Educational Seminars

Local trade shows

Telemarketing

Public Relations

INTERFACING TECHNOLOGIES

Optical Disks

CD - ROM

Electronic Imaging

Microcomputers

Bar Coding

CAR Systems

Database Software

I AM ALSO INTERESTED IN THE FOLLOWING TOPICS:
(Write in your own topics)

SPECIAL   OFFER

I WISH TO SAVE $30.00 BY ACCEPTING THIS SPECIAL OFFER. ENCLOSED IS MY CHECK FOR $95.00 MADE PAYABLE TO TECHNOLOGY DATABASE ASSOCIATES FOR 12 ISSUES OF THE SERVICE BUREAU NEWSLETTER

NAME_____
TITLE_____
COMPANY_____
ADDRESS _____
CITY _____
STATE_____ ZIP _____
PHONE _____( )_____

_____
(SIGNATURE)

_____
(DATE)

MAIL THIS ENTIRE PAGE AND CHECK TO:

TECHNOLOGY DATABASE ASSOCIATES
P.O. BOX 3161
WESTPORT, CONNECTICUT 06880

CALL ME IF YOU HAVE ANY QUESTIONS -----

CHUCK MILES, EDITOR 203-222-9310

PAGE 8

The body copy on the makeover has been replaced by a friendlier letter-from-the-editor type of motif.

The check-boxes over-whelm the type on the original.

MAKEOVER

Do you read us?

The Service Bureau Newsletter is dedicated to publishing information that is of practical value to micrographic executives in the operation of their businesses. So that we can be sure that we include articles you want to read, please check the topics which interest you most. Call me at 203/222-9310 if you have any questions.

Chuck Miles, Editor

Market Planning
- ❑ Local market survey
- ❑ Market testing
- ❑ Market strategy

Product Planning
- ❑ Building a profitable product mix
- ❑ Maximizing vendor relationships

Sales Promotion
- ❑ Direct mail
- ❑ Educational seminars
- ❑ Local trade shows
- ❑ Telemarketing
- ❑ Public relations

Interfacing Technologies
- ❑ Optical disks
- ❑ CD-ROM
- ❑ Electronic imaging
- ❑ Microcomputers
- ❑ Bar coding
- ❑ CAR systems
- ❑ Database software

. . . And Especially . . . Write in your own topics:

_____

_____

_____

_____

Read us for less!

I accept your special offer to save $30 on my next 12 issues of **The Service Bureau Newsletter**. Enclosed is my check for $95, payable to Techology Database Associates.

Name

Title

Company

Address

City   *State*   *Zip*

Phone

Signature

Date

Return this page with your check to:
Technology Database Associates
P.O. Box 3161
Westport, Connecticut 06880

Return address information should be well positioned, but not necessarily large. Once a reader has decided to purchase, he or she will find the mail-back data.

Note how adding the headline, coupon and bold type makes the piece look less like a survey and more like an ad.

Organization and layout can make or break a survey—particularly among busy readers who shouldn't have to think twice as they answer questions.

ORIGINAL

Media Action Project Survey

DATE: _____

Check at least two:
☐ a. Actively working as a producer or co-producer with a work in progress
☐ b. Have been a producer or co-producer with producer credits
☐ c. Have production experience and actively seeking funds
☐ d. Have been denied funding for a majority of funding proposals

1. What areas of media do you work in?
☐ TELEVISION   ☐ Commercial   ☐ STATION:
☐ VIDEO PRODUCTION ☐ Corporate-Industrial ☐ Local
☐ CABLE   ☐ Independent**   ☐ Network
☐ AUDIO/RADIO PRODUCTION ☐ Public
                    ☐ Public Access
                    ** Independent: having artistic control of your work

2. Indicate your principal areas of work by ranking them in priority of involvement from number 1 to 3.
___ TELEVISION   ___ Commercial   ___ STATION:
___ VIDEO   ___ Corporate-Industrial ___ Local
___ AUDIO/RADIO   ___ Independent   ___ Network
___ CABLE   ___ Public
                    ___ Public Access

3. Do you have film-making experience? ☐ Yes ☐ No In what formats? ☐ 8mm 16mm ☐ 35mm

4. Do you have video-making experience? In what formats? ☐ 1/2" ☐ 3/4" ☐ 1" ☐ 8mm

5. What media production experience do you have? specify
☐ TELEVISION   ☐ Producer   ☐ Engineer
☐ VIDEO   ☐ Director   ☐ Camera
☐ PRODUCTION   ☐ Manager   ☐ Sound
☐ AUDIO/RADIO PRODUCTION   ☐ Lights
☐ CABLE   ☐ Editing
other: _____

6. How long have you been producing? ☐ 1-3 years ☐ 3-6 years ☐ 6-10 years ☐ 10-20 years ☐ 20+

7. What influenced you to enter the media field?
☐ formal education   ☐ friends/family   ☐ community interests
☐ selected courses   ☐ mentors   ☐ arts background
other: _____

8. In what styles of media are you producing/have you produced?
☐ documentary ☐ narrative/fiction ☐ experimental other: _____

9. What areas have you had experience with?   Contract Negotiations:
☐ Production contracts ☐ Equipment/Insurance ☐ Distribution ☐ Exhibition ☐ None of the above
other:
If you have worked with unions, which ones? _____

10. What subject areas best describe the focus of the majority of your work?
☐ Social concerns: ☐ local ☐ national ☐ global   }
☐ Politics: ☐ local ☐ national ☐ global   } other: _____
☐ Culture/the arts: ☐ performing ☐ literary ☐ visual ☐ folk }

11. Are you producing a project now? ☐ Yes ☐ No

12. What stage is the project in? ☐ Pre-production ☐ Production ☐ Post-production ☐ Distribution
other: _____

Always be consistent in design style; here, boxes and dashes were used to solicit the same information, discouraging readership.

Information is spread across the page and questions aren't differentiated from answers or from other questions.

MAKEOVER

MEDIA ACTION PROJECT SURVEY

Date: _____

Check at least two:

❑ a. Actively working as a producer or co-producer with a work in progress
❑ b. Have been a producer or co-producer with producer credits
❑ c. Have production experience and actively seeking funds
❑ d. Have been denied funding for a majority of funding projects

1. What areas of media do you work in?

❑ TELEVISION ❑ Commercial
❑ VIDEO PRODUCTION ❑ Corporate-Industrial
❑ CABLE ❑ Independent**
❑ AUDIO/RADIO PRODUCTION ❑ Public
❑ Public Access
❑ STATION: ❑ Local ❑ Network
**Independent: having artistic control of your work

2. Indicate your principal areas of work by ranking them in priority of involvement from number 1 to 3.

❑ TELEVISION ❑ Commercial
❑ VIDEO ❑ Corporate-Industrial
❑ AUDIO/RADIO ❑ Independent**
❑ CABLE ❑ Public
❑ Public Access
❑ STATION: ❑ Local ❑ Network

3. Do you have film-making experience?

❑ Yes ❑ No
In what formats? ❑ 8mm ❑ 16mm ❑ 35mm

4. Do you have video-making experience?

❑ Yes ❑ No
In what formats? ❑ 1/2" ❑ 3/4" ❑ 1" ❑ 8mm

5. What media production experience do you have?

❑ TELEVISION ❑ Producer
❑ VIDEO ❑ Director
❑ PRODUCTION ❑ Manager
❑ AUDIO/RADIO PRODUCTION ❑ Engineer
❑ CABLE ❑ Camera
❑ Sound
❑ Lights
❑ Editing
Other: _____

6. How long have you been producing?

❑ 1-3 years ❑ 3-6 years ❑ 6-10 years ❑ 10-20 years ❑ 20+

7. What influenced you to enter the media field?

❑ Formal education ❑ Friends/family
❑ Community interests ❑ Selected courses
❑ Mentors ❑ Arts background
Other: _____

8. In what styles of media are you producing/ have you produced?

❑ Documentary ❑ Narrative/fiction ❑ Experimental
Other: _____

9. What areas have you had experience with? Contract Negotiations:

❑ Production contracts ❑ Equipment/insurance
❑ Distribution ❑ Exhibition
❑ None of the above
Other _____
If you have worked with unions, which ones? _____

10. What subject areas best decribe the focus of the majority of your work?

❑ Social concerns: ❑ local ❑ national ❑ global
❑ Politics: ❑ local ❑ national ❑ global
❑ Culture/the arts: ❑ performing ❑ literary
❑ visual ❑ folk
Other subject areas: _____

11. Are you producing a project now?

❑ Yes ❑ No

12. What stage is the project in?

❑ Pre-production ❑ Production
❑ Post-production ❑ Distribution
Other: _____

The two-column format tightens the white space and allows readers to quickly grasp and respond to information in blocks.

Lightly screened rules separate the question blocks without harshly weighting the page.

Price lists are often hard to read simply because most companies pay little attention to their design and effectiveness—a mistake that can result in lost sales.

ORIGINAL

ENSEMBLES WITH PIANO: 15% OFF SELECTED EDITIONS

COMPOSER	PUBLISHER		YOUR COST
ARENSKY	KAL	Piano Trio,op32: vn,vc,pf	5.95
BERWALD	BAR	Piano Quartet,Eb: cl,hrn,bsn,pf	13.75
CHAUSSON	INT	Piano Quartet,op30: vn,va,vc,pf	17.00
COLERIDGE-TAYLOR	KAL	Valse de la Rheine: 2vn,va,vc,pf	5.10
FAURE	INT	Piano Quartet #2,op45: vn,va,vc,pf	15.30
MENDELSSOHN,FANNY	KNZ	Piano Trio,op11: vn,vc,pf	24.45
RACHMANINOFF	KAL	Trio Elegiaque, op.9: vn,vc,pf	9.75
SCHUMANN,CLARA	KNZ	Piano Trio,op17: vn,vc,pf	26.50
SCHUBERT	INT	Trout Quintet: vn,va,vc,bass(2nd vc),pf	11.70
WEBER	INT	Piano Trio,op63: vn,vc,pf	9.35

ENSEMBLES WITH FLUTE: 15% OFF SELECTED EDITIONS

COMPOSER	PUBLISHER		YOUR COST
BACH	BAR	Musical Offering: fl,vn,pf	8.15
DANZI	MR	Sinf.Conc.,op41: fl,cl,pf	13.80
DANZI	INT	Quintet,op67,#2:fl,ob,cl,bsn,hrn	11.00
HAYDN	INT	London Trios: 2fl,vc	8.50
PLEYEL	INT	3 Quartets,op41: fl,vn,va,vc	11.70
RAMEAU	BAR	Pieces de Clavecin: fl,vc,pt	25.50
REICHA	KNZ	Grand Quat.Conc,op104: fl,bsn,vc,pf	26.75
SHOSTAKOVICH	MR	Four Waltzes: fl,cl,pf	7.40
SPOHR	MR	Quintet,op52: fl,cl,bsn,hrn,pf	19.15

PUBLISHER CODES:

BAR=BAERENREITER	KAL=KALMUS
BEN=BENLE	KNZ=KUNZELMANN
INT=INTERNATIONAL	MR=MUSICA RARA

Always align numbers on price lists around the decimal.

Placing prices inside the box and off to the right makes it difficult to match the edition with the cost.

MAKEOVER

ENSEMBLES WITH PIANO: *15% OFF SELECTED EDITIONS*

COMPOSER	PUBLISHER		YOUR COST
Arensky	KAL	Piano Trio, op.32: vn, vc, pf	5.95
Berwald	BAR	Piano Quartet, Eb: cl, hrn, bsn, pf	13.75
Chausson	INT	Piano Quartet, op.30: vn, va, vc, pf	17.00
Coleridge-Taylor	KAL	Valse de la Rheine: 2vn, va, vc, pf	5.10
Faure	INT	Piano Quartet #2,op.45: vn, va, vc, pf	15.30
Mendelssohn, Fanny	KNZ	Piano Trio, op.11: vn,vc, pf	24.45
Rachmaninoff	KAL	Trio Elegiaque, op.9: vn, vc, pf	9.75
Schumann, Clara	KNZ	Piano Trio, op.17: vn, vc, pf	26.50
Schubert	INT	Trout Quintet: vn, va, vc, bass (2nd vc), pf	11.70
Weber	INT	Piano Trio, op.63: vn, vc, pf	9.35

Rules serve the dual purpose of off-setting the products and allowing the eye to easily scan for prices.

ENSEMBLES WITH FLUTES: *15% OFF SELECTED EDITIONS*

COMPOSER	PUBLISHER		YOUR COST
Bach	BAR	Musical Offering: fl, vn, pf	8.15
Danzi	MR	Sinf.Conc., op.41: fl, cl, pf	13.80
Danzi	INT	Quintet, op.67, #2:fl, ob, cl, bsn, hrn	11.00
Haydn	INT	London Trios: 2fl, vc	8.50
Pleyel	INT	3 Quartets, op.41: fl, vn, va, vc	11.70
Rameau	BAR	Pieces de Clavecin: fl, vc, pf	25.50
Reicha	KNZ	Grand Quat. Conc., op.104: fl, bsn, vc, pf	26.75
Shostakovich	MR	Four Waltzes: fl, cl, pf	7.40
Spohr	MR	Quintet, op. 52: fl, cl, bsn, hrn, pf	19.15

Publisher Codes: **BAR**=Baerenreiter, **HEN**=Henle, **INT**=International, **KAL**=Kalmus, **KNZ**=Kunzelmann, **MR**=Musica Rara

Bold type and horizontal formatting make the codes at the bottom easier to scan.

Avoid typewritten formats when creating visually complex documents such as price lists—Courier and Prestige typefaces don't offer enough sizes and styles to highlight important information.

ORIGINAL

CENTURY
offers the best buys in Music

with an 'INTERNATIONAL FLAVOR'........
(music/words/chords)
....."Hard To Be A Jew"/Vocal Selection 3.95
.....Hebrew Festival Melodies-EZ Pa./Voc.2.95
.....Israeli&Jewish Song Hits-EZ Pa./Voc 5.95
.....Israel In Song   6.95
.....Jewish Nostalgia-EZ Pa./Voc.   6.95
.....Jewish Song Hits-EZ Pa./Voc.   5.95
.....Jewish Theatre Songs - Vol.1   5.95
.....Kammen Favorite Jewish Songs Vol.2 5.95
.....International Dance Folio No.1   5.95
.....International Dance & Concert
     Folio No. 9   5.95
.....Lichvad Ha Shabbat/A Contemporary
     Sabbat Service-Sholom Secunda   3.00
.....New York Times Great Songs Of The
     Yiddish Theatre/Norman Warembud
     (Hard Cover)   14.95
.....Russian Songs/Ed.Henry Lefkowitch   6.95
              JEWISH SONG HITS
(World Famous Songs Made EZ To Play/Estella)
.....Accordion   5.95
.....Guitar or Violin   4.95
.....Clarinet-Tenor Saxophone   4.95
.....Eb Alto Saxophone   4.95
.....Trumpet   4.95
        ISRAELI & JEWISH SONG HITS
           (EZ To Play/Jaffe&Kammen)
.....Accordion   4.95
.....Guitar or Violin   4.95
.....Clarinet-Tenor Saxophone   4.95
.....Eb Alto Saxophone   4.95
.....Trumpet   4.95
KAMMEN INTERNATIONAL DANCE FOLIO NO. 1
.....Accordion   4.95
.....Guitar or Violin   4.95
.....Clarinet-Tenor Saxophone   4.95
.....Eb Alto Saxophone   4.95
.....Trumpet   4.95
KAMMEN INTERNATIONAL DANCE&CONCERT FOLIO NO9
.....Accordion   4.95
.....Guitar or Violin   4.95
.....Clarinet-Tenor Saxophone   4.95
.....Eb Alto Saxophone   4.95
.....Trumpet   4.95

.....Hebrew Festival Melodies-Finest collection of its kind!For elementary pianists and
organists with guitar symbols...........2.95
.....Pictures At An Art Exhibition-A beautiful edition of Moussorgsky's masterpiece,
explained and presented in its entirety.2.95

"MOST POPULAR" Piano Books $4.95 each
....MP 1-PIANO PIECES
....MP 2-PIANO PIECES IN SIMPLIFIED FORM
....MP 3A-TUNES YOU LIKE TO PLAY(large notes) *
....MP 3B-TUNES YOU LIKE TO PLAY(large notes)
....MP 4-EASY PIECES FOR PIANO AND ALL ORGANS
....MP 5-MUSIC FROM THE MASTERS TO THE MINORS *
....MP 6-EASY DUETS FOR PIANO *
....MP 7-93 SHORT CLASSICS
....MP 8-90 TRI-CHORD TUNES
....MP 9-107 EASY TO PLAY HYMNS
....MP 10-FINEST PIANO SOLOS
....MP 11-BEAUTIFUL STRAUSS WALTZES
....MP 12-STANDARD PIANO PIECES
....MP 13-MUSIC OF THE GREAT MASTERS
....MP 14-CHILDREN'S PIANO PIECES
             (*$5.95 each)
....BLANK STOCK WRAPPERS FOR FILING SHEET MUSIC.
Sturdy grey kraft, with space for sales record
of number. 6¢ each.

CENTURY MUSIC PUBLISHING CO.,INC.
263 Veterans Blvd.,Carlstadt,N.J. 07072

NAME_____
ADDRESS_____
CITY_____STATE_____ZIP_____

Although only one typeface was used, creative use of bold and type sizes effectively separates categories, making it easy to read the prices.

Never use leader lines or broken lines when information is to be completed.

MAKEOVER

C E N T U R Y
THE BEST BUYS IN MUSIC

INTERNATIONAL FLAVOR

____	"Hard To Be A Jew"/Vocal Selection	3.95
____	Hebrew Festival Melodies–EZ Pa./Voc.	2.95
____	Israeli & Jewish Song Hits–EZ Pa./Voc.	5.95
____	Israel In Song	6.95
____	Jewish Nostalgia–EZ Pa./Voc	6.95
____	Jewish Song Hits–EZ Pa./Voc	5.95
____	Jewish Theatre Songs Vol. 1	5.95
____	Kammen Favorite Jewish Songs Vol. 2	5.95
____	International Dance Folio No. 1	5.95
____	International Dance & Concert Folio No. 9	5.95
____	Lichvad Ha Sabbat/A Contemporary Sabbat Service-Sholom Secunda	3.00
____	New York Times Great Songs of The Yiddish Theatre/Norman Warembud (Hard Cover)	14.95
____	Russian Songs/Ed. Henry Lefkowitch	6.95

Jewish Song Hits
(World Famous Songs Made EZ to Play/Estella)

____	Accordion	5.95
____	Guitar or Violin	4.95
____	Clarinet–Tenor Saxophone	4.95
____	Eb Alto Saxophone	4.95
____	Trumpet	4.95

Israeli & Jewish Song Hits (EZ to Play/Jaffe & Kammen)

____	Accordion	4.95
____	Guitar or Violin	4.95
____	Clarinet–Tenor Saxophone	4.95
____	Eb Alto Saxophone	4.95
____	Trumpet	4.95

Kammen International Dance Folio No. 1

____	Accordion	4.95
____	Guitar or Violin	4.95
____	Clarinet–Tenor Saxophone	4.95
____	Eb Alto Saxophone	4.95
____	Trumpet	4.95

Kammen Int'l Dance & Concert Folio No. 9

____	Accordion	4.95
____	Guitar or Violin	4.95
____	Clarinet–Tenor Saxophone	4.95
____	Eb Alto Saxophone	4.95
____	Trumpet	4.95

Hebrew Festival Melodies

____	Finest collection of its kind! For elementary pianists and organists with guitar symbols	2.95

"MOST POPULAR" Piano Books

$4.95 each (with * $5.95 each)

____	MP 1	Piano Pieces
____	MP 2	Piano Pieces in Simplified Form
____	MP 3A	Tunes You Like to Play (large notes)*
____	MP 3B	Tunes You Like to Play (large notes)
____	MP 4	Easy Pieces for Piano and All Organs
____	MP 5	Music from the Masters to the Minors*
____	MP 6	Easy Duets for Piano*
____	MP 7	93 Short Classics
____	MP 8	90 Tri-Chord Tunes
____	MP 9	107 Easy to Play Hymns
____	MP 10	Finest Piano Solos
____	MP 11	Beautiful Strauss Waltzes
____	MP 12	Standard Piano Pieces
____	MP 13	Music of the Great Masters
____	MP 14	Children's Piano Pieces

Pictures At An Art Exhibition

____	A beautiful edition of Moussorgsky's masterpiece, explained and presented in its entirety.	2.95

Blank stock wrappers for filing Sheet Music

____	sturdy grey kraft, with space for sales record of number.	6 cents each

CENTURY MUSIC PUBLISHING CO., INC.
263 Veterans Blvd., Carlstadt, N.J. 07072

Name _____

Address _____

City _____ State _____ Zip _____

A bold rule anchors the top and bottom, and complements the bold type.

Use boxes "popped" from a light background screen to distinguish categories, coupons and other distinct blocks of copy.

Forms, such as invoices and price lists, can now be an integral part of the corporate image at no extra cost.

ORIGINAL

DON'S MASONRY CO.
Don & Rusty Sparrow
209 E. Main St.
Carrboro, N. C. 27510

JOB NAME: _____   DATE: _____

MASONRY UNITS	UNITS DELIVERED	LEFT ON JOB	UNITS LAID	UNIT PRICE		AMOUNT
Face Brick — Reg.						
Face Brick — Oversize						
Cull:						
Solite Brick						
Fill Brick						
Block: 4"						
6"						
8"						
12"						
Caps						
				TOTAL		

SIGNATURE: _____
DON'S MASONRY

A poorly organized invoice might reflect the same of a business.

As cottage industries grow up, and desktop publishing proliferates, the public will be less willing to accept messy documents.

MAKEOVER

DON'S MASONRY
DON & RUSTY SPARROW

209 East Main Street
Carrboro, NC 27510

Job

Date

Masonry Units	Units Delivered	Left on Job	Units Laid	Unit Price		Amount	
Face Brick – Regular							
Face Brick – Oversize							
Culls							
Solite Brick							
Fill Brick							
Block: 4"							
6"							
8"							
12"							
Caps							

TOTAL

Signature

The "brick" motif nicely reflects the line of business—while remaining functional!

A bolder box highlights the all-important "total."

Because they're not sales pieces per se, spec sheets and product listings often omit logo and address information—just when the customer may be ready to buy!

ORIGINAL

STANDARD SPECIFICATIONS - All Models

California Valley Homes

Walls

☐ Exterior: 2" x 6" studs 16" on center.
☐ 3/8" plywood sheathing.
☐ Interior: 2" x 4" studs 16" on center.
☐ 1/2" sheetrock throughout, taped and painted off-white.
☐ All corners and wall/ceiling joints taped and compounded –no beads of caulk or moldings.
☐ Plywood under sheetrock joints.
☐ Sheetrock glued and nailed to studs.
☐ Sheathing locked to floor and plates.
☐ 6" insulation (see insulation).

Floors

☐ 2" x 10" joists 16" on center.
☐ Center carrying beam: Six 2" x 10"s bolted and glued.
☐ Sub Floors: 1" plywood (two 1/2" layers) glued and nailed.
☐ Metal cross bridging.
☐ Outside band joist: 2" x 10".
☐ 6" insulation (see insulation)

Roof and Ceilings

☐ 2" x 6" roof rafters and ceiling joists spaced 16"

on center (patented roof system). Meets or exceeds 40 lb. snow load.
☐ 1/2" plywood roof sheathing.
☐ 5/12 pitch standard; higher roof pitches optional.
☐ 10 3/4" overhang front and rear; 12" on sides.
☐ 225 lb. spec. self-seal fiberglass asphalt shingles over felt.
☐ Ridge vent and vented soffit.
☐ 1/2" sheetrock on ceilings, taped and painted with sand finish.
☐ 7'6" ceiling height except in cathedral areas.
☐ *Optional:* 8' ceiling height.
☐ 12" insulation (see insulation).

Insulation

☐ Ceiling: R-38; 12" fiberglass installed in two 6" layers overlapped to eliminate gaps.
☐ Floor: R-19; 6" fiberglass installed locally.
☐ Wall: R-19; 6" fiberglass in a 2" x 6" wall (R-21 total wall structure)
☐ *Optional:* 3/4" layer of polystyrene foam with foil back sheetrock. (R-25 total wall structure)

Siding

☐ Standard: Maintenance-free vinyl or aluminum siding.
☐ *Optional:* Cedar clapboard, board & batten, cedar shingle, or other siding.

☐ *Optional:* Various exterior trim packages.

Windows

☐ Andersen High Performance windows; double hung, vinyl clad.
☐ Window screens
☐ Front shutters
☐ Interior window sash natural wood ready for staining.
☐ *Optional:* Any Anderson window; bow, sliding, arch, crankout etc.

Doors and Trim

Interior
Choice of:
☐ Wood Luan doors, unstained.
☐ 6-panel colonial doors, primed.
☐ Natural colonial wood trim ready for staining.
☐ Privacy lock door knobs on bathroom and master bedroom doors.
☐ Passage door knobs on all other interior doors.
☐ *Optional:* 6-panel solid wood doors, unstained.
☐ *Optional:* Stained interior woodwork and trim.

Exterior
☐ 6 panel metal clad front door with foam insulation and thermal break.
☐ Crossbuck metal clad kitchen door with foam insulation, insulated glass, and thermal break.

Vertical rules in this piece fight with bullets and bolding. They're best used to off-set large, unbroken blocks of text.

The bullets look like check-boxes, sending a confusing message to readers.

MAKEOVER

California Valley Homes

STANDARD SPECIFICATIONS FOR ALL MODELS

Walls

- **Exterior:**
  2" x 6" studs
  16" on center
- **Sheathing:**
  3/8" plywood
- **Interior:**
  2" x 4" studs
  16" on center
- **Sheetrock:**
  1/2" throughout
  Taped and painted off-white
- **All corners and wall/ceiling joints:**
  Taped and compounded
  No beads of caulk or moldings
- **Plywood:**
  Under sheetrock joints
- **Sheetrock glued and nailed to studs**
- **Sheathing:**
  Locked to floor and plates
- **Insulation:**
  6" insulation
  (For further information, see Insulation)

Floors

- **Joists:**
  2" x 10" joists
  16" on center
- **Center carrying beam:**
  Six 2" x 10"s
  Bolted and glued
- **Sub Floors:**
  1" plywood (two 1/2" layers)
  Glued and nailed
- **Metal cross bridging**
- **Outside band joist:**
  2" x 10"
- **Insulation:**
  6" insulation
  (For further information, see Insulation)

Roof and Ceilings

- **Roof rafters and ceiling joists:**
  2" x 6" roof rafters
  Ceiling joists 16" on center
  (Patented roof system)
- **Snow load:**
  Meets or exceeds 40 lb.
- **Roof sheathing:**
  1/2" plywood
- **Pitch:**
  5/12 pitch standard
  Higher pitches optional
- **Overhang:**
  10 3/4" front and rear
  12" on sides
- **Shingles:**
  225 lb.
  Spec. self-seal fiberglass
  Asphalt shingles over felt
- **Venting:**
  Ridge vent
  Vented soffit
- **Ceilings:**
  1/2" sheetrock
  Taped and painted
  Sand finish
- **Ceiling height:**
  7'6" except in cathedral areas
- **Optional:**
  8' ceiling height
- **Insulation:**
  12" insulation
  (For further information, see Insulation)

Insulation

- **Ceiling:**
  R-38
  12" fiberglass
  Installed in two 6" layers
  overlapped to eliminate gaps
- **Floor:**
  R-19
  6" fiberglass
  Installed locally
- **Wall:**
  R-19
  6" fiberglass in 2" x 6" wall
  (R-21 total wall structure)
- **Optional:**
  3/4" layer
  Polystyrene foam with foil back sheetrock
  (R-25 total wall structure)

Siding

- **Standard:**
  Maintenance-free vinyl or aluminum siding
- **Optional:**
  Cedar clapboard, board & batten, cedar shingle, or other siding
  Various exterior trim packages

Windows

- **Manufacturer:**
  Andersen High Performance windows
  Double hung
  Vinyl clad.
- **Window screens**
- **Front shutters**
- **Sashes:**
  Interior window sash
  natural wood ready for staining
- **Optional:**
  Any Andersen window —
  bow, sliding, arch,
  crankout, etc.

Doors and Trim

Interior

- **Doors:**
  Choice of —
  - Unstained Wood Luan
  - Primed 6-panel colonial
- **Trim:**
  Natural colonial wood trim
  ready for staining
- **Door knobs:**
  - Privacy lock door knobs on bathroom and master bedroom doors
  - Passage door knobs on all other interior doors
- **Optional:**
  - 6-panel solid wood doors, unstained
  - Stained interior wood work and trim

Exterior

- **Front door:**
  6 panel metal clad front door with foam insulation and thermal break
- **Kitchen door:**
  Crossbuck metal clad kitchen door with foam insulation, insulated glass and thermal break

California Valley Homes
76 Madison Avenue
Santa Barbara, CA 93101
805/966-1234

A four-column format helps tighten the type and open up white space between categories.

Thick rules and more liberal use of bold type let readers more easily scan the page for specific information.

The appropriate placement of a few rules and screens can make forms, surveys and other "action" documents vastly more readable—and easier to complete.

ORIGINAL

BRANCH ORIENTATION
TRAINEE EVALUATION REPORT
CONFIDENTIAL

NAME _____ DEPARTMENT _____

BRANCH _____ DATE OF HIRE _____

TRAINING PERIOD COVERED _____ DATE OF LAST EVALUATION _____
(if applicable)

NAME OF EVALUATOR _____ DATE OF THIS EVALUATION _____

I. MAJOR SKILL/BEHAVIORAL INDICATORS
Rating of each behavior according to the **KEY** below reflects trainee performance during the Branch Orientation Training Program.

II. RESULTS
Zone Training Coordinator | Branch Department Manager

A. *PERFORMANCE IN THE CLASSROOM*
- Gives correct answers when questioned — N/A
- Completes assignments on time — N/A
- Participates - asks questions to further understanding — N/A
- Volunteers answers — N/A

B. *PERFORMANCE IN THE DEPARTMENT*
- Completes assignments on time — N/A
- Asks questions to further understanding — N/A

C. *COMMUNICATION SKILLS*
- Writes in clear, concise organized manner
- Makes clear, organized, accurate presentations
- Uses platform skills in speaking to group

D. *INTERPERSONAL SKILLS*
- Interacts effectively with peers (gives constructive feedback, demonstrates respect for ideas and opinions of others, gives support and help when appropriate)
- Interacts effectively with instructors

E. *TEST SCORES/GRASP OF MATERIAL*
- Demonstrates grasp of material through passing test scores

QUIZ 1 | QUIZ 2 | FINAL EXAM

Individual score

Class Average

ZONE TRAINING COORDINATOR _____ DATE

BRANCH DEPARTMENT MANAGER _____ DATE

TRAINEE _____ DATE

KEY
++ = Demonstrates excellent skills (cite examples on back of page)
+ = Satisfactory performance of skill
– = Needs improvement (cite examples on back of page)
0 = Not observed

©Copyright 1988

The bullets in the body copy are too large, over-whelming the type and distracting the reader.

The name of the form should be prominently featured so that it can be easily discerned from other, similar documents.

MAKEOVER

TRAINEE EVALUATION REPORT

BRANCH ORIENTATION PHASE   **CONFIDENTIAL**

Name _____ Department _____
Branch _____ Date of Hire _____
Training Period Covered _____ Date of Last Evaluation _____
      (if applicable)
Name of Evaluator _____ Date of This Evaluation _____

I. MAJOR SKILL/BEHAVIORAL INDICATORS	II. RESULTS	
Rating of each behavior according to the **KEY** below reflects trainee performance during the Branch Orientation Training Program.	Zone Training Coordinator	Branch Department Manager
A. PERFORMANCE IN THE CLASSROOM		
• Gives correct answers when questioned	☐	N/A
• Completes assignments on time	☐	N/A
• Participates - asks questions to further understanding	☐	N/A
• Volunteers answers	☐	N/A
B. PERFORMANCE IN THE DEPARTMENT		
• Completes assignments on time	N/A	☐
• Asks questions to further understanding	N/A	☐
C. COMMUNICATION SKILLS		
• Writes in clear, concise, organized manner	☐	☐
• Makes clear, organized, accurate presentations	☐	☐
• Uses platform skills in speaking to group	☐	☐
D. INTERPERSONAL SKILLS		
• Interacts effectively with peers (gives constructive feedback, demonstrates respect for ideas and opinions of others, gives support and help when appropriate)	☐	☐
• Interacts effectively with instructors	☐	☐
E. TEST SCORES/GRASP OF MATERIAL		
• Demonstrates grasp of material through passing test scores		

                                 Quiz 1 Quiz 2 Final Exam
                Individual Score ☐   ☐   ☐
                Class Average ☐   ☐   ☐

		KEY
Zone Training Coordinator	Date	**++** Demonstrates excellent skills (cite examples on back of page)
Branch Department Manager	Date	**+** Satisfactory performance of skill
Trainee	Date	**-** Needs improvement (cite examples on back of page)
		0 Not observed

Desktop publishing lets you use screens and rules as tools of emphasis.

Two boxes at the bottom give weight to the piece and add balance.

Because information handwritten on purchase orders and invoices is usually transferred to a computer by someone else, forms must be easy to complete and interpret.

ORIGINAL

PURCHASE ORDER

Job NUMBER

Vendor NUMBER   Vendor reference NUMBER

Vendor name   Date ordered

Purchasing Agent   Order Type   RO#

Terms_____

FOB Point_____

Ship VIA_____

Conf. Needed_____ (N-Original order, Y-Confirming copy, X-No confirmation)

Order Taken By_____

Date Requred_____

References: _____
_____
_____
_____
_____

Quantity	PM#	Vendor Part#	Description	SO#	Unit Cost

Ship to: NAME _____
            ATTENTION_____
            STREET_____
            P.O. BOX _____
            CITY_____ STATE_____ ZIP_____

Make form headings large and easy to iden-tify, particularly if your company uses a number of similar forms.

MAKEOVER

PURCHASE ORDER

VENDOR # ☐☐☐☐ VENDOR REF# ☐☐☐☐☐ ORDER TYPE: ☐S ☐D RO#

VENDOR NAME ☐☐☐☐☐☐☐☐☐☐ DATE ORDERED ☐☐☐☐☐☐

JOB # ☐☐☐☐☐☐

SHIP TO: NAME ☐☐☐☐☐☐☐☐☐☐☐

ATTN. ☐☐☐☐☐☐☐☐☐☐☐

STREET ☐☐☐☐☐☐☐☐☐☐☐

P.O. BOX ☐☐☐☐☐☐☐☐☐☐☐

C-S-Z ☐☐☐☐☐☐☐☐☐☐☐

QTY	PM#	VENDOR PART#	DESCRIPTION	SO#	UNIT COST

PURCHASING AGENT ☐☐☐

TERMS ☐☐☐

FOB POINT ☐☐☐

SHIP VIA ☐☐☐

CONF. NEEDED ☐ (N-original order, Y-confirming copy, X-no confirmation)

ORDER TAKEN BY ☐☐☐

DATE REQUIRED ☐☐☐☐☐☐

REFERENCES
_____
_____
_____
_____
_____
_____
_____

Use boxes instead of rules, so there's no confusion about whether required information goes above or below the question.

A larger work space makes writing more legible—your data entry person will be forever grateful!

Keep writing to a minimum by offering choices the reader can check rather than fill in a written response.

Most word processing software now carries basic desktop publishing features, so even the most modest forms can be more readable and look better.

ORIGINAL

Evaluation

I. GENERAL SESSION — Keynote Speaker
Please circle one

Strongly Agree — Strongly Disagree

5	4	3	2	1	(1) The information presented increased my knowledge of secondary education in Howard County.
5	4	3	2	1	(2) The presentation was relevant and well presented.
5	4	3	2	1	(3) I would recommend this speaker for future conferences.

Other Comments or Observations: _____

II. SESSION I— TITLE: _____
Please circle one

Strongly Agree — Strongly Disagree

5	4	3	2	1	(1) The information presented increased my knowledge of secondary education in Howard County.
5	4	3	2	1	(2) The presentation was relevant and well presented.
5	4	3	2	1	(3) I would recommend this speaker for future conferences.

Other Comments or Observations: _____

III. SESSION II — TITLE: _____
Please circle one

Strongly Agree — Strongly Disagree

5	4	3	2	1	(1) The information presented increased my knowledge of secondary education in Howard County.
5	4	3	2	1	(2) The presentation was relevant and well presented.
5	4	3	2	1	(3) I would recommend this speaker for future conferences.

Other Comments or Observations: _____

Page 15

Multiple rules serving different purposes create visual distractions, particularly when the reader has to write on the form.

The "Strongly Agree-Strongly Disagree" copy is repeated needlessly on the page.

MAKEOVER

Evaluation

Please circle one.

Strongly agree				Strongly disagree	*General Session*/Keynote Speaker
5	4	3	2	1	1. The information presented increased my knowledge of secondary education in Howard County.
5	4	3	2	1	2. The presentation was relevant and well presented.
5	4	3	2	1	3. I would recommend this speaker for future conferences.

Other comments or observations: _____

_____

Session One/Title:

5	4	3	2	1	1. The information presented increased my knowledge of secondary education in Howard County.
5	4	3	2	1	2. The presentation was relevant and well presented.
5	4	3	2	1	3. The presentation will enable me to share the content with others.

Other comments or observations: _____

_____

Session Two/Title:

5	4	3	2	1	1. The information presented increased my knowledge of secondary education in Howard County.
5	4	3	2	1	2. The presentation was relevant and well presented.
5	4	3	2	1	3. The presentation will enable me to share the content with others.

Other comments or observations: _____

_____

One rule serves the dual purpose of visually separating the copy blocks and eliciting written comments and suggestions from the reader.

Thick rules further define copy blocks.

While documents such as resumes shouldn't be overdesigned or "cute," basic modifications can improve readability—and employment opportunities!

ORIGINAL

RESUME

GEORGE TCHOBANOGLOUS

Address

662 Diego Place
Davis, California 95616
(916) 756-5747

Education

Ph.D., (Civil Engineering) Stanford University, 1969
M.S., (Sanitary Engineering) University of California, Berkeley, 1960
B.S., (Civil Engineering) University of the Pacific, 1958

Present Position

Professor of Environmental Engineering, Department of Civil Engineering, University of California, Davis. Research areas include solid waste management, innovative water and wastewater treatment systems, wastewater filtration, small wastewater treatment systems, on-site systems, and aquatic treatment systems.

Honors, Awards

Blue Key
Who's Who in America
Outstanding Teacher Award, 1980, School of Engineering, University of
California, Davis
Gordon Maskew Fair Medal, 1985, Water Pollution Control Federation
Distinguished Alumnus of the Year for Public Service, 1985,
University of the Pacific, Stockton, CA.

Society Memberships

Association of Environmental Engineering Professors
Diplomat, American Association of Environmental Engineers
American Society of Civil Engineers
Water Pollution Control Federation
American Water Works Association
International Association on Water Pollution Research and Control
California Water Pollution Control Federation
American Association for the Advancement of Science
Sigma Xi
World Mariculture Society
American Fisheries Associaton

Registration

Registered Civil Engineer in California

Employment Record

1976 - Present: Professor
University of California, Davis, CA
1971 - 1976: Associate Professor
University of California, Davis, CA
1970 - 1971: Assistant Professor
University of California, Davis, CA

Avoid using too much Helvetica—this versatile and readable typeface has been overused by desktop publishers.

Note how a lack of attention to leading makes the piece difficult to scan.

MAKEOVER

GEORGE TCHOBANOGLOUS

662 Diego Place
Davis, California 95616
916/756-5747

Education

PhD., Civil Engineering, Stanford University, 1969
M.S., Sanitary Engineering, University of California, Berkeley, 1960
B.S., Civil Engineering, University of the Pacific, 1958

Present Position

Professor of Environmental Engineering, Department of Civil Engineering, University of California, Davis.

Research areas include solid waste management, innovative water and wastewater treatment systems, wastewater filtration, small wastewater treatment systems, on-site systems, and aquatic treatment systems.

Honors/Awards

Blue Key

Who's Who in America

Outstanding Teacher Award, 1980, School of Engineering, University of California, Davis

Gordon Maskew Fair Medal, 1985, Water Pollution Control Federation

Distinguished Alumnus of the Year for Public Service, 1985, University of the Pacific, Stockton, CA

Society Memberships

Association of Environmental Engineering Professors

Diplomat, American Association of Environmental Engineers

American Society of Civil Engineers

Water Pollution Control Federation

American Water Works Association

International Association on Water Pollution Research and Control

California Water Pollution Control Federation

American Association for the Advancement of Science

Sigma Xi

World Mariculture Society

American Fisheries Association

Registration

Registered Civil Engineer in California

Employment

1976-Present: **Professor**
University of California, Davis, CA

1971-1976: **Associate Professor**
University of California, Davis, CA

1970-1971: **Assistant Professor**
University of California, Davis, CA

1967-1969: **Acting Assistant Professor**
Stanford University, Stanford, CA

Boldface type "pops" key information, and rules separate categories.

The addition of a serif typeface helps readers quickly differentiate between headers and body text, and provides diversity.

Although resumes generally should be simple and unadorned, desktop publishing lets you easily create, update and tailor resumes as needed.

ORIGINAL

```
Andrew Becker
220 Millbrook Ct.
Milford, PA 77022
(521) 577-0225

Personal:
    Born, Newport News, Va., 5/5/49
    Married, wife, Cathy, son, Andrew, 3
    Excellent health

Education:
    High Point Central High School, High Point,
    N.C., diploma, June 1968
    Furman University, Greenville, S.C., BA
    December, 1971
    Expect M.A. UNC-CH December 1988

Employment History:
    While in graduate school my income has come
    from teaching assistantships and various
    outside employment. In 1986 my wife and
    I began the Applejack riding school in Chapel
    Hill.
    July 1983 - September 1977, reporter for The
    Charlotte Observer, Charlotte, N.C.
    July 1977 - June 1975, reporter for the
    Wilmington Star News, Wilmington, N.C.
    June 1975 - June 1973, reporter for the Monroe
    (N.C.) Enquirer-Journal

References:
    Stan Smith, night editor of the
    Charlotte Observer, 600 South Tryon Street
    Charlotte, N.C., (704) 379-6426
    Bill Elliot, Textbook Dept., University of
    North Carolina, Chapel Hill, (919) 962-5024
```

Dot matrix-generated materials are fine for some timely documents—but not for resumes, which should be both eye-catching and easy to read at a glance.

MAKEOVER

Andrew Becker

220 Millbrook Ct., Milford, PA 77022
(521) 577-0225

Personal
Born: Newport News, VA, 5/5/49
Married, wife, Cathy, son, Andrew, 3
Excellent health

Education
High Point Central High School, High Point, NC
Diploma—June l968

Furman University, Greenville, SC
BA—December l977

Employment History
While in graduate school, my income came from teaching assistantships and various outside employment. In l986, my wife and I began the Applejack riding school in Chapel Hill.

July 1983-September l977, reporter for *The Charlotte Observer*, Charlotte, NC

July l977-June l975, reporter for the *Wilmington Star News*, Wilmington, NC

June 1975-June l973, reporter for the *Monroe Enquirer-Journal*, Monroe, NC

References
Stan Smith, night editor of *The Charlotte Observer*, 600 South Tryon Street, Charlotte, NC, (704) 379-6426

Bill Elliott, Textbook Department
University of North Carolina at Chapel Hill, Chapel Hill, NC
(919) 962-5024

Rules of varying thicknesses can effectively highlight headlines and subheads.

A two-column format helps separate categories.

CATALOGS & BOOKLETS

Catalogs and booklets are two of desktop publishing's most satisfying and challenging applications. Suddenly, you're publishing on a much larger scale: You're presenting more of a story and are producing documents that will have a longer life.

Catalogs and booklets require far more attention to the details of layout and production than the publications discussed so far. You're competing with catalogs and booklets produced by large publishers with virtually unlimited design resources. To succeed in such a competitive environment, you have to capture your readers' attention with a strong cover and hold their attention on every page.

Judging Books by Their Covers

The cover of your publication is likely to appear in a visually busy environment—a mailbox, a cluttered desktop or a kitchen table—so it has to be strong enough to compete with other publications and capture your readers' interest.

The cover may also help to prolong the life of what's inside. People do judge books by their covers, and a cheap cover ensures an early trip to the wastebasket. On the other hand, readers respect quality and are likely to keep a publication with a simple, arresting cover around much longer.

One of the first cover considerations is positioning—creating an appropriate image of the inside copy in the reader's mind. In the Library of Michigan example, the original cover's outline type and rounded border project a dated image. Notice how elements on the page compete with each other: The visual's border "fights" the page border.

Now look at the more contemporary makeover. Notice that the important word "Acquisitions" has become the dominant visual on the page, set in bold uppercase type with "Recent" tucked vertically out of the way.

Note also how "Acquisitions" is balanced by the enlarged illustration in the lower left corner of the page.

The contemporary feeling of the makeover also comes from the increased white space surrounding both "Acquisitions" and the illustration. Moving the body copy to its own column surrounds it with white space, too. In addition, the illustration in the left-hand column anchors the left and bottom of the page, and makes the cover look larger.

The open left-hand column also emphasizes the folio information—publication date and issue number—which was lost in the clutter of the original.

The "Insurance as an Investment" cover illustrates several similar points. Once again, we see the detrimental effect of using a double border around the page. The cover becomes far more contemporary when the border is replaced by a heavy horizontal rule at the top, which bleeds off to the right. The visual gains importance when it's enlarged—on the original, it lacks impact because of the grid behind it. The revised cover also shows how much easier it is to read a title set flush-left on one line, rather than on three centered lines.

You can also learn several lessons from the cover of the "How to Computerize and Maintain Your Mailing List for Greater

Profit." The keys to its makeover include choosing a design that reinforces its content, having strong control over typography and eliminating visual elements that compete with each other.

The original title is difficult to read, because it's set on long lines in uppercase type. The title also competes with the Dependable logo and the repeated title set vertically to the right.

In the makeover, the long title is made easier to read by isolating "helping" phrases like "How to" and "for Greater Profit." The Dependable logo is reduced and placed at the bottom left of the page, where the reader logically sees it after reading the title. Publication price and mission statement now balance each other on the diagonal.

The background design of the revised cover is also more appropriate to the brochure's subject matter. The vertical rules suggest computer printout paper. They unify the publication by reinforcing the margins of the grid used inside.

Inside Pages

A catalog's success is determined by how easily readers can find the information they need. This is especially true of long, copy-filled reference publications, such as the Library of Michigan Recent Acquisitions catalog.

The original publication is set in relatively large type on a two-column grid. The grid is retained for the makeover, but columns of unequal width are used. The narrow column to the left holds category headings and are set flush-right to link them with the publications they introduce. Surrounded above, below and to the left with white space, these subheads are far more readable, even though they're set in a slightly smaller type size than in the original.

Bibliographic entries run the full length of the second wider column. Now you can read them easily and naturally rather than having to jump from line to line.

Publication numbers are set in bold type. "Recent Acquisitions" is repeated at the top of each page and aligned with the second column. A different style separates the qualifying term "Recent" from the key word "Acquisitions."

A glance at both the original and the makeover shows that the same amount of information is contained on both pages. Yet the makeover's is more accessible—even though smaller type is used—and the catalog looks more contemporary.

Emphasis Through Simplicity

The inside pages of the "Insurance as an Investment" booklet present a strong case for simplicity.

As the "before" and "after" examples indicate, relatively simple changes in page border and type create a totally different impression. The message becomes clearer and the publication's image is updated.

Compare the old-fashioned image of the original boxed page to the open, contemporary feeling of the makeover. Notice how the change from serif to sans-serif headings makes each letter easier to read, without the distractions of the thick diagonal strokes. Widening the columns lets the subheads run on one line instead of being broken over two.

Most important, notice how strong each paragraph's introductory statement becomes when the ellipses are omitted and the statement is set in boldface type on a line by itself. In the original, the first full sentence is set bold, as are the key words "Safety," "Liquidity," etc. In the makeover, however, the preliminary statements are distinct, giving "punch" to the introductory sentences.

Finally, notice how the important "For example" paragraph, lost in the second column of the original, becomes a dominant visual on the page when set narrower and reversed.

Many of the same techniques are used to improve the "Questions to ask" page. The key word "Questions" in the headline is emphasized. Body copy becomes easier to read when the distracting "Q"s and "A"s are eliminated and boldface type is used for the questions. Finally, notice how replacing the box border with a strong horizontal rule opens up the page and creates a more contemporary appearance.

Readability

The inside pages of "How to Computerize and Maintain Your Mailing List" show the importance of choosing a grid that works with your publication's content. The original page has an extremely dense appearance. Reader cues are set in uppercase type and separated from the copy by deep indents. The copy is hard to read because the columns are too wide and the left-hand margins "float," due to the wide indents.

In the makeover, it's easier to scan the subheads and then read the body copy. Subheads have their own column to the left and are emphasized by strong horizontal rules and white space. The subheads are also set off by upper- and lowercase type and wide line spacing. The body copy is set in a clear, serif typeface with uniform left margins.

Since the catalog is likely to be copied, its title is now repeated in the header of each page. Note how the rules in the subhead column echo the rule under the header. The header rule matches the column width of the body copy, creating a unified page design.

Visuals and Clip Art

"Hints for Your Wedding" proves that it's possible to be both contemporary and old-fashioned at the same time. It also shows how you can personalize a publication with commercially available clip art.

Page 20 of the original wedding booklet doesn't look old-fashioned. It looks dated and lacks character. Elements contributing to this include: a rounded double border, wide columns of type with tight line spacing and insufficient contrast between elements of page architecture, such as type style.

Look at the heading: "Hints for Your Wedding." In the original, all four words are set in the same size and style. Compare this to the makeover, where "Wedding" stands out from the less-important introductory words.

Continuing to analyze the type, notice how the second-level subheads stand out in the makeover. The first-level subheads (Engagement, Invitations and Wedding) are set in a typeface that contrasts well with the upper- and lowercase italics of the second-level subheads.

Notice how replacing the boxed/double-line border with strong horizontal rules at top and bottom creates a contemporary appearance. The page number and footer are easier to find when set below the border instead of within it.

Finally, notice how the large illustration unifies the page and adds visual interest by breaking the border at the top. The overall effect of these changes transforms a dated work to a highly stylized publication that's both romantic and readable.

Page 21 of the wedding booklet repeats several of these changes, such as the subhead treatments and the improved border. Notice how the illustration in the original floats on the page. In the makeover, however, the illustration is allowed to break over the vertical rule between the columns and the horizontal border at the bottom of the page. This anchors the illustration to the page. Finally, the narrower columns in the revised booklet make the copy easier to read.

Take Another Look

As you evaluate your catalogs and booklets, ask yourself these questions:

- ✔ Is the cover simple and uncluttered?
- ✔ Does the cover communicate the content of the inside pages?
- ✔ Have distracting elements been removed from the cover to strengthen the remaining elements?
- ✔ Does the cover design establish a theme or format that's maintained on the inside pages?
- ✔ Have subheads and other reader cues been emphasized for easy reading?
- ✔ Has body copy been set in columns wide enough for comfortable reading?
- ✔ Has clutter, such as unnecessary indents and ellipses, been omitted?
- ✔ Has important information, such as page numbers and titles, been repeated on every page?
- ✔ Have appropriate page borders been used?
- ✔ Do illustrations float, or are they an integral part of page layout?

Take the time to create a well-designed style for periodicals such as newsletters and catalogs.

ORIGINAL

Recent
Acquisitions

March 1986   Number 23

The books listed here have been selected with state government employees in mind. No matter what your agency, one or more of these titles may be valuable to you in your work.

Most books at the Library of Michigan may be borrowed for four weeks with an optional renewal period. Because of the high demand for books on this list, the loan period for recent acquisitions is limited to two weeks with no renewals. Books can be sent to you via ID mail, or they may be picked up at the Library between 8:00 and 5:00 p.m. weekdays. All listed books can be loaned except those whose call number is preceded by "Ref."; such titles must be used in the Library.

Books on this list may be reserved. If a state employee wishes to reserve one of these titles, please supply the Circulation Unit at the Library with the title and call number along with the patron's name, ID address and telephone number.

Each entry contains four elements: author, title, publication date, and call number. When requesting books from this list, include all four of these elements. You may submit requests by ID mail (attention: Circulation Unit), or by phone (3-1593). To ensure accuracy, requests for three or more items at a time are best sent by ID mail.

Library of Michigan

Avoid outline serif type—the serifs usually are difficult to read.

The sans-serif, condensed typeface used in the text creates a "run-on" look and is hard to read.

MAKEOVER

ACQUISITIONS

March 1986   The books listed here have been selected with state government employees in mind.
Number 23   No matter what your agency, one or more of these titles may be valuable to you in your
              work.

Library Loan Policy

Most books at the Library of Michigan may be borrowed for four weeks with an
optional renewal period. Because of the high demand for books on this list, the loan
period for recent acquisitions is limited to two weeks with no renewals. Books can be
sent to you via ID mail, or they may be picked up at the Library between 8 a.m. and 5
p.m. weekdays. All listed books can be loaned except those whose call number is
preceded by "Ref."; such titles must be used in the Library.

Reserving Titles

Books on this list may be reserved. If a state employee wishes to reserve one of these
titles, please supply the Circulation Unit at the Library with the title and call number
along with the patron's name, ID address and telephone number.

Each entry contains four elements: author, title, publication date and call number.
When requesting books from this list, include all four of these elements.

You may submit requests by ID mail (attention: Circulation Unit), or by phone
(3-1593). To ensure accuracy, requests for three or more items at a time are best sent
by ID mail.

Library of **MICHIGAN**

Better leading and selection of a serif face can improve even the most basic documents.

Use subheads to organize information.

Presenting long lists of information skillfully used to be difficult for nonprofit or low-budget institutions. But desktop publishing makes it easy to create and update "agency quality" material.

ORIGINAL

RECENT ACQUISITIONS

AGING
1) Depression in the elderly: an interdisciplinary approach. G. Maureen Chaisson-Stewart, ed. 1985. 377p.
RC 537 .D4434 1985

2) Elder neglect and abuse: an annotated bibliography. Tanya F. Johnson, ed. 1985. 223p.
Ref. HV 1461 .J56 1985

3) Site planning and design for the elderly: issues, guidelines, and alternatives. 1985. 170p.
NA 7195 .A4 C3 1985

4) Wellness and health promotion for the elderly. Ken Dychtwald, ed. 1985. 378p.
RA 564.8 .W45 1985

AGRICULTURE
5) Agricultural chemicals: book I, insecticides, acaricides and ovicides. W. T. Thompson. 1985/86 revision. 255p.
SB 951 .T488z 1985 Bk. 1

6) Agricultural chemicals: book IV, fungicides. W. T. Thomson. 1985 revision. 181p.
SB 951 .T488z 1985 Bk. 4

AIDS
7) AIDS issues: hearings...on research and treatment..., protection of confidentiality of records of research subjects and blood donors, cost of AIDS care and who is going to pay. U.S. GPO. 1985.
Govt. Docs. Y4.En2/3:99-45

8) Focus: AIDS in the workplace. Richard H. Wexler. 1986. 32p.
RA 644 .A25 W48 1986

ARCHIVES
9) Native American archives: an introduction. John A. Fleckner. 1984. 69p.
E 97.9 .F54 1984

BIOTECHNOLOGY
10) Biotechnology: implications for public policy. Sandra Panem, ed. 1985. 99p.
TP 248.2 .B56 1985

COAST GUARD
11) Coast Guard stations and user fee:hearings...on proposed closure and consolidation of Coast Guard stations on the Great Lakes; establishing fees for certain Coast Guard services. U.S. GPO. 1986.
Govt. Docs. Y4.M53:99-13

COMMERCE
12) Forging a new era for United States-Japan trade: companion statements by the Program Committee of the Committee for Economic Development and trustees of Keizai Doyukai. 1985. 13p.
HF 3127 .C65 1985

COMMUNICATIONS
13) Simple & direct: a rhetoric for writers. Rev. ed. Jacques Barzun. 1985. 291p.
PE 1408 .B436 1985

14) That's not what I meant! How conversational style makes or breaks your relations with others. Deborah Tannen. 1986. 214p.
P 95.45 .T364 1986

COMPUTERS
15) Assembly language programming for the IBM personal computer. David J. Bradley. 1984. 340p.
QA 76.8 .I2594 B7 1984

16) Cleaning up a computer mess: a guide to diagnosing and correcting computer problems. William E. Perry. 1986. 255p.
HF 5548.2 .P47279 1986

17) dBASE III tips and tricks. David Jenkins. 1985. 160p.
QA 76.9 .D3 J46 1985

18) Guide to local area networks. T. J. Byers. 1984. 182p.
TK 5105.7 .B94 1984

19) Local area networks: an introduction to the technology. John E. McNamara. 1985. 165p.
TK 5105.7 .M36 1985

20) Personal computing with the UCSD p-System. 2d ed. Mark Overgaard. 1986. 315p.
QA 76.76 .O63 O84 1986

21) Project management software directory. Jack Gido. 1985. 251p.
Ref. T 56.8 .G54 1985

22) Reading between the lines: an introduction to bar code technology. Craig K. Harmon. 1984. 253p.
HF 5416 .H288 1984

1

Type styles and typefaces aren't varied enough to let you quickly find categories ("Aging," "Agriculture," etc.) and other important information.

Underlining and punctuation (periods and commas) make numbers hard to read.

MAKEOVER

Recent **ACQUISITIONS**

AGING **1** Depression in the elderly: an interdisciplinary approach. G.Maureen Chaisson-Stewart, ed. 1985. 377p. *RC 537 .D4434 1985*
2 Elder neglect and abuse: an annotated bibliography. Tanya F. Johnson, ed. 1985. 223p. *Ref. HV 1461. J56 1985*
3 Site planning and design for the elderly: issues, guidelines, and alternatives. 1985. 170p. *NA 7195 .A4 C3 1985*
4 Wellness and health promotion for the elderly. Key Dychtwald, ed. 1985. 378p. *RA 564.8 .W45 1985*

AGRICULTURE **5** Agriculture chemicals: book I, insecticides, acaricides and ovicides. W.T. Thompson. 1985/86 revision. 255p. *SB 951. T488z 1985 Bk. 1*
6 Agricultural chemicals: book IV, fungicides. W.T. Thompson. 1985 revision. 181p. *SB 951. T488z 1985 Bk. 4*

AIDS **7** Aids issues: hearings...on research and treatment...,protection of confidentiality of records of research subjects and blood donors, cost of AIDS care and who is going to pay. U.S. GPO. 1985. *Govt. Docs. Y4.En2/3:99-45*
8 Focus: AIDS in the workplace. Richards H. Wexler. 1986. 32p. *RA 644.A25W48 1986*

ARCHIVES **9** Native American archives: an introduction. John A. Fleckner. 1984. 69p. *E97.9.F54 1984*

BIOTECHNOLOGY **10** Biotechnology: implications for public policy. Sandra Panem, ed. 1985. 99p. *TP248.2.B56 1985*

COAST GUARD **11** Coast Guard stations and user fee: hearings...on proposed closure and consolidation of Coast Guard stations on the Great Lakes; establishing fees for certain Coast Guard services. U.S. GPO. 1986. *Govt. Docs. Y4.M53:99-13*

COMMERCE **12** Forging a new era for United States-Japan trade: companion statements by the Program Committee of the Committee for Economic Development and trustee of Keizai Doyukai. 1985. 13p. *HF 3127 .C65 1985*

COMMUNICATIONS **13** Simple & direct: a rhetoric for writers. Rev. ed. Jacques Barzun. 1985. 291p. *PE 1408 .B436 1985*
14 That's not what I meant! How conversational style makes or breaks your relations with others. Deborah Tannen. 1986. 214p. *P95.45.T364 1986*

COMPUTERS **15** Assembly language programming for the IBM personal computer. David J. Bradley. 1984. 340p. *QA 76.8.J2594 B7 1984*
16 Cleaning up a computer mess: a guide to diagnosing and correcting computer problems. William E. Perry. 1986. 255p. *HF5548.2.P47279 1986*
17 dBASE III tips and tricks. David Jenkins. 1985. 160p. *QA 76.9.D3 J46 1985*
18 Guide to local area networks. T.J. Byers. 1984. 182p. *TK 5105.7.B94 1984*
19 Local area networks: an introduction to the technology. John E. McNamara. 1985. 165p. *TK5105.7.M36 1985*
20 Personal computing with the UCSD p System. 2d ed. Mark Overgaard. 1986. 315p. *QA76.76.O63 O84 1986*
21 Project management software directory. Jack Gido. 1985. 251p. *Ref. T56.8.G54 1985*
22 Reading between the lines: an introduction to bar code technology. Craig K. Harmon. 1984. 253p. *HF5416.H288 1984*

The title, "Recent Acquisitions," reflects the look of the nameplate.

Placing the categories in the left margin lets readers quickly find the topic they're looking for.

Italicizing ID numbers helps distinguish them from the rest of the text—handy when ordering by number.

Order forms and coupons form the heart of any catalog; an otherwise interested reader can be easily discouraged if information isn't well presented and easy to complete.

ORIGINAL

Forcing readers to write at an angle will hurt response.

The "Order Form" is unnecessarily large, while the type in the form itself is too small.

MAKEOVER

ASHLEY
DEALERS SERVICE, INC.
133 Industrial Ave. Box 337
Hasbrouck Heights, NJ 07604

(201) 288–8080

IN ENGLAND:
Ashley–Fields (Music Distributors)

Ashley Publications, Inc.
Century Music Publishing Co., Inc.
Ethnic Music Publishing Co., Inc.
Heritage Music Publishing Co., Inc.
J. & J. Hammen Music Co.
Larrabee Publications
Lewis Music Publishing Co., Inc.
Misirlou Corporation
Edward Schuberth and Company, Inc.
Treasure Chest Publications, Inc.

ORDER FORM

Use this catalog as your order blank. Another will be sent with your order.

Please send items indicated in this catalog via _____

Name _____

Address _____

City _____ State _____ Zip Code _____

Thank you,
Al Ashley

Prices subject to change   Printed in USA   ISBN Prefix 0-8611

Remember to make telephone numbers large when asking for response.

Solid lines replace the leader lines in the order form—your order entry people will appreciate it, as well as the reader!

Acluttered catalog invokes nightmarish visions of the company's shipping room—can you imagine getting your order fulfilled correctly when the mail order piece itself is not well organized?

ORIGINAL

The oversized prices don't reflect special savings—they only clutter the piece and confuse the reader.

The vertical rules create a fragmented effect.

Too many typefaces and styles create an environment of disarray.

MAKEOVER

PIANO BOOKS

$2.25	**The Barrett Theory Papers**
	____Level One (356-4)
	____Level Two (357-2)
	____Level Three (358-0)
	____Level Four (359-9)
$2.25	**The Barrett Note Speller**
	____Book One (360-2)
	____Book Two (361-0)
$3.95	**Easy to Play Well Known Melodies**
	____Vol. 1 (363-7)
	____Vol. 2 (364-5)
	____Vol. 3 (365-3)
	____Vol. 4 (366-1)
	____Vol. 5 (367-X)
	____Vol. 6 (368-8)
	____Vol. 7 (369-6)
	____Vol. 8 (370-X)
$2.95	**Everybody Likes the Piano-Estella**
	____Preparatory Book (371-8)
	____Book 1 (372-6)
	____Book 2 (373-4)
$3.95	____Book 3 (374-2)
	____Book 4 (375-0)
	____Book 5 (376-9)
$3.95	**Hilde B. Kreutzer's The Young Pianist Series**
	____Elementary Book I (377-7)
	____Elementary Book II (378-5)
	____Elementary Book III (379-3)
	____Book IV (380-7)
	____Book V **(New)** (381-5)
	____Book VI **(New)** (382-3)

Supplementary Books

$3.95	**(The Young Pianist)**
	____For A Young Pianist-Book I (383-1)
	____For A Young Pianist-Book II (383-X)
$4.95	**Learn to Play a Tune a Day for Piano -By Betty Bryan**
	____Book 1 (383-8)
	____Book 2 (386-6)
	____Book 3 (383-4)
$5.95	**Modern Piano Method by Lee Sims**
	____Book 1 (Beginners) (388-2)
$4.95	**Playing Piano for Pleasure-Spivak, etc.**
	____Book 1 (391-2)
	____Book 2 (392-0)
	____Book 3 (393-9)
	____Playing Classics for Pleasure (394-7)
$2.95	**The Play-Way to Music Series by Fay Templeton Frisch**
	____Fun All Day: Introductory Book (395-3)
	____Happily Playing: Book 1 (396-3)
	____Skip Along: Book 2 (397-1)
	____Play Along: Book 3 **(New)** (398-X)
	____See And Play: Book 4 **(New)** (399-8)
	____By Myself: Book One (400-5)
	____By Myself: Book Two (401-3)
$2.95	**The Little Treasury Series Edited by C. Lambert**
	____Classics: One (402-1)
	____Classics: Two (403-X)
	____Classics: Three (404-8)
	____Classics: Four (405-6)
	____Sonatinas: One (407-2)
	____Folk Songs and Dances: One (408-0)
	____Folk Songs and Dances: Two (409-9)
	____Recital Classics: One (410-2)
	____Recital Classics: Two (411-0)

$2.95	**The Little Treasury Series Edited by C. Lambert (continued)**
	____Polyphonic Pieces: One (413-9)
	____Polyphonic Pieces: Two (413-7)
	____Etudes: One (414-5)
	____Etudes: Two (415-3)
	____Playtime: One (416-1)
	____Piecetime (417-X)
$6.95	____Enjoy Debussy (473-0)
$7.95	____My Favorite Chopin (474-9)
$3.95	**For Sight Reading-Leonard Deutsch**
	____Vol. 1 (425-0)
	____Vol. 2 (426-9)
$8.95	____Bach:Cothen Suites (427-7)
$4.95	____Hymns with easy chords-Grant (428-5)
	____Junior Hymnal for Piano-Barrett (429-3)
	____Pictures at an Art Exhibition-Moussorgsky (430-7)

Outstanding Publications for Piano

$4.95	____Chord Instructor for Popular Piano Playing (418-8)
	____How to Play Popular Piano-McGowan (419-6)
	Pop Style Piano Playing
	____1 (420-X)
	____2 (421-8)
	____3 (422-6)
	____Czerny Germer Vol. I (423-4)
	____Czerny Germer Vol. II (424-2)
$6.95	____Scott Joplin-King of Ragtime Piano (431-5)
$3.95	____Scott Joplin-King of Ragtime EASY Piano (432-3)
	____Children's Christmas Party (433-1)
	____Children's Very First Piano Pieces (434-4)
	____Chopin Music To Remember (435-8)
	____48 Tuneful Technical Studies (436-6)
	____58 Tuneful Technical Studies-Bk. 1-Spivak (437-4)
$1.95	____Hymns (Giant Note Series) (438-2)
	____Marches (Giant Note Series) (439-0)
	____Waltzes (Giant Note Series) (440-4)
$4.95	____61 Easy to Play Hymns for Piano (441-2)
	____Sousa's 21 Best Marches-Piano (442-0)
$29.95	____Piano Masterpieces (443-9)
$3.95	____Woodland Sketches-MacDowell (444-7)
	____The World's Most Famous Folio of Christmas Songs & Carols Made Easy to Play (445-5)
$4.95	____Best of Boogie and Blues (446-3)
$3.95	____Nanerl Mozart's Piano Book (Ed. H. Kreutzer)(447-1)
	____Ada Richter-Just for Me (Grade 2) (448-X)
	____Beethoven-The Bonn Sonatas (Grade 4) (449-8)
	____The First Haydn Book-Memories of Old Vienna (450-1)
	____Great Masters (Editor David Hirschberg) (451-X)
	____Great Music (Ed.Minniberg & Eckhardt) (452-8)
	____The Holiday Book (Arranged by Ruth Post) (453-6)
	____Mozart, Nanner 1-21 Original Piano Pieces (454-4)
	____Mozart-Six Viennese Sonatinas (Grade 3-4) (455-2)
$2.95	____Sea-Going Time (Selma Seider) (456-0)
$4.95	____A Treasury of Easy Classics (Grade 2-3) (457-9)
$2.95	____So Easy (Samuel Wilson) (448-7)
	____Tuneful Technic (King & Minnieberg) (459-5)
$3.95	____Very Easy Piano Pieces for Children-Vol.1 (Agay) (460-9)
	____Easy Piano Pieces for Children-Vol.2 (Agay) (461-7)
$2.95	____Let's Play Hymns (Hilde B. Kruetzer) (462-5)

PIANO DUETS COLLECTIONS

$3.95	**Duet Albums: One Piano-Four Hands**
	____Schubert: Dances (Grade 2-3) (475-7)
	____Mozart: Sonata in D (K381) (Grade 4) (476-5)
	____Mozart: Sonata in B (K358) (Grade 4) (477-3)
	____Schumann: Pictures from the East (Grade 4) (478-1)
$2.95	____One Plus One (Elizabeth E. Rogers) (479-X)
	____Classics as Duets: One (Edited Marion Bauer) (480-3)
	____Classics as Duets: Two (Edited Marion Bauer) (481-1)
	____The Adventures of Primo & Segundo (E. Rogers) (482-X)

SELECTED DUETS for Various Like Instruments

$5.95	**Book 1-Easy/Intermediate Book 2-Intermediate/Advanced by J. Arnold**
	____50 Selected Duets-Clarinet Book 1 (483-8)
	____31 Selected Duets-Clarinet Book 2 (484-6)
	____44 Selected Duets-Flute Book 1 (485-4)
	____34 Selected Duets-Flute Book 2 (486-2)
	____30 Selected Duets-Saxophone Book 1 (487-0)
	____28 Selected Duets-Saxophone Book 2 (488-9)
	____78 Selected Duets-Trumpet Book 1 (489-7)
	____38 Selected Duets-Trumpet Book 2 (490-0)

A staggered two-column format helps break up type.

Price categories are separated by thin rules, eliminating the need for multiple typefaces and sizes.

Don't be afraid to make a splash on booklet covers. Oversized type, large icons and other attention-getters help your piece stand out, even in stacks of unsolicited direct mail.

ORIGINAL

The serif typeface appears textbook-ish and uninviting.

The placement of the graphic makes it look like an afterthought.

MAKEOVER

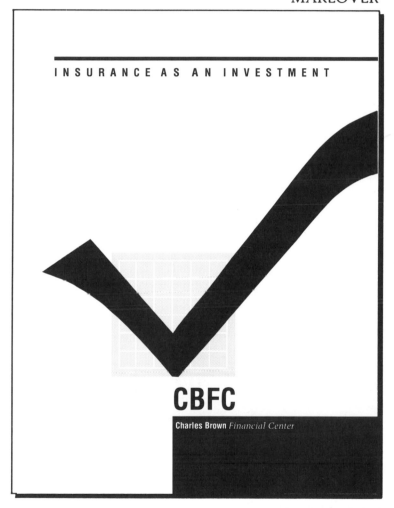

A sans-serif typeface lends a contemporary feel to the cover.

The check mark has been enlarged to further the "rising curve" concept.

A lightly screened grid helps unite the type with the graphic and balance the entire piece.

Subtle changes in typefaces and sizes can alter the tone and mood of a page. Here, replacing serif headlines and subheads with sans-serif creates a contemporary, corporate image that matches its content.

ORIGINAL

DID YOU KNOW THAT...

Municipal Bonds...

...do not provide **Safety. The definition of safety is that anytime you want your funds you will always get back at least the amount you originally invested.** This disqualifies municipal bonds. For, except at the time of maturity, the value of municipal bonds fluctuate according to interest rates. Their value increases when interest rates decrease. Their value decreases when interest rates increase.

...do not provide **Liquidity. Liquidity is defined as you being able to access your funds** anytime **you want, again never getting back less than what you originally invested.** You can sell your Municipal Bonds at anytime, but you may not receive the same amount of money you used to purchase them. Again, municipal bonds increase in value when interest rates decrease. They decrease in value when interest rates increase. If you need to liquidate at a time of high interest rates, you could lose money.

...do not provide **Flexibility. You don't have the choice to leave your income in a Municipal Bond,** therefore giving up the advantages of compounded interest. This is an especially dangerous situation in a declining interest rate environment.

...do not provide **Resistance to Inflation. All income is fixed until the bond matures.** This fixed aspect makes it impossible for your income to increase as inflation increases, offering you no protection against rising expenses.

Certificates of Deposit...

...do not provide **Safety.** Our definition of safety is the ability to get back your funds at anytime. **With a CD, if you need your money shortly after you have deposited it, the bank will charge you a six month interest penalty for withdrawing your funds.** That penalty can, for the first several months, cut into your principal.

For example: if you deposited $100,000 at 10% into a CD and two months later withdraw your CD you would be penalized 6 months interest and receive back only $96,666; a loss of $3,334.

...do not provide **Liquidity. Liquidity is defined as you being able to access your funds anytime you want, again never getting back less than what you originally invested.** If you need to liquidate a CD unexpectedly within the first six months, you could end up with less money than you invested originally.

...do not provide **Tax Free Income.** Very simply, the income **earned on Certificates of Deposit is taxable.**

Long blocks of bold type within body copy usually defeat the impact of bold type.

Never underline when you can use italics.

The border is uninteresting and creates a too-symmetrical, boxy effect.

MAKEOVER

DID **YOU** KNOW THAT...

MUNICIPAL BONDS...

✔ **Do not provide Safety.**
The definition of safety is that anytime you want your funds you will always get back at least the amount you originally invested. This disqualifies municipal bonds. For, except at the time of maturity, the value of municipal bonds fluctuates according to interest rates. Their value increases when interest rates decrease. Their value decreases when interest rates increase.

✔ **Do not provide Liquidity.**
Liquidity is defined as you being able to access your fund *anytime* you want, again never getting back less than what you originally invested. You can sell your municipal bonds at any time, *but* you may not receive the same amount of money you used to purchase them. Again, municipal bonds increase in value when interest rates decrease. They decrease in value when interest rates increase. If you need to liquidate at a time of high interest rates, you could lose money.

✔ **Do not provide Flexibility.**
You don't have the choice to leave your income in a municipal bond, therefore giving up the advantages of compounded interest. This is an especially dangerous situation in a declining interest rate environment.

✔ **Do not provide Resistance to Inflation.**
All income is fixed until the bond matures. This fixed aspect makes it impossible for your income to increase as inflation increases, offering you no protection against rising expenses.

CERTIFICATES OF DEPOSIT...

✔ **Do not provide Safety.**
Our definition of safety is the ability to get back your funds at any time. With a CD, if you need your money shortly after you have deposited it, the bank will charge you a six month interest penalty for withdrawing your funds. That penalty can, for the first several months, cut into your principal.

> If you deposited $100,000 at 10% into a CD and two months later withdrew your CD, you would be penalized 6 months interest and receive back only $96,666: a loss of $3,334!

✔ **Do not provide Liquidity.**
Liquidity is defined as your being able to access your funds anytime you want, again never getting back *less* than what you originally invested. If you need to liquidate a CD unexpectedly within the first six months, you could end up with less money than you invested originally.

✔ **Do not provide Tax Free Income.**
Very simply, the income earned on Certificates of Deposit is taxable.

Bullets in the shape of check marks focus the reader on the message's main points, and continue the theme from the front cover.

Important statements have been converted to subheads, making the message more persuasive.

A "Q & A" format appeals to a customer's natural sense of curiosity—but it must be designed for easy reading.

ORIGINAL

Questions to ask the Sales Agent when purchasing a Single Premium Whole Life policy, and the best answers.

Q) - What is the A.M. Best Rating of the Insurance Company?

A) - A+ or A, depending on your situation. If safety is a prime feature then you want to stick to the higher rating.

Q) - What is my net loan cost to borrow out my interest?

A) - 0%

Q) - Can I take out all my interest, anytime I want to after the first year, with a 0% charge?

A) - Yes

Q) - Can I loan my funds out more than once a year for no charge?

A) - Yes

Q) - Can that 0% net loan charge ever be raised?

A) - It is written in the contract, for the life of the contract, that the 0% net loan charge will not be raised, or if it is, not past 1/2 of a percent.

Q) - What is the net loan charge to take out my principal?

A) - Anywhere from 2% up to 3.5%, depending on the company.

Q) - Can the 2% - 3.5% net loan charge on principal ever be raised?

A) - No. It is written in the contract for the life of the contract that the net loan charge on principal will never be raised past these amounts.

Q) - Can part of my principal be withdrawn without any cost to me?

A) - Yes.

Q) - How long has the company been selling SPWL's?

A) - At least 3 years.

Q) - Does the company absorb the State Premium Tax?

A) - Yes.

Q) - Are there any fee's, charges, or hidden costs down the line?

A) - No.

Q) - How well known is the parent company you are purchsing the policy from?

A) - Extremely well known.

Q) - Does 100% of my funds go to work for me with absolutely zero going to pay for the insuance of the policy?

A) - Thats right.

Q) - What is the quality of the bond portfolio backing this investment?

A) - 100% A rated bonds or better.

Q) - Can I see in writing a history of renewal rates?

A) - Yes.

Q) - How familiar are you with this investment and how carefully do you monitor it after I purchase it?

A) - It is the area I specialize in and your investment is constantly being monitored.

Avoid long, centered headlines—and unsightly widows.

The lack of differentiation between questions and answers makes this piece uninteresting and difficult to read.

MAKEOVER

Bold, sans-serif questions off-set serif answers for an easier read.

QUESTIONS TO ASK ABOUT
A SINGLE PREMIUM WHOLE LIFE POLICY
. . . AND THE BEST ANSWERS

What is the A.M. Best Rating of the Insurance Company?
✔ A+ or A, depending on your situation. If safety is prime feature then you want to stick to the higher rating.

What is my net loan cost to borrow out my interest?
✔ 0%.

Can I take out all my interest any time I want to after the first year, with a 0% charge?
✔ Yes.

Can I loan my funds out more than once a year for no charge?
✔ Yes.

Can that 0% net loan charge ever be raised?
✔ It is written in the contract, for the life of the contract, that the 0% net loan charge will not be raised, or if it is, not past 1/2 percent.

What is the net loan charge to take out my principal?
✔ Anywhere from 2% up to 3.5%, depending on the company.

Can the 2% -3.5% net loan charge on principal ever be raised?
✔ No. It is written in the contract for the life of the contract that the net loan charge on principal will never be raised past these amounts.

Can part of my principal be withdrawn without any cost to me?
✔ Yes.

How long has the company been selling SPWLs?
✔ At least 3 years.

Does the company absorb the State Premium Tax?
✔ Yes.

Are there any fees, charges, or hidden costs down the line?
✔ No.

How well known is the parent company you are purchasing the policy from?
✔ Extremely well known.

Does 100% of my funds go to work for me with absolutely zero going to pay for the issuance of the policy?
✔ That's right.

What is the quality of the bond portfolio backing this investment?
✔ 100% A-rated bonds or better.

Can I see in writing a history of renewal rates?
✔ Yes.

How familiar is my sales agent with this investment and how carefully will he/she monitor it after I purchase it?
✔ It is the area our agents specialize in and your investment is constantly being monitored.

Because questions and answers are brief, the repetitive Q's and A's can be eliminated for a cleaner presentation.

Better leading between question-and-answer blocks helps readers scan for important data.

O ne of the most important steps for any design project involves placing the message in a proper setting. Content should match purpose, making readers feel "at home" with the piece.

ORIGINAL

Hints For Your Wedding
• Engagement • Invitations • Wedding • Reception • Honeymoon • Coming Home •

• Engagement

When you decide to marry, you and your fiancée should first inform all of your parents, preferably in person. If your families don't know each other, arrange a meeting as soon as possible. Generally the bride's parents are responsible for the announcement, either by sending a detailed release to the newspapers, or at a party, or both. An engagement party is an ideal way of telling relatives and friends. If there is to be no engagement party, write or telephone relatives and friends before your announcement is released. Check local and hometown requirements in advance and announce within one year of your engagement.

• Invitations

The bride's family determines the number of guests. They should, however, consult the groom and his family before determining the number. The groom and his family are entitled to invite one-half of the total. Less is permissible and usually the outcome.

Who is invited?

Usually it is only close friends and family. Business acquaintances are not invited unless the wedding is to be extremely large. If all friends are not invited, wedding announcements should be mailed to those not invited within two days after the wedding.

Your wedding list should include:

1. Those who receive invitations to the wedding.
2. Those who receive wedding and reception invitations.
3. Those who will receive announcements after the wedding.

Wedding invitations are sent out approximately six weeks prior to the wedding. Informal wedding invitations should be short personal notes, telegrams, or telephone calls. If an engagement is broken, all gifts should be returned, except perishable ones. Legally the engagement ring is yours, but tradition calls for you to return it.

• Wedding

Arranging the wedding

No bride should make plans for a formal wedding unless her groom accepts all it entails. If your wedding is to be an elaborate formal affair, professional management should be retained if possible.

Working with the professionals

For either a formal or informal wedding, there is no substitute for a professional. It is very necessary that you make certain decisions and arrangements before consulting professional firms for details. You should know your budget, the style of your wedding, date, time, location, number of guests, attendants, and have fabric swatches for coordinating the color scheme.

Page 20 — *The Wedding Planner*

The bullet lists and floating subheads create unsightly white space.

Undifferentiated type styles produce a gray look that readers tend to avoid.

The border is inappropriate, making the piece look like an advertisement.

MAKEOVER

HINTS FOR YOUR
Wedding

*Engagement | Invitations |
Wedding | Reception |
Honeymoon | Coming Home*

ENGAGEMENT

As soon as you decide to marry, you and your fiancee should inform all of your parents, preferably in person. If your families don't know each other, arrange a meeting as soon as possible. Generally the bride's parents are responsible for the announcement, either by sending a detailed release to the newspapers, or at a party, or both. An engagement party is an ideal way of telling relatives and friends. If there is to be no engagement party, write or telephone relatives and friends before your announcement is released. Check local and hometown requirements in advance and announce within one year of your engagement.

INVITATIONS

The bride's family determines the number of guests. They should, however, consult the groom and his family before determining the number. The groom and his family are entitled to invite one-half of the total. Less is permissible and usually the outcome.

Who is invited?
Usually it is only close friends and family. Business acquaintances are not invited unless the wedding is to be extremely large. If all friends are not invited, wedding announcements should be mailed to those not invited within two days after the wedding.

Your wedding list should include:
1. Those who receive invitations to the wedding.
2. Those who receive wedding and reception invitations.
3. Those who will receive announcements after the wedding.

Wedding invitations are sent out approximately six weeks prior to the wedding. Informal wedding invitations should be short personal notes, telegrams, or telephone calls. If an engagement is broken, all gifts should be be returned, except perishable ones. Legally the engagement ring is yours, but tradition calls for you to return it.

WEDDING

Arranging the wedding
No bride should make plans for a formal wedding unless her groom accepts all it entails. If your wedding is to be an elaborate formal affair, professional management should be retained if possible.

20 | *The Wedding Planner*

The world of clip art and scanning technology allows desktop publishers easy access to a wide variety of illustrations, photography and other graphic tools.

Wraparound type, which follows the contours of an illustration, was once tedious and expensive to produce. It can now be used effectively to enhance nearly any document.

Two rules help contain the graphics—note how the illustration "pops" through the top rule, creating a lively three-dimensional effect.

U sing white space effectively is one of the most overlooked tools of the trade—and there are no set rules for its use and abuse.

ORIGINAL

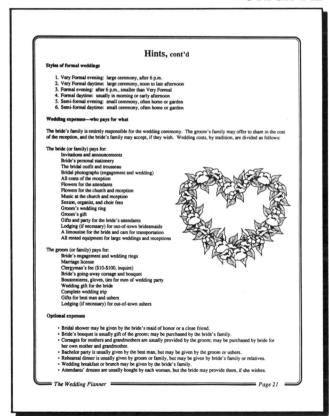

Hints, cont'd

Styles of formal weddings

1. Very Formal evening: large ceremony, after 6 p.m.
2. Very Formal daytime: large ceremony, noon to late afternoon
3. Formal evening: after 6 p.m., smaller than Very Formal
4. Formal daytime: usually in morning or early afternoon
5. Semi-formal evening: small ceremony, often home or garden
6. Semi-formal daytime: small ceremony, often home or garden

Wedding expenses—who pays for what

The bride's family is entirely responsible for the wedding ceremony. The groom's family may offer to share in the cost of the reception, and the bride's family may accept, if they wish. Wedding costs, by tradition, are divided as follows:

The bride (or family) pays for:
Invitations and announcements
Bride's personal stationery
The bridal outfit and trousseau
Bridal photographs (engagement and wedding)
All costs of the reception
Flowers for the attendants
Flowers for the church and reception
Music at the church and reception
Sexton, organist, and choir fees
Groom's wedding ring
Groom's gift
Gifts and party for the bride's attendants
Lodging (if necessary) for out-of-town bridesmaids
A limousine for the bride and cars for transportation
All rented equipment for large weddings and receptions

The groom (or family) pays for:
Bride's engagement and wedding rings
Marriage license
Clergyman's fee ($10-$100, inquire)
Bride's going-away corsage and bouquet
Boutonnieres, gloves, ties for men of wedding party
Wedding gift for the bride
Complete wedding trip
Gifts for best man and ushers
Lodging (if necessary) for out-of-town ushers

Optional expenses

• Bridal shower may be given by the bride's maid of honor or a close friend.
• Bride's bouquet is usually gift of the groom; may be purchased by the bride's family.
• Corsages for mothers and grandmothers are usually provided by the groom; may be purchased by bride for her own mother and grandmother.
• Bachelor party is usually given by the best man, but may be given by the groom or ushers.
• Rehearsal dinner is usually given by groom or family, but may be given by bride's family or relatives.
• Wedding breakfast or brunch may be given by the bride's family.
• Attendants' dresses are usually bought by each woman, but the bride may provide them, if she wishes.

The Wedding Planner ———————————————————— *Page 21*

The space between numbers and letters makes this page difficult to read. The same is true for the bullets below.

The illustration stands by itself with nothing tying it to the total message.

The severe left margin creates a cramped effect, despite all the white space on the right!

MAKEOVER

Wedding Hints

STYLES OF FORMAL WEDDINGS

1. Very Formal evening: large ceremony, after 6 p.m.
2. Very Formal daytime: large ceremony, noon to late afternoon
3. Formal evening: after 6 p.m., smaller than Very Formal
4. Formal daytime: usually in morning or early afternoon
5. Semi-formal evening: small ceremony, often home or garden
6. Semi-formal daytime: small ceremony, often home or garden

WEDDING EXPENSES—WHO PAYS FOR WHAT

The bride's family is entirely responsible for the wedding ceremony. The groom's family may offer to share in the cost of the reception, and the bride's family may accept, if they wish. Wedding costs, by tradition, are devided as follows:

The bride (or family) pays for:
Invitations and announcements
Bride's personal stationery
The bridal outfit and trousseau
Bridal photographs (engagement and wedding)
All costs of the reception
Flowers for the attendants
Flowers for the church and reception
Music at the church and reception
Sexton, organist, and choir fees
Groom's wedding ring
Groom's gift
Gifts and party for the bride's attendants
Lodging (if necessary) for out-of-town bridesmaids
A limousine for the bride and cars for transportation
All rented equipment for large weddings and receptions

The groom (or family) pays for:
Bride's engagement ring and wedding rings
Marriage license
Clergyman's fee ($10-$100, inquire)
Bride's going-away corsage and bouquet
Boutonnieres, gloves, ties for men of wedding party
Wedding gift for the bride

Complete wedding trip
Gifts for best man and ushers
Lodging (if necessary) for out-of-town ushers

Optional expenses
Bridal shower may be given by the bride's maid of honor or a close friend.

Bride's bouquet is usually gift of the groom; may be purchased by the bride's family.

Corsages for mothers and grandmothers are usually provided by the groom; may be purchased by the bride for her own mother and grandmother.

Bachelor party is usually given by the best man, but may be given by the groom or ushers.

Rehearsal dinner is usually given by groom or family, but may be given by bride's family or relatives.

Wedding breakfast or brunch may be given by the bride's family.

Attendants' dresses are usually bought by each woman, but the bride may provide them, if she wishes.

The Wedding Planner | 21

A two-column format and a vertical rule between columns make the list more readable.

Note how the illustration effectively pops out of both the vertical and horizontal rules, creating an illusion of motion.

Design your booklet covers to resemble books or magazines—particularly when the information purports to be objective.

ORIGINAL

This mall marketing guide has been designed to help you understand and improve your direct marketing results.

How TO COMPUTERIZE AND MAINTAIN YOUR MAILING LIST FOR GREATER PROFIT

Dependable
L I S T S, I N C.

2^{00}

HOW TO COMPUTERIZE AND MAINTAIN YOUR MAILING LIST FOR GREATER PROFIT

Long blocks of vertical type are hard to read.

The title appears twice on the page—a waste of valuable space.

MAKEOVER

Pin stripes reversed from a dense screen create a no-nonsense, professional image.

Long headlines often can be broken up with innovative visual techniques.

Logos need not be big to be prominent—this smaller logo is very visible and doesn't overwhelm the rest of the copy.

A few simple touches can make a booklet look like a professionally designed book. Headers, footers, chapter heads and other traditional book design techniques create a serious, informative reading environment.

ORIGINAL

tape is not unrelated to costs, because there's a charge for every stroke of the typewriter, every punch of a key. You'd be wise to discuss all this with your advisor and make sure you have a good idea of what each method costs before you make your decision.

CREATING YOUR "MATCH CODE" As mentioned earlier, one of the uses you will want to make of the computer when you put your names on tape is the *elimination of duplicate names and addresses.* For this your system will have to create your *match code.* Match codes come in two types: a) more complex codes, used for billing and other special services; b) simpler codes, used to locate and eliminate duplicates. In all likelihood, you'll be using a simple match code for the elimination of duplicate names.

To create a match code, the first requirement is that all your data input to the computer should be *consistent:* designators, prefix and suffix titles, compound names, two-word names, abbreviations and zip codes. You have to see to it that all of these are handled in the same way, or your system just won't function. While you won't be doing the actual work yourself (your service bureau will), you should have the details clearly in mind, and, most important, *ask to see several tests* in order to be sure that the code developed will properly serve your purposes. What you have to remember in dealing with the computer is that poorly handled or incorrect programming duplicates itself throughout the computer and keeps coming back to haunt you like a bad dream. You'll never spend time or money more wisely than in seeing to it that, right from the outset, the data input to your computer is completely consistent and that your match code works to suit your needs.

HOW TO MAINTAIN YOUR LIST Computerized lists are like children. You have to maintain them after you've brought them into the world. This is no place for a discussion on raising children, but perhaps a few words on computer list maintenance might not be out of order.

List maintenance is principally a matter of *adding new names, deleting "nixes"* (undeliverable mail) and *entering changes of address* as customers move. None of this is difficult, of course, but all of it is highly necessary if computer lists are to live and thrive.

The thing about maintaining computer lists is that you can't do it when the spirit moves you or when you've nothing else to do. Computer time is expen-

14

Sans-serif type set in long blocks is generally more difficult to read than serif type.

Use different type styles to off-set subheads and body copy.

MAKEOVER

tape is not unrelated to costs, because there's a charge for every stroke of the typewriter, every punch of a key. You'd be wise to discuss all this with your advisor and make sure you have a good idea of what each method costs before you make your decision.

Creating your "match code"

As mentioned earlier, one of the uses you will want to make of the computer when you put your names on tape is the elimination of duplicate names and addresses. For this your system will have to create your match code. Match codes come in two types: a) more complex codes, used for billing and other special services; b) simpler codes, used to locate and elimiate duplicates. In all likelihood, you'll be using a simple match code for the elimination of duplicate names.

To create a match code, the first requirement is that all your data input to the computer should be consistent: designators, prefix and suffix titles, compound names, two-word names, abbreviations and zip codes. While you won't be doing the actual work yourself (your service bureau will), you should have the details clearly in mind, and most important, ask to see several tests in order to be sure that the code developed will properly serve your purposes. What you have to remember in dealing with the computer is that poorly handled or incorrect programming duplicates itself throughout the computer and keeps coming back to haunt you like a bad dream. You'll never spend time or money more wisely than in seeing to it that, right from the outset, the data input to your computer is completely consistent and that your match code works to suit your needs.

How to maintain your list

Computerized lists are like children. You have to maintain them after you've brought them into the world. This is no place for a discussion on raising children, but perhaps a few words on computer list maintainance might not be out of order.

List maintenance is principally a matter of adding new names, deleting "nixes' (undeliverable mail) and entering changes of address as customers move. None of this is difficult, but all of it is highly necessary if computer lists are to live and thrive.

The thing about maintaining computer lists is that you can't do it when the spirit moves you or when you've nothing else

14

Flush-left subheads reduce the line lengths of the body copy, making it easier to read.

A full-justified type treatment creates a cleaner look.

Headers and footers help readers quickly locate information and make your publication look more professional.

CHARTS & GRAPHS

Charts and graphs let you breathe life into complex relationships between numbers. They replace unappealing tables of numbers with highly visual graphics, adding interest to your documents. Best of all, they let you clearly show even the most detailed relationships between numbers.

Using charts and graphs effectively is based on several key considerations. One is that you choose the right type for the numeric relationships you want to communicate. For example, an effective technique for communicating figure relationships would probably not be suitable for presenting trends.

How you place a chart or graph on a page is equally important. It must relate to the other material but not overpower it. Conversely, charts and graphs are more readable when separated from surrounding text.

Labeling is another important consideration. Ideally, there should be a heading or caption that summarizes what the graph or chart represents and the information within. Readers should be able to find the less obvious information as well; for example, the horizontal and vertical axes of charts and graphs should always be clearly marked.

The communicating power of a chart or graph is often enhanced by a background grid, which helps readers relate the visuals to the numbers involved.

Design Tips and Tricks

The importance of choosing the right type of chart or graph is illustrated by the "PM Interval Affects PM Cost" graph. The original is a line graph that relates cost to mileage. This graph also communicates the contributions made by factors A, B and C. The original chart is difficult to interpret because it lacks a background grid. Also, too much space separates the graphs from the explanatory legend.

The makeover is easier to understand: the grid links cost to mileage and the screens make the meaning of the A, B and C graphically obvious.

This graph also shows the importance of clear labels. In the "before" example, the heading extends nearly the width of the graph, detracting from it. The expanded type also attracts undue attention. In the makeover, however, the heading is set using a condensed typeface that takes up less horizontal space. Thus, the heading complements the labels and other graphic elements.

The original graph lacks strong boundaries. As a result, it just floats on the page. The makeover, however, is contained within a simple strong border.

A final improvement is the bold sans-serif type that identifies the A, B and C data. Also notice how the information is visually coded with screened boxes, connecting the labels to the larger screens. The use of contrasting type sizes in the graph's legend makes the whole thing more legible and interesting.

Multidimensional Charts and Graphs

Anyone who's bored by a graphic probably won't study it long enough to comprehend the data it represents. Charts and graphs are at their best when information is related as pictorially as possible. This is illustrated by the "Comparative Maintenance Cost & Frequency by Vehicle System" graph. Here, a vertical bar graph has been replaced by a horizontal graph that effectively uses visual images to communicate two different types of data: costs and frequency of repair.

The original vertical graph is difficult to understand because it lacks a background grid showing relative scale. The extreme contrast between the black bars and white bars also makes it hard to review the original for any length of time without eye strain.

The revised graph communicates more information at a glance. Flipping the horizontal and vertical axes makes the labels clearer. Labels that were set in small type, like "Cooling System," can now be set in a larger, more readable size. Equally important, the data become more meaningful when rearranged to read from lowest to highest figures.

The revision also unifies the top and bottom of the graph with gray screens that make the type stand out.

Organization Charts

The "Maintenance Council Organizational Chart" also illustrates how reverses and background screens can distinguish a chart or graph from its surroundings and simultaneously improve its communicating power.

A reversed background is used to emphasize the heading and also to highlight the first steps in the chain of command. Gray screens are then used to highlight areas of responsibility. Notice how the horizontal rule at the bottom balances the reversed text at the top, creating a unified whole.

The "Maintenance Council Organizational Chart" also shows the importance of typography in headings and legends. The chart becomes more effective by using sans-serif type; italics emphasize the parenthetical subhead.

Visual Symbols

There's no practical limit to the size of a chart or graph, as long as it communicates as effectively as possible. This is illustrated by the chart that correlates inquiries with ad size. The original didn't succeed in making the point because it didn't visually relate to the subject. Truly effective charts can immediately convey a message, even if readers don't take the time to read the labels.

In the original chart, the height of the bars indicates only the level of response. In order to make the comparisons, you have to search below for the corresponding ad size.

In the revised chart, however, you can easily grasp the relationship between ad size and response because the bars have been replaced by illustrations that show the ad sizes as gray screens against a white background. The horizontal arrangement of the labels to the right, using larger type, reinforces the illustrations.

Typography and background grids have also been refined. A more prominent background grid serves to integrate the components, helping your eye relate the sizes of the drawings to the totals. Finally, freeing up a full column for the copy provides room for a larger heading. A sans-serif italic type with exaggerated line spacing adds further impact. In addition, the heading is linked to the chart by the wide screened rules at the top and bottom.

In contrast to the usual style, the zero reference point is placed at the right-hand side of the chart. This moves interest toward the heading. Consider how the chart would lose impact if the zero point were on the left.

Many of these same points are illustrated by the "Hyundai Excel Purchase Price" graph. Once again, a dull bar graph is given new life by the use of symbols that represent the product. In this case, the graphs total 100 percent. Screens ranging from light gray to black represent different price categories.

The original chart is hard to understand because the legend doesn't make clear what the different types of screens signify. The makeover clarifies the connection between screen shades and the categories they represent.

The use of screens to integrate a chart or graph with overall page design is illustrated by the "Test Results" example. The original scattergraphs are simply dropped into white space; there's little to visually connect them to the page. In the makeover, however, identical background screens highlight the subheads as well as the graphs. The typography is unified, too; note how text and graph headings are of equal size, implying equal importance.

A lot of detailing takes place in this makeover. Notice how "% of sales" is moved from the top of the vertical axis to the bottom. Note also how much more distinguishable from the body copy the headings and labels are when serif type is replaced with sans-serif.

Finally, notice how the text that introduces the graphs is placed on top instead of below them. Introductions now come logically before the visuals, instead of after.

Take Another Look

Ask yourself these questions as you review the charts and graphs you include in your projects:

✔ Are charts and diagrams large enough to be easily read without overwhelming adjacent text?

✔ Have I accented charts and graphs with appropriate backgrounds and borders?

✔ Did I choose the type of chart that best communicates the points I want to make?

✔ Can readers understand the chart or graph at a glance?

✔ Did I choose symbols that appropriately reflect the product category being described?

✔ Are headings, labels and explanations of data sources easy to find?

✔ Are totals and other important data summarized for fast comprehension?

✔ Do charts and diagrams inadvertently distort the data?

Take care to contain information within charts and graphs, particularly scattergrams and line charts, so that readers can easily discern where visual information begins and ends.

ORIGINAL

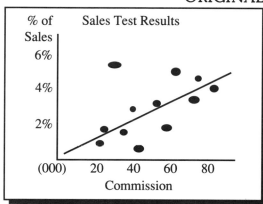

The chart floats freely with no border to de-fine its limits.

Scatter dots are not well executed.

MAKEOVER

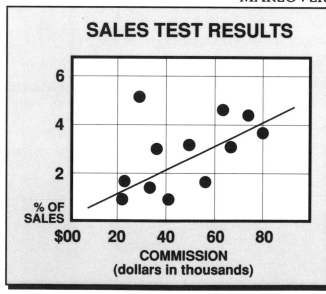

The simple addition of a screen helps focus attention on the data.

A grid helps readers to easily grasp relation-ships between elements.

A chart or graph should let the reader grasp complex data quickly. Always keep the reader in mind when you're displaying quantitative information visually.

Data appear to float off the page.

Too many leaders on the left make it hard to find information.

ORIGINAL

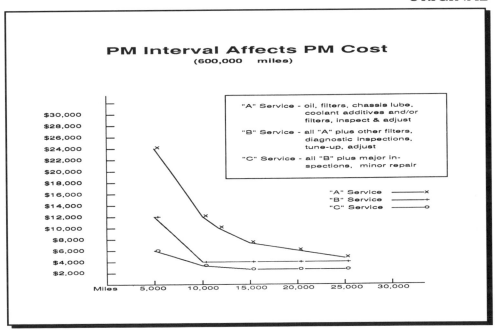

Blocks of information can be off-set by using screens of different values.

Borders and boxes are important tools in defining the parameters of charts and graphs.

MAKEOVER

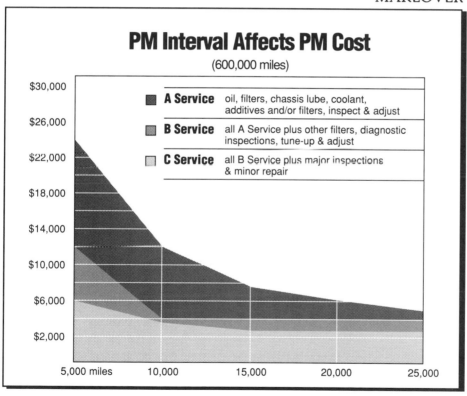

Using screens and reverses on visual material often compounds the gray, monotonous effect of surrounding text.

This chart is too "white," and the reader's eyes aren't properly directed to important data.

Leader lines often clutter the graphics and distract the reader.

ORIGINAL

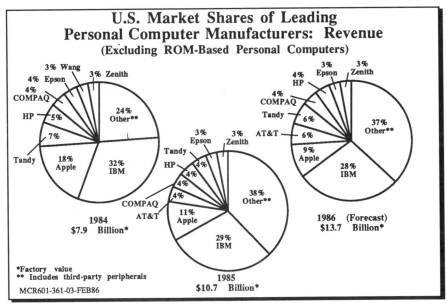

U.S. Market Shares of Leading Personal Computer Manufacturers: Revenue
(Excluding ROM-Based Personal Computers)

3% Wang
4% Epson
4% COMPAQ
3% Zenith
HP 5%
24% Other**
7%
Tandy
18% Apple
32% IBM
1984 $7.9 Billion*

Tandy
HP
3% Epson
3% Zenith
4%
4%
4%
4%
COMPAQ
AT&T
11% Apple
38% Other**
29% IBM
1985 $10.7 Billion*

4% HP
3% Epson
3% Zenith
4% COMPAQ
Tandy 6%
AT&T 6%
9% Apple
37% Other**
28% IBM
1986 (Forecast) $13.7 Billion*

*Factory value
** Includes third-party peripherals
MCR601-361-03-FEB86

Placing the pie charts within boxes helps to organize the information and redirect the reader's eyes.

Moving the year and revenue figure outside the related pie-chart box makes that information more accessible and gives the charts a less cluttered look.

MAKEOVER

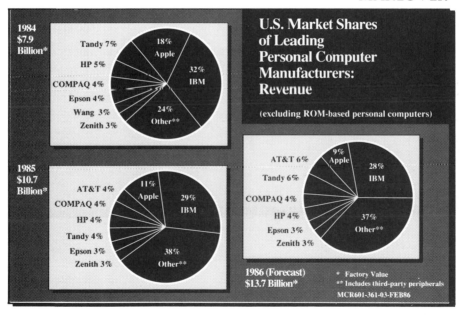

U.S. Market Shares of Leading Personal Computer Manufacturers: Revenue

(excluding ROM-based personal computers)

1984 $7.9 Billion*

Tandy 7%
HP 5%
COMPAQ 4%
Epson 4%
Wang 3%
Zenith 3%
18% Apple
32% IBM
24% Other**

1985 $10.7 Billion*

AT&T 4%
COMPAQ 4%
HP 4%
Tandy 4%
Epson 3%
Zenith 3%
11% Apple
29% IBM
38% Other**

AT&T 6%
Tandy 6%
COMPAQ 4%
HP 4%
Epson 3%
Zenith 3%
9% Apple
28% IBM
37% Other**

1986 (Forecast) $13.7 Billion*

* Factory Value
** Includes third-party peripherals
MCR601-361-03-FEB86

Through desktop publishing, the ability to develop, import and manipulate graphics creates opportunities to make dry statistical information more appealing and persuasive.

ORIGINAL

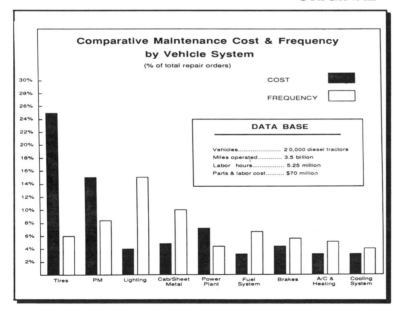

A vertical orientation results in small, un-readable type in the categories ("Tires," "PM," etc.).

When possible, place reader information within the confines of one inset, for easy scanning.

MAKEOVER

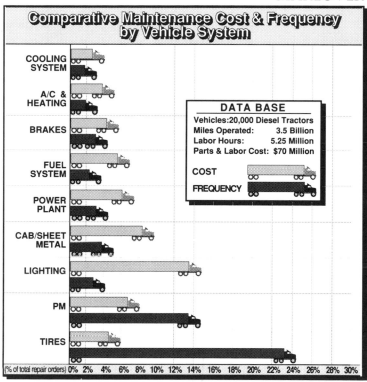

Comparative Maintenance Cost & Frequency by Vehicle System

COOLING SYSTEM

A/C & HEATING

BRAKES

FUEL SYSTEM

POWER PLANT

CAB/SHEET METAL

LIGHTING

PM

TIRES

DATA BASE

Vehicles: 20,000 Diesel Tractors
Miles Operated: 3.5 Billion
Labor Hours: 5.25 Million
Parts & Labor Cost: $70 Million

COST

FREQUENCY

(% of total repair orders) 0% 2% 4% 6% 8% 10% 12% 14% 16% 18% 20% 22% 24% 26% 28% 30%

Drop shadows and/or reverse rules can enhance insets without unduly distracting readers.

A horizontal orientation allows larger, more readable type for categories.

A light background grid lets readers scan accurate data at a glance.

Even a simple schematic or flowchart can be enhanced quickly and inexpensively by using screens and reverses.

ORIGINAL

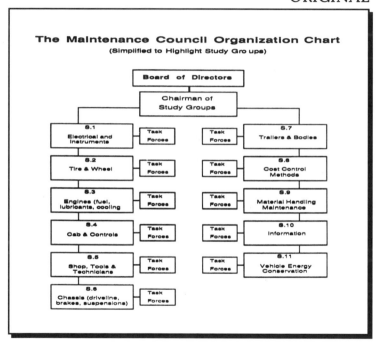

The white space on the left and right is unnecessary. The space would be better used to make the chart wider and more readable.

MAKEOVER

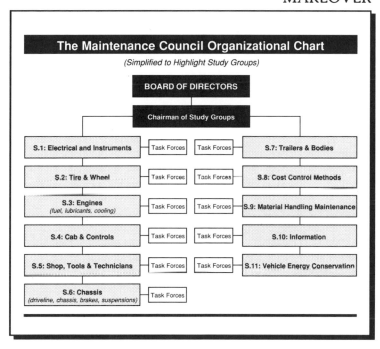

The wider boxes let you set the type larger for easy scanning.

Screens off-set repetitive information so the eyes can easily make the connection.

V isual information must be presented clearly—
that's why it was highlighted in the first place!

The legend is crowded
and difficult to read.

The symbols don't give
readers a quick base of
comparison between
models and price ranges.

ORIGINAL

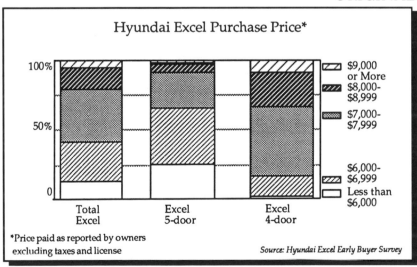

Hyundai Excel Purchase Price*

*Price paid as reported by owners
excluding taxes and license

Source: Hyundai Excel Early Buyer Survey

Increments of 10 percent, around which the data are based, are clearly delineated by the icons.

Graduated screens of varying density let readers make quick comparisons.

Simple icons often add visual appeal.

MAKEOVER

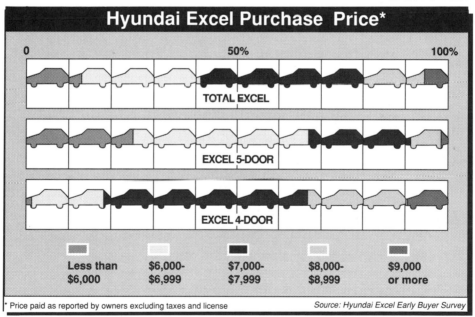

Hyundai Excel Purchase Price*

0   50%   100%

TOTAL EXCEL

EXCEL 5-DOOR

EXCEL 4-DOOR

Less than $6,000 | $6,000-$6,999 | $7,000-$7,999 | $8,000-$8,999 | $9,000 or more

* Price paid as reported by owners excluding taxes and license

Source: Hyundai Excel Early Buyer Survey

CHARTS & GRAPHS

Avoid frivolous design when creating charts and graphs. Statistical information should first inform, then entertain.

The wildly varying patterns within the bars don't correspond to changes in data. Nor do they reflect anything about the subject matter.

ORIGINAL

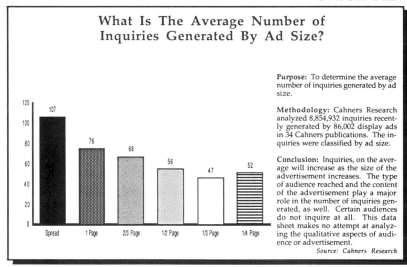

What Is The Average Number of Inquiries Generated By Ad Size?

Purpose: To determine the average number of inquiries generated by ad size.

Methodology: Cahners Research analyzed 8,854,932 inquiries recently generated by 86,002 display ads in 34 Cahners publications. The inquiries were classified by ad size.

Conclusion: Inquiries, on the average will increase as the size of the advertisement increases. The type of audience reached and the content of the advertisement play a major role in the number of inquiries generated, as well. Certain audiences do not inquire at all. This data sheet makes no attempt at analyzing the qualitative aspects of audience or advertisement.

Source: Cahners Research

MAKEOVER

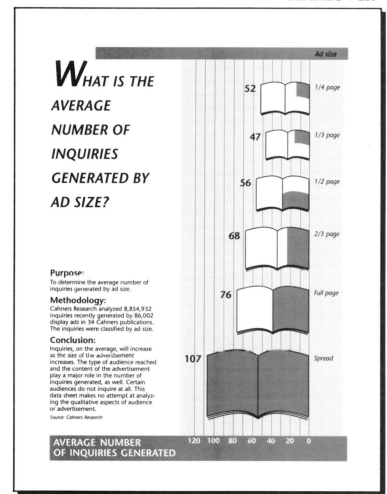

WHAT IS THE AVERAGE NUMBER OF INQUIRIES GENERATED BY AD SIZE?

Purpose:
To determine the average number of inquiries generated by ad size.

Methodology:
Cahners Research analyzed 8,854,932 inquiries recently generated by 86,002 display ads in 34 Cahners publications. The inquiries were classified by ad size.

Conclusion:
Inquiries, on the average, will increase as the size of the advertisement increases. The type of audience reached and the content of the advertisement play a major role in the number of inquiries generated, as well. Certain audiences do not inquire at all. This data sheet makes no attempt at analyzing the qualitative aspects of audience or advertisement.

Source: Cahners Research

Ad size

52 — 1/4 page
47 — 1/3 page
56 — 1/2 page
68 — 2/3 page
76 — Full page
107 — Spread

AVERAGE NUMBER OF INQUIRIES GENERATED

120 100 80 60 40 20 0

Icons not only add interest, but also let the reader more quickly grasp data.

Often, light background screens subtly define the parameters of charts and graphs. Be sure that type is large and bold enough to be easily read.

It's appropriate to add visual interest to charts and graphs as long as the supporting data are clear and readers aren't misled.

ORIGINAL

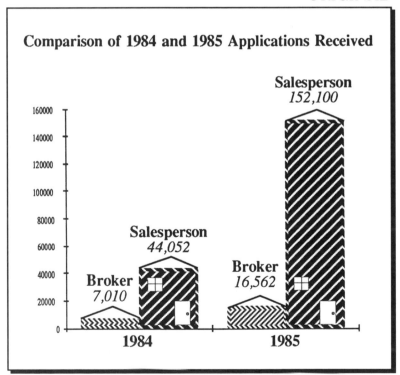

Avoid unnecessary flourishes (doors and windows) that force readers to question their meaning.

Zigzags and other complex visualizations further confuse readers.

MAKEOVER

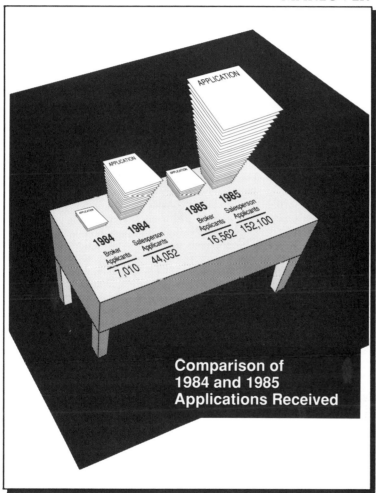

An exaggerated perspective gives readers a heightened sense of contrast.

Use "trick" charts and graphs only when the base data are uncomplicated and easily supported; otherwise, there's nothing wrong with tried-and-true pie, bar and line charts.

Maps and other complex illustrations are available in clip-art and graphics programs—a worthwhile investment.

Try to avoid the "dot-matrix" school of cartography—the jaggies are difficult to read and small type often is lost on the reader.

ORIGINAL

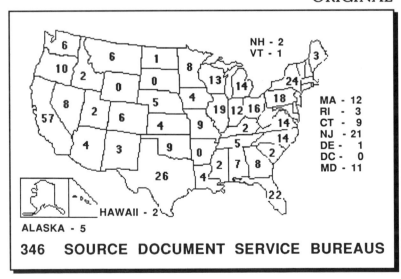

A more elongated map allows enough space for state names as well as numbers—a benefit for readers who flunked geography.

MAKEOVER

WA 6
OR 10
ID 2
MT 6
ND 1
MN 8
NH - 2
VT - 1
ME 3
NY 24
SD 0
WI 13
MI 14
PA 18
WY 0
IA 4
NV 8
UT 2
CO 6
NE 5
IL 19
IN 12
OH 16
WV
CA 57
KS 4
MO 9
KY 2
VA 14
A7 4
NM 3
OK 9
AR 0
IN 5
NC 14
SC 2
MS 2
AL 7
GA 8
TX 26
LA 4
HAWAII 2
ALASKA 5
FL 22

MA - 12
RI - 3
CT - 9
NJ - 21
DE - 1
DC - 0
MD - 11

346 TOTAL
UNITED STATES
SOURCE DOCUMENT
SERVICE BUREAUS

CHAPTER

10

ESTABLISHING A CORPORATE IDENTITY

By giving all your print communications an integrated look, or "family resemblance," you can establish a consistent corporate image. Distinctive design elements repeated on all your documents—from invoices and price lists to letterhead and brochures—give your message more clout and your company more stature.

This chapter describes the importance of developing a distinct corporate identity for a variety of projects. Key considerations include:

- Consistent placement of a logo (a unique graphic treatment of your firm's name) in each project.
- Consistent use of typography and white space on all projects.
- Consistent use of graphic accents, such as rules and screens.

The key word for all these, of course, is "consistent." Consistency simplifies the design of each project, speeds up production and builds reader confidence.

Consistency eliminates the need to reinvent the wheel each time you begin a new project. By designing each new project on the same pattern, you'll find that decisions, such as which typeface and type size to use, are already settled.

Consistency expedites production when you use your desktop publishing or word processing program in an informed way. In many cases, this involves making the most of your program's stylesheet feature.

Stylesheets are electronic files that specify typeface, type size, type style, line spacing and other typographic details. In fact, some programs let you include graphic accents, such as rules and predetermined amounts of white space, in your style definitions.

Stylesheets are templates that can be used over and over again. Once you establish stylesheets for one project—a product sheet, for example—you can reuse the same ones for other product sheets. Without them, not only must you start every project from scratch, but your readers will be confused and wonder how many firms share the same name!

A strong corporate identity program gives readers a reassuring feeling of familiarity and dependability, making them more receptive to your communications.

Start with the Logo

Develop a strong logo for your firm and use it on all your print communications. Some firms inadvertently use several logos at once; each project or department may use a slightly different logo and at a slightly different size! Those firms lack a coherent corporate identity.

Start by creating an official logo for all your firm's documents. Whenever possible, store it as an encapsulated PostScript file. This will let you increase or decrease the size of the logo without sacrificing quality. When redesigning a logo, try to develop an image strong enough to be distinctive even when reduced to fairly small sizes. Ideally, your new logo should incorporate some characteristics of previous logos.

As the System Three example illustrates, the revised logo strongly resembles its predecessor, but it's been simplified and enhanced—simplified by a uniform type treatment for "The Boatbuilder's Epoxy" slogan, and enhanced by adding a background screen. The three horizontal rules and reverse type have been retained.

As you'll see in several of the following examples, the three bars of the System Three logo are sometimes used alone to provide continuity on multi-page documents.

As you look at the originals and makeovers on the following pages, notice the logo's major role in creating and maintaining a distinctive look for all of System Three's print communications. Even when the logo is relatively small, it still provides continuity and reinforces System Three's corporate identity.

The "before" and "after" examples also show how pieces as diverse as invoices, product sheets, letterhead and step-by-step instruction sheets become unified by the consistent placement of the System Three logo, often balanced by the placement of the firm's address and phone number. This design even extends to System Three's envelopes and business cards.

Courier & Other Image-Busters

After standardizing your logo, the next step in establishing a corporate identity might involve replacing typewritten forms—predictably done in bland Courier type—with image-building, typeset ones.

To understand the importance of this, compare the original System Three "Build a Lighter Boat" order form with the makeover.

The revised form offers three things not found in the original: the strength of typefaces other than Courier, creative use of white space and an easy-to-use coupon.

ESTABLISHING A CORPORATE IDENTITY

Looking at the original form, would you feel comfortable with their products? The wide typewritten, justified columns are intimidating; they don't offer much information about what the products are or how they work. The makeover, on the other hand, projects a competent, professional image. The bold headings engage your attention. Liberal use of white space opens up the page.

Notice in the original how the firm's address and phone number are placed at the top of the page. This is information you don't really need until you've decided to buy. The makeover puts it in a more appropriate place—at the bottom.

Also notice the revised heading placement. In the "before" sample, headings are centered over their wide blocks of copy. Your eye has to travel from the end of a heading to the extreme left margin of the page. In the "after" example, however, there's a smooth transition into the text.

Another advantage of the makeover is its emphasis on customer response. The original order form uses a separate coupon, which readers could easily lose. The revised version, however, builds the coupon right into the form, where it anchors the piece. Now filling out the coupon becomes a simple extension of reading the form.

Notice how using the same typeface and type size for most headings, subheads and body copy provides important continuity throughout the makeovers.

Desktop publishing's role in pre-selling customers and improving the communicating power of even prosaic projects is shown in the System Three Price List "before" and "after" samples—one of the most dramatic makeovers in this book.

In the original, notice how difficult it is to find specific products. Because typewritten projects can't make the graphic distinctions typeset ones can, it's hard to tell the difference between categories and products. The only typographic enhancement available on typewriters is uppercase type—which, in this case, hinders legibility. The makeover, however, uses a contrasting typeface and thick and thin rules to visually separate the categories. Now it's easy to find Cab-O-Sil among the fillers.

In addition, the typewritten price list—which is "gray," or too dense to read—discourages buyers. The makeover, however, makes response easy by clearly presenting all important buying information, such as quantities, shipping weights and price breaks.

The White-Space Remedy

You've seen the improvements resulting from the consistent use of a few typefaces and establishing a hierarchy of type sizes that relate to the importance of the information being communicated. Now notice how the revised samples demonstrate a similar use of white space.

The originals, dense with copy and with little relieving white space, are monotonous; there's little, if any, visual contrast. The makeovers, however, are accented by generous use of white space. This provides dramatic contrast between the System Three logo, the headings and the copy.

Moving On

After comparing the originals to the makeovers, notice how the revised documents inspire more confidence and are easier to read. They're also easier to produce because logo placement, typeface and type size decisions have already been made!

As you become more comfortable with your desktop publishing or word processing program, you'll find it easier to create and maintain a distinct corporate identity, which will make your message more effective—even before your clients read it.

Because readers tend to scan messages in copy blocks, too much information crammed into a small area discourages response.

ORIGINAL

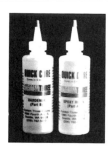

NEW! FROM

SYSTEM THREE !

QUICK CURE

THE EPOXY GLUE THAT
LETS YOU KEEP ON WORKING!

- Cures tack free in five minutes.
- Cures to full strength in fifteen minutes.
- Handy squeeze bottle plastic dispensers.
- Easy to "eyeball" one to one mix ratio.
- Most jobs don't require the addition of fillers.
- Mixes with standard fillers for tough jobs.

We first used "five minute" epoxy resins several years ago while building a strip planked dingy. For $2.98 at the local hardware store we'd get a dual syringe dispensing system containing one fluid ounce of glue — quite handy but at the cost of almost one hundred dollars per quart of fast glue!

The temptation to produce and improve upon the product for ourselves became irresistible. Soon friends asked for some. "Quick Cure" is the result. We wouldn't build a boat or run a wood shop today without it.

Quick Cure is a one-to-one volume mix of fairly thick epoxy and hardener packaged in polyethylene squeeze bottles with spout caps — just like the ones on ketchup and mustard dispensers. To use Quick Cure just squeeze equal size puddles of resin and hardener next to each other on a scrap of wood. Fold the two puddles into each other, mix for a few seconds and use. The ratios are not critical so this "eyeball" measuring method works very well.

In about five minutes Quick Cure will solidify. The glue line is strong in 15 minutes. Quick Cure is highly resistant to water but not waterproof, so don't expose the cured epoxy to constant immersion in water. Most Quick Cure joints are sealed with System Three epoxy so this factor is not a problem.

Today, we mix Quick Cure with wood flour, microballoons and several other fillers as well as use it "straight". It has some gap filling ability without the use of fillers.

John Marples describes some excellent uses for Quick Cure on the reverse side of this sheet. We've also used it to fill screw holes that were somehow missed when microballooning but found right when ready to begin 'glassing. (Imagine being able to sand an epoxy/microballoon mixture in 15 minutes!) Quick Cure makes great "lock tight" to keep nuts on bolts that are subject to vibration. We use it to glue plywood perimeter patterns for fitting inside panels, counter tops, bulkheads, thwarts, etc. Having a super fast setting epoxy around simply makes the boat building job go faster and easier.

We're sure that you'll come up with new uses around your shop, too. Try some now.

QUART KIT $28.00 • PINT KIT $15.00 • ½ PINT KIT $8.00

SYSTEM THREE RESINS • P.O. BOX 70436 • SEATTLE, WASHINGTON 98107 • (206) 782-7976

Centered type, set ragged-right and fully justified on one page, forces readers' eyes to work needlessly.

Sans-serif type generally is harder to read than serif, particularly when large copy blocks aren't off-set by subheads.

MAKEOVER

QUICK CURE

The epoxy glue that lets you keep on working!

NEW!

- Cures tack free in five minutes.
- Cures to full strength in fifteen minutes.
- Handy squeeze bottle plastic dispensers.
- Easy to "eyeball" one-to-one mix ratio.
- Most jobs don't require adding fillers.
- Mixes with standard fillers for tough jobs.

We first used "five minute" epoxy resins several years ago while building a strip planked dingy. For $2.98 at the local hardware store we'd get a dual syringe dispensing system containing one fluid ounce of glue quite handy but at the cost of almost one hundred dollars per quart of fast glue!

The temptation to produce and improve upon the product for ourselves became irresistible. Soon friends asked for some. "Quick Cure" is the result. We wouldn't build a boat or run a wood shop today without it.

Quick Cure is a one to one volume mix of fairly thick epoxy and hardener packaged in polyethylene squeeze bottles with spout caps—just like the ones on ketchup and mustard dispensers. To use Quick Cure, just squeeze equal size puddles of resin and hardener next to each other on a scrap of wood. Fold the two puddles into each other, mix for a few seconds and use. The ratios are not critical so this

"eyeball" measuring method works very well.

In about five minutes Quick Cure will solidify. The glue line is strong in 15 minutes. Quick Cure is highly resistant to water but not waterproof, so don't expose the cured epoxy to constant immersion in water. Most Quick Cure joints are sealed with System Three epoxy, so this factor is not a problem.

Today, we mix Quick Cure with wood flour, microballoons and several other fillers as well as use it "straight." It has some gap filling ability without the use of fillers.

John Marples describes some excellent uses for Quick Cure on the reverse side of this sheet. We've also used it to fill screw holes that were somehow missed when microballooning but found right when ready to begin 'glassing.' (Imagine being able to sand an epoxy/microballoon mixture in 15 minutes!) Quick Cure makes great "lock tight" to keep nuts on bolts that are

subject to vibration. We use it to glue plywood perimeter patterns for filling inside panels, counter tops, bulkheads, thwarts, etc. Having a super fast setting epoxy around simply makes the boat building job go faster and easier.

We're sure that you'll come up with new uses around your shop, too. Try some now.

Quart kit
$28.00

Pint kit
$15.00

Half-pint kit
$8.00

Telephone:
206/762-5313

System Three Resins
PO Box 70436
Seattle, WA 98107
206/762-5313

A three-column format reduces line length for easier reading.

More effective use of white space off-sets messages and reduces visual clutter.

Important price information deserves a prominent position, and the nearby phone number encourages response.

Because price lists and other order forms contain so much information, graphic emphasis helps readers make decisions more easily.

ORIGINAL

A lack of differentiation in type size and style makes this document nearly impossible to read—just when the buyer is most interested!

Remember to double-check that all numbers are properly aligned.

MAKEOVER

THE BOATBUILDER'S EPOXY

SYSTEM THREE

Price List
6/15/85

- $20 minimum order.
- Prices FOB Seattle, WA.
- Prices subject to change without notice.
- Shipment via UPS or most convenient carrier.
- All orders shipped COD unless prepaid by check, money order, VISA or Mastercard.

Epoxy Resin

Item	Net contents U.S. measure	Shipping wt. Pounds	Price U.S. $
System Three standard resin	Quart	3	15.00
	Gallon	10	35.00
	2.5 gallon	25	75.00
	5 gallon	48	135.00
	3x5 gallon	144	390.00
	55 gallon (drum)	541	1,075.00

Hardeners
- 1. Fast
- 2. Medium
- 3. Slow

Item	Net contents U.S. measure	Shipping wt. Pounds	Price U.S. $
All hardeners	Quart	3	15.00
	Gallon	9	35.00
	2.5 gallon	23	75.00
	5 gallon	44	135.00
	3 x 5 gallon	132	390.00
	55 gallon (drum)	494	1,075.00

Fillers

Item	Net contents U.S. measure	Shipping wt. Pounds	Price U.S. $
Wood flour	1 pound bag	1.5	2.00
	50 pound bag	55	65.00
Cab-O-Sil	4 ounce bag	1.5	7.00
	10 pound bag	13	60.00
Phenolic microballoons	1 pound bag	1.5	8.50
	17 pound bag	22	125.00
Quartz microspheres	1 pound bag	1.5	4.50
	10 pound bag	13	40.00
Plastic thickener (Replaces asbestos)	1 pound bag	1.5	4.50
	10 pound bag	13	42.00
1/4 inch chopped glass strands	1 pound bag	1.5	2.00
Milled glass fibers	1 pound bag	1.5	3.00
	25 pound box	25	50.00
Aluminum powder	1 pound bag	1.5	4.00
Graphite powder	1 pound bag	1.5	2.25
White epoxy paste pigment	4 pound (quart can)	5	15.00

Combinations

Buy a half-drum of hardener (27.5 gallons) at half the full drum price when also buying a full drum of resin.

Combine resin and hardener in 5-gallon containers for the 3 x 5 price break:
- 2 fives of resin and 1 five of hardener, or
- 2 fives of resin and two 2.5 gallon containers of hardener.

System Three Resins
PO Box 70436
Seattle, WA 98107
206/762-5313

Important purchasing information is featured prominently.

Rules can be used as effective leaders, so that readers can quickly skim long horizontal blocks of information.

Thick rules effectively call attention to the various categories while reinforcing the company's logo.

One of desktop publishing's most cost-effective tools is inexpensive access to a variety of typefaces and styles. These can dramatically enhance the traditional Courier type presentation.

ORIGINAL

THE BOATBUILDER'S EPOXY

SYSTEM THREE

SYSTEM THREE RESINS
5965 FOURTH AVENUE, SOUTH
SEATTLE, WASHINGTON 98108
(206) 762-5313

BUILD A LIGHTER BOAT

That's right, a lighter boat! SYSTEM THREE RESIN AND HARDENER have a mixed system weight per gallon of 8.81 pounds. One nationally advertised wood/epoxy system has a mixed system weight per gallon of 9.60 pounds. SYSTEM THREE is over three quarters of a pound per gallon LIGHTER. As an example, a 4,000 pound hull which uses 50 gallons of epoxy will weigh 40 pounds less with SYSTEM THREE. A full 1% of of total hull weight!. A 60 pound strip planked canoe could weigh as much as 3% less when built with SYSTEM THREE EPOXY. These savings in weight occur because epoxies are used by volumetric measure in boat construction - not by weight!

BUILD A LESS EXPENSIVE BOAT

Comparing the drum prices from price lists in effect as of February 1, 1985, the mixed system cost per gallon of SYSTEM THREE EPOXY is $2.95 LESS than the mixed system cost per gallon of a nationally advertised 5:1 product. In gallon containers the difference is $6.86 LESS per gallon!

BUILD A BETTER BOAT

SYSTEM THREE EPOXY is designed to exhibit a tough resilience giving it excellent resistance to stress cracking and "star" breaks along with unequaled fatigue strength. Stiffer, more brittle epoxy systems can't match these features. SYSTEM THREE EPOXY resin and hardeners are formulated and modified here at our Seattle plant under the constant control and supervision of W. Kern Hendricks, chemical engineer and inventor of the system. To insure against acquiring a "we know it all" attitude we have on retainer as consultant a leading reinforced plastics engineer who is very active in the Aero-Space industry. The formulation and sales of complete epoxy systems is our ONLY business.

BUILD YOUR BOAT WHEN OTHERS CAN'T

SYSTEM THREE RESIN AND HARDENERS RESIST moisture before cure. Clear coats won't "white out" or "blush" when applied under highly humid conditions. With some other systems the builder must wait until conditions are "ideal" or be faced with possible dissappointment. SYSTEM THREE'S wide range of hardeners allow the builder to work under extreme temperature conditions - from the harsh winters of Alaska and New England to the humid heat of Guatemala and the South Pacific.

WE'RE HERE TO HELP

Here at SYSTEM THREE RESINS our purpose has a narrow focus. We want you, our customer, to build the best boat you can. To this end we strive to manufacture and make available the best epoxy resin system possible with today's technology. We stay in constant contact with

The logo is too large and bold, overwhelming the message below.

A traditional typewritten piece gives too few clues about what's important or what to read first.

MAKEOVER

THE BOATBUILDER'S EPOXY
SYSTEM THREE

Build a lighter boat

That's right, a lighter boat! System Three resin and hardener have a mixed system weight per gallon of 8.81 pounds. One nationally advertised wood/epoxy system has a mixed system weight per gallon of 9.60 pounds. System Three is over three quarters of a pound per gallon *lighter*. As an example, a 4,000 pound hull that uses 50 gallons of epoxy will weigh 40 pounds less with System Three. A full 1% of the total hull weight! A 60 pound strip planked canoe could weigh as much as 3% less when built with System Three Epoxy. These savings in weight occur because epoxies are used by volumetric measure in boat construction — not by weight!

Build a less expensive boat

Comparing the drum prices from price lists in effect as of February 1, 1985, the mixed system cost per gallon of System Three Epoxy is $2.95 *less* than the mixed system cost per gallon of a nationally advertised 5:1 product. In gallon containers the difference is $6.86 less per gallon!

Build a better boat

System Three Epoxy is designed to exhibit a tough resilience, giving it excellent resistance to stress cracking and "star" breaks along with unequaled fatigue strength. Stiffer, more brittle epoxy systems can't match these features. System Three Epoxy resin and hardeners are formulated and modified here at our Seattle plant under the constant control and supervision of W. Kern Hendricks, chemical engineer and inventor of the system. To insure against acquiring a "we-know-it-all" attitude we have on retainer as consultant a leading reinforced plastics engineer who is very active in the Aero-Space industry. The formulation and sales of complete epoxy systems is our *only* business.

Build your boat when others can't

System Three resin and hardeners *resist* moisture before cure. Clear coats won't "white out" or "blush" when applied under highly humid conditions. With some other systems, the builder must wait until conditions are "ideal" or be faced with possible disappointment. System Three's wide range of hardeners allow the builder to work under extreme temperature conditions — from the harsh winters of Alaska and New England to the humid heat of Guatemala and the South Pacific.

We're here to help

Here at System Three Resins our purpose has a narrow focus. We want you, our customer, to build the best boat you can. To this end we strive to manufacture and make available the best epoxy resin system possible with today's technology. We stay in constant contact with both our professional and amateur builder/customers; the knowledge we gain from these associations, coupled with our collective backgrounds in and around boats, gives us the ability to help *you* with your problems. We even answer our own phones. Call Kern or Tom at 206/762-5313.

System Three Resins
PO Box 70436
Seattle, WA 98107
206/762-5313

Logo, address and telephone information have been reduced and repositioned to allow a clear visual path to the selling message.

Headlines off-set to the left of the copy help emphasize the effective, repetitive "Build" copy.

The rules in the body copy not only help emphasize subheads, but also help tie the message to the company's logo.

Careful selection of type styles and sizes usually lets you fit more copy in less space; not only is your piece more attractive and persuasive, but you save money in production and printing.

ORIGINAL

both our professional and amatuer builder/customers; the knowledge we gain from these associations, coupled with our collective backgrounds in and around boats, gives us the ability to help YOU with YOUR problems. We even answer our own phones. Call Kern or Tom at (206) 762-5313.

TRY US!

The right way to for us to convince you we know what we're talking about is to get you to try SYSTEM THREE EPOXY. We don't think you should have to spend a small fortune just to sample our product, but we can't just give it away, either. So, we're introducing the SYSTEM THREE RESINS TRIAL KIT. This kit contains 8 fluid oz. of SYSTEM THREE EPOXY, 4 fluid oz. of SYSTEM THREE HARDENER, disposable gloves, common fillers, 'glass cloth, measuring cups, and stir sticks. All this for just ten bucks and we'll pay the freight. Send in the special trial kit order form and "try us."

SYSTEM·THREE EPOXY SPECIFICATIONS
MIX RATIO

The proper mixing ratio of two parts SYSTEM THREE EPOXY RESIN to one part SYSTEM THREE HARDENER BY VOLUME must be maintained. Epoxy resins are not at all like polyesters and cure times cannot be adjusted by varying the mix ratio.

COVERAGE

Because of the wide variety of woods and working conditions, coverage figures are, at best, a general approximation.

	SQUARE FEET PER GALLON
Saturation coat on softwood	250 - 300
Saturation coat on hardwood	300 - 350
Subsequent coats on wood	500 - 525
Laminating 4 oz. cloth	250 - 300
Fill coats on cloth	425 - 500

POT LIFE AND CURE TIME

These numbers are averages, as pot life is VERY dependant upon the amount in the pot and its' mass. Pot life times are given for 100 grams (about 3 fluid ounces) at 77°.

each 18° drop in
In practice, pot
flat tray (such
the temperature
upon which the e

HARDENER #1
HARDENER #2
HARDENER #3

OKAY, SYSTEM THREE, SHOW ME! ENCLOSED IS MY TEN BUCKS

SEND MY SYSTEM THREE EPOXY TRIAL KIT TO:

NAME: _____

STREET OR P.O. BOX: _____

CITY: _____

STATE: _____ZIP:_____

EVENING (HOME) PHONE: (_____) _____-_____

Typewritten brochures don't allow the flexibility to present a sales message effectively.

Too often, coupons are created as an afterthought, resulting in a cramped or awkward presentation.

The "Try us!" close is followed by the anticlimactic specifications, a guaranteed response-fizzler.

MAKEOVER

Try us!

The right way for us to convince you we know what we're talking about is to get you to try System Three Epoxy. We don't think you should have to spend a small fortune just to sample our product, but we can't just give it away, either. So, we're introducing the System Three Resins *trial kit*. This kit contains 8 fluid oz. of System Three Epoxy, 4 fluid oz. of System Three Hardener, disposable gloves, common fillers, glass cloth, measuring cups, and stir sticks. All this for just ten bucks and we'll pay the freight. Send in the special trial kit order form and "try us."

System Three Epoxy specifications

■ **Mix ratio**

The proper mixing ratio of two parts System Three epoxy resin to one part System Three hardener *by volume* must be maintained. Epoxy resins are not at all like polyesters and cure times cannot be adjusted by varying the mix ratio.

■ **Coverage**

Because of the wide variety of woods and working conditions, coverage figures are, at best, a general approximation.

	s.f./gal.
Saturation coat on softwood	250 - 300
Saturation coat on hardwood	300 - 350
Subsequent coats on wood	500 - 525
Laminating 4 oz. cloth	250 - 300
Fill coats on cloth	425 - 500

■ **Pot life and cure time**

These numbers are averages, as pot life is VERY dependant upon the amount in the pot and its mass. Pot life times are given for 100 grams (about 3 fluid ounces) at 77 degrees. A good rule of thumb is that pot life and cure time double for each 18 degree drop in temperature and halve for every 18 degree increase in temperature. In practice, pot life may be extended by pouring the mixture out into a large, flat tray (such as one for paint rollers). Cure times will vary not only with the temperature of the room but also with the temperature and mass of the part upon which the epoxy is applied.

	Pot life	Thin film Tack free cure
Hardener #1 (Fast)	15 minutes	2 to 2 1/2 hours
Hardener #2 (Medium)	30 minutes	4 to 5 hours
Hardener #3 (Slow)	70 minutes	10 to 12 hours

OK

System Three, show me! Enclosed is my ten bucks. Send my System Three epoxy trial kit to:

Name:

Street or P.O. Box:

City:

State: _____ Zip: _____

Evening (home) phone:

System Three Resins
PO Box 70436
Seattle, WA 98107
206/762-5313

System Three Resins
PO Box 70436
Seattle, WA 98107
206/762-5313

The coupon, formerly an awkward stand-alone flyer, has now been incorporated into the main message.

Coupons can make or break a response rate—design them so they're attractive and easy to complete.

Not only are typefaces more readable than typewriter print, they often save invaluable space that can be used for illustrations, bigger headlines and other important visual aids.

ORIGINAL

THE BOATBUILDER'S EPOXY

SYSTEMTHREE

SYSTEM THREE RESINS
5965 FOURTH AVENUE, SOUTH
SEATTLE, WASHINGTON 98108
(206) 762-5313

SYSTEM THREE MEASURING TOOLS

METERING PUMP, MODEL "M". The new model "M" metering dispensing pump was designed for us and is manufactured especially for use with SYSTEM THREE RESINS. It replaces the old style model "A" pump. Features of the model "M" pump are a lower center of gravity, cleaner operation, and a larger amount of resin/hardener mix dispensed per stroke.

GEAR PUMPS. We have gear pumps available on special order, but most customers find that with SYSTEM THREE'S two to one mix ratio it's faster to use graduated cups to measure large batches, and use the model "M" pump for the smaller batches.

CONVERSION KIT - OLD STYLE 5:1 METER PUMPS. If you have an older style 5:1 ratio model "A" pump we can convert it to a 2:1 ratio pump for a small fee. Prices quoted on request.

GRADUATED PAPER CUPS. Available in both 3 ounce and 14 ounce sizes, these cups are printed for the health industry, but make excellent measuring and mixing pots for epoxy resin. If they were custom printed they would cost a lot more, so for the savings we just put up with the words "Barium" and "Medicine".

SYSTEM THREE FILLERS

Cab-O-Sil
A brand name for coloidal silica, Cab-O-Sil is a fine powder used to control viscosity. In large filler to resin ratios, Cab-O-Sil can provide a non-sag high strength mixture.

PHENOLIC MICROBALLONS
Tiny, hollow spheres, brownish-purple in color, when mixed with SYSTEM THREE makes an inexpensive fairing compound or putty of excellent compressive strength and light weight.

QUARTZ MICROSPHERES
Commonly called "Q cells". Hollow glass spheres, lightweight and tough are used much the same as phenolic microballoons but are harder to sand after cure.

PLASTIC THICKENER
Replaces asbestos powder. Has the same gluing properties as asbestos but is a bit harder to mix. Tends to lump up in the dry state so it requires some crumbling before blending with epoxy. Superior to linen fiber as a thickener for glue.

½" CHOPPPED GLASS STRANDS
An additive of chopped fiberglass for adding structural strength and viscosity.

Logos should be seen and not heard; readers immediately should be able to identify a corporate image without being visually overwhelmed while reading the piece.

MAKEOVER

System Three measuring tools

■ **Metering pump, model M**
The new model M metering dispensing pump was designed for us and is manufactured especially for use with System Three resins. It replaces the old style model A pump. Features of the model M pump are a lower center of gravity, cleaner operation and a larger amount of resin/hardener mix dispensed per stroke.

■ **Gear pumps**
We have gear pumps available on special order, but most customers find that with System Three's two-to-one mix ratio it's faster to use graduated cups to measure large batches, and use the model M pump for the smaller batches.

■ **Conversion kit — old style 5:1 meter pumps**
If you have an older style 5:1 ratio model "A" pump, we can convert it to a 2:1 ratio pump for a small fee. Prices quoted on request.

■ **Graduated paper cups**
Available in both 3 ounce and 14 ounce sizes, these cups are printed for the health industry, but make excellent measuring and mixing pots for epoxy resin. If they were custom-printed they would cost a lot more, so for the savings we just put up with the words "Barium" and "Medicine."

System Three fillers

■ **Cab-O-Sil**
A brand name for coloidal silica, Cab-O-Sil is a fine powder used to control viscosity. In large filler to resin ratios, Cab-O-Sil can provide a non-sag, high-strength mixture.

■ **Phenolic microballoons**
Tiny, hollow spheres, brownish-purple in color, when mixed with System Three make an inexpensive fairing compound or putty of excellent compressive strength and light weight.

■ **Quartz microspheres**
Commonly called "Q cells." Hollow glass spheres, lightweight and tough are used much the same as phenolic microballoons but are harder to sand after cure.

■ **Plastic thickener**
Replaces asbestos powder. Has the same gluing properties as asbestos but is a bit harder to mix. Tends to lump up in the dry state so it requires some crumbling before blending with epoxy. Superior to linen fiber as a thickener for glue.

■ **1/4" Chopped glass strands**
An additive of chopped fiberglass for adding structural strength and viscosity.

■ **Milled glass fibers**
Makes a thick, jelly like paste for use as a filler for large areas where maximum strength is required.

■ **Aluminum powder**
Added to epoxy resin in a ratio of 5% to 10% this gives some ultra-violet protection for subsequent painting. Increases hardness of coated surface.

System Three Resins
PO Box 70436
Seattle, WA 98107
206/762-5313

When possible, break up visuals horizontally and vertically for contrast.

Although the type is smaller, the narrower columns make the piece more readable.

Even mundane documents such as invoices can be enhanced inexpensively to make them more readable and create a unified corporate image.

ORIGINAL

THE BOATBUILDER'S EPOXY

SYSTEM THREE

SYSTEM THREE RESINS
5965 FOURTH AVENUE, SOUTH
SEATTLE, WASHINGTON 98108
(206) 762-5313

DATE

Sold To:

Name _____

Address _____

City _____

State _____ Zip _____

Phone _____

Ship To:

_____

_____

_____

_____ Zip _____

ITEM	SIZE	QUANTITY	UNIT PRICE	TOTAL	WEIGHT
EPOXY RESIN					
HARDENER #					

SUBTOTAL			
WA SALES TAX			
SHIPPING COST			
TOTAL			shipping weight

When documents are typeset (instead of typewritten), space is usually available for important information; in this case, there wasn't room to include payment terms and minimum order requirements.

Because the sale has already been made, large logos aren't necessary on materials such as invoices and statements.

MAKEOVER

Drop shadows around check-boxes add emphasis.

Short, thick rules call attention to key blocks of information.

Using screens instead of rules is sometimes a good way to provide vertical or horizontal orientation.

When laying out photographs, illustrations and other visuals, take care to avoid too much symmetry, which leads to visual boredom.

ORIGINAL

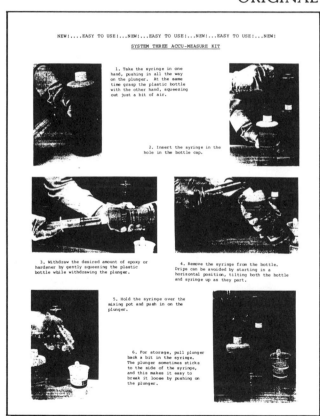

Superlatives aren't neces-sary on an instruction sheet—the client has already been sold.

Typewritten captions usually look stark and unprofessional with photographs.

MAKEOVER

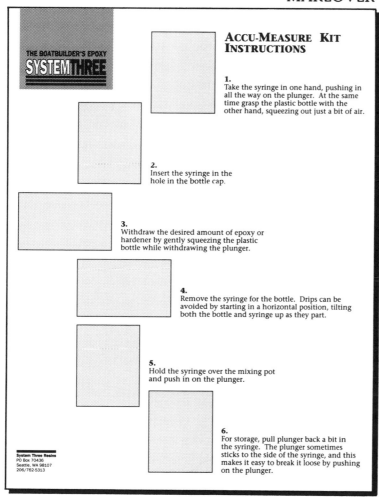

THE BOATBUILDER'S EPOXY
SYSTEM THREE

ACCU-MEASURE KIT INSTRUCTIONS

1.
Take the syringe in one hand, pushing in all the way on the plunger. At the same time grasp the plastic bottle with the other hand, squeezing out just a bit of air.

2.
Insert the syringe in the hole in the bottle cap.

3.
Withdraw the desired amount of epoxy or hardener by gently squeezing the plastic bottle while withdrawing the plunger.

4.
Remove the syringe for the bottle. Drips can be avoided by starting in a horizontal position, tilting both the bottle and syringe up as they part.

5.
Hold the syringe over the mixing pot and push in on the plunger.

6.
For storage, pull plunger back a bit in the syringe. The plunger sometimes sticks to the side of the syringe, and this makes it easy to break it loose by pushing on the plunger.

System Three Resins
PO Box 70436
Seattle, WA 98107
206/762-5313

A new layout forces the reader's eyes down the page in the correct sequence.

The hype has been replaced with address and telephone information for customer service problems—or reorders!

Computer-aided design lets you experiment with a variety of motifs...

MAKEOVER

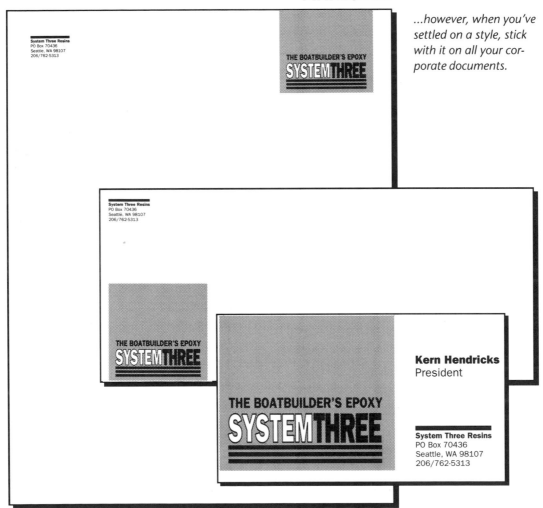

...however, when you've settled on a style, stick with it on all your corporate documents.

System Three Resins
PO Box 70436
Seattle, WA 98107
206/762-5313

THE BOATBUILDER'S EPOXY
SYSTEM THREE

Kern Hendricks
President

System Three Resins
PO Box 70436
Seattle, WA 98107
206/762-5313

MAKEOVER

The ability to move elements around successfully is a good "acid test" of a logo's flexibility.

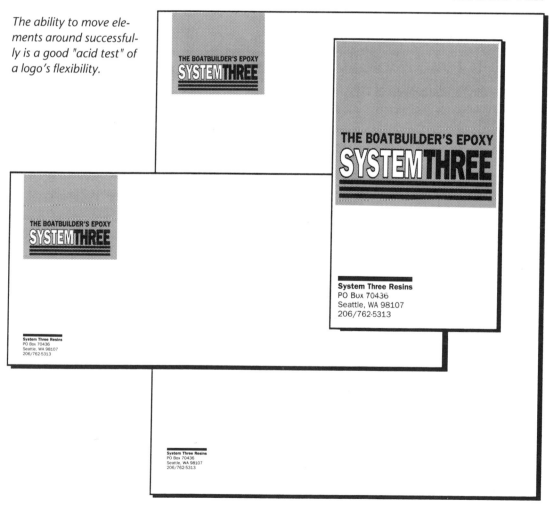

CONCLUSION: FOUR STEPS TO SUCCESS

So, what are the keys to creating a successful makeover? After analyzing 101 "before" and "after" examples, you've probably noticed how a few basic themes are repeated throughout this book. Indeed, it appears that all makeovers are ultimately based on four basic concepts: simplicity, contrast, organization and image.

Keep It Simple

Virtually every original was improved by eliminating "clutter." Major improvements in project quality were achieved by removing distractions and excessive visual elements.

Often, simplicity was achieved by eliminating page borders. Borders, especially box borders around all four sides of a page, often compete with the contents of the page.

In other cases, simplicity was achieved by removing or reducing the size of "empty" words like "Page" in front of numbers or "The" in front of a publication name. Removing redundancies also simplified documents, such as eliminating the Q)'s and A)'s in the "Insurance As An Investment" example in Chapter Eight.

Simplicity was achieved also by removing backgrounds, such as the grid behind the checkmark on the cover of "Insurance As An Investment."

All of these examples demonstrate that less is often more when it comes to design.

The Importance of Adding Contrast

Another key ingredient in the makeovers involves increasing the contrast between elements on a page. This was accomplished in several ways.

Changes in typography can be very effective in creating contrast. In some cases, publications gained a distinct identity when visuals were replaced by contrasting typefaces and type sizes to distinguish key phrases from less important elements.

Lack of contrast in an advertisement or publication makes it harder to read. As the Seattle Design Store advertisement in Chapter Three shows, when all the type on a page "shouts," it's hard to pay attention to what it's saying. The revised ad, with its strongly contrasting type sizes, is far more readable. So is the new nameplate for "Updater," a newsletter in Chapter Two.

In addition, you probably noticed that the smaller type in the makeovers was much more readable than the larger type in the originals. This is because smaller type allows additional white space.

Contrast also comes from the skillful use of white space to highlight headings and visuals, or using grids of different column widths. Examples of these include the makeovers for the library of Michigan catalog and the Dependable booklet, both in Chapter Eight.

Finally, reverses and shaded backgrounds were often used to emphasize headings, visuals or charts and graphs. Many of the makeovers in Chapter Nine, achieved contrast with the use of screened backgrounds.

Overall, contrast adds tension and interest to a page, ensuring that readers will sit up and notice.

Organizing Information

The third basic makeover device found throughout this book is the use of design to guide the reader's eye.

For example, mixing type and graphics to present information in a desired sequence helps readers move through a document.

Likewise, many of the documents in this book were improved when reverses and screens were used to distinguish important information. The front cover of the SAE Technical Paper Series in Chapter Five illustrates how reverses and screens can organize type. Organization also makes the purpose of a publication clearer, removing ambiguity about what you want your readers to do. Perhaps the best example of this is the coupon with System Three's "Build a Lighter Boat" order form in Chapter Ten. There's no doubt that System Three wants you to send in ten dollars for an epoxy trial kit!

Establishing a hierarchy of importance makes your documents all the more effective by eliminating confusion and encouraging response.

Projecting an Image

A final concept involves choosing and using appropriate type and visuals. Often, 20th century firms and associations use 19th century typefaces! The revised cover for the Library of Michigan catalog illustrates how a type style can update a publication's image.

Visual imagery plays an important role in establishing the right atmosphere. Good examples of this are the waves in the Swimex brochure in Chapter Three and the bricks in the Don's Masonry business correspondence in Chapter Six.

Moving On

As you review the originals and the makeovers in this book, you'll discover other examples of how simplicity, contrast, organization and image were achieved. Get in the habit of consciously analyzing simplicity, contrast, organization and image as you read the ads in your favorite magazine or newspaper and the flyers that appear in your mailbox.

Most important, get in the habit of reviewing your own work—as you're working and after it's printed. We all have a lot to learn from past design mistakes.

Achieving success in desktop publishing is an ongoing process based on attention to detail and constant self-improvement. You'll get there if you pass the tests of simplicity, contrast, organization and image.

BIBLIOGRAPHY

Books

Adobe Systems, Inc. **The Adobe Type Catalog**, Adobe Systems, Inc., Palo Alto, CA, 1987.

The Adobe Type Catalog shows typefaces you can add to your laser printer as downloadable fonts. Each typeface is illustrated, along with suggested applications.

Bauermeister, Benjamin. **A Manual of Comparative Typography: The PANOSE System**, Van Nostrand Reinhold, New York, NY, 1988.

One of the most practical books on typography available. Characteristics distinguishing one typeface from another are described and coded; the book then lists over 240 alphabet sets, referenced by code. Even if you don't know Times Roman from Helvetica, this book will help you find the right typeface if you can describe the characteristics you're looking for.

Beach, Mark. **Editing Your Newsletter: A Guide to Writing, Design and Production**, Coast to Coast Books, Portland, OR, 1982.

A straightforward introduction to the field, written during pre-desktop publishing days. Contains numerous sample layouts.

Beaumont, Michael. **Type: Design, Color, Character & Use,** North Light Publishers, Cincinnati, OH, 1987.

This book summarizes the basics of typeface architecture and illustrates successful applications of the principles. It lives up to its title by analyzing the emotional effects colors have on readers. Includes a good glossary of typographic terms.

Bly, Robert W. **The Copywriter's Handbook: A Step-By-Step Guide to Writing Copy that Sells**, Dodd, Mead & Company, New York, NY, 1986.

This book helps you choose the right words and organize them in a logical fashion—even if you're preparing your first advertisement, brochure, or newsletter. It updates and expands upon the "classic" rules of copywriting of an earlier generation of advertising professionals like David Ogilvy and John Caples.

BIBLIOGRAPHY

Brigham, Nancy. **How To Do Leaflets, Newsletters and Newspapers**, Hastings House, New York, NY, 1982.

Written in pre-desktop publishing days, this remains a useful introduction to the correct use of the various formats.

Carter, Rob, Day, Ben and Meggs, Phillip. **Typographic Design: Form and Communication,** Van Nostrand Reinhold, New York, NY, 1985.

This book combines a historical perspective on typeface development with descriptions and examples of the typefaces available to desktop publishers from Adobe and Bitstream. It provides a perspective on the use of type in page design, with numerous examples of type in action.

Craig, James. **Designing with Type**, Watson-Guptil, New York, NY, 1980.

A comprehensive coverage of the characteristics of the various typefaces and how they can be best used. Special sections devoted to display type, bold copy and copyfitting.

Danuloff, Craig and McClelland, Deke. **The Typefaces of Desktop Publishing**, Publishing Resources, Boulder, CO, 1987.

A catalog illustrating virtually every PostScript font available for Apple Macintosh computers. A full alphabet of each typeface is shown, including bold and italic variations. It includes useful hints, technical data and vendor/pricing information.

Gedney, Karen and Fultz, Patrick. **The Complete Guide to Creating Successful Brochures**, Asher-Gallant, Westbury, NY, 1988.

This combines a marketing approach with good advice on design. Topics include post-production, printing and scheduling.

Gosney, Michael and Dayton, Linnea. **Making Art on the Macintosh II**, Scott, Foresman, Glenview, IL, 1989.

This book describes in detail the major Macintosh drawing, painting and illustration programs. Even if you use an MS-DOS computer, you'll find information and concepts that you can translate to your specific software.

Holmes, Nigel. **Designer's Guide to Creating Charts & Diagrams**, Watson-Guptill, New York, NY, 1984.

Written by a *Time* magazine professional, this book describes how art can be used to communicate numbers. Contains numerous color illustrations.

Hudson, Howard Penn. **Publishing Newsletters: A Complete Guide to Markets, Editorial Content, Design, Printing, Subscriptions, Management, and Much More...**, Charles Scribner's Sons, New York, NY, 1982.

A standard in the field, **Publishing Newsletters** is written by the publisher of the popular *Newsletter on Newsletters*. Contains numerous layout ideas and an extensive bibliography and glossary.

Hurlburt, Alan. **The Grid**, Van Nostrand Reinhold, New York, NY, 1982.

Illustrates how grids can be used in developing page layouts for newspapers, magazines and books.

Kelly, Kevin, ed. **Signal: Communication Tools for the Information Age, A Whole Earth Catalog**, Whole Earth Access, Berkeley, CA, 1988.

An invaluable reference for anyone interested in cultivating new markets for their desktop publishing skills. This large-format book contains hundreds of references—books, audio and video tapes, and computer hardware and software—that will help you make the most of your talents.

BIBLIOGRAPHY

Kleper, Michael L. **The Illustrated Handbook of Desktop Publishing and Typesetting**, Tab Books, Blue Ridge Summit, PA, 1987.

This book is the best introduction to the wide range of hardware and software options available for both MS-DOS and Apple Macintosh computers. Contains more than 700 pages of information.

Middleton, Tony. **A Desktop Publisher's Guide to Pasteup: A Do-It-Yourself Guide to Preparing Camera-Ready Pasteups and Mechanicals**, Plusware, Colorado Springs, CO, 1987.

This guide provides a practical answer to the question, "What do you do with the pages which come out of your laser printer?" It describes the tools needed to prepare paste-ups and how to use them. It also explains how to choose the right commercial printers to duplicate your job and how to deal with them.

Nelson, Roy Paul. **The Design of Advertising**, Wm. C. Brown Co., Dubuque, IA, 1985.

A classic college text, this book succeeds because of its many examples and "hands-on" conversational style. Fourteen of its 16 chapters are devoted to print advertising.

Nelson, Roy Paul. **Publication Design**, Wm. C. Brown Co., Dubuque, IA, 1987.

This companion volume concentrates on magazine, newspaper and newsletter design. Chapter 11, "Miscellaneous Publications," describes brochures and direct mail.

Makuta, Daniel J. and Lawrence, William F. **The Complete Desktop Publisher**, "Compute!" Publications, Greensboro, NC, 1986.

An informed overview of the field, this book places emphasis on function rather than on specific hardware or software.

New York Art Directors Club. **The One Show**, Watson-Guptil Publications, New York, NY. Annual.

The One Show is a one-stop source for viewing the nation's finest advertising. Each year, the nation's leading art directors submit their best work to a jury of their peers. **The One Show** includes the entries in each category and showcases the winners. Because of its inspirational value, this book is an important addition to your collection.

Pattison, Polly. **How to Design a Nameplate: A Guide for Art Directors and Editors**, Ragan Communications, Chicago, IL, 1982.

Although written in pre-desktop publishing days, this concise volume can serve as an excellent source for ideas when you begin to design your newsletter. It contains numerous illustrations of how changes in typography can alter a newsletter's appearance and emotional appeal.

Perfect, Christopher and Rookledge, Gordon. **Rookledge's International Typefinder: The Essential Handbook of Typeface Recognition & Selection**, PBC International, Glen Cove, NY, 1986.

An excellent complement to Bauermeister's **Manual of Comparative Typography**, this book contains samples of literally hundreds of alphabet sets, organized by primary design and historical characteristics.

Pickens, Judy E. **The Copy-to-Press Handbook: Preparing Words and Art for Print**, John Wiley & Sons, New York, NY, 1985.

Although written in pre-desktop publishing days, this book provides a good perspective on book and brochure publishing by combining an overview of traditional methods of phototypesetting and pasteup with a detailed examination of the printing process.

BIBLIOGRAPHY

Romano, Frank J. **The TypEncyclopedia: A User's Guide to Better Typography**, R.R. Bowker, New York, NY, 1984.

A starting point for making better use of your type library. Alphabetically organized from "Accents" through "Zero," this book is both concise and complete. Each topic has its own page. It combines sparse text with numerous illustrations and diagrams. Contains a strong index and a handy type cross-reference that helps you find typefaces with characteristics similar to the ones you're familiar with.

Seybold, John and Dressler, Fritz. **Publishing from the Desktop**, Bantam Books, New York, NY, 1987.

A technical overview of the various aspects of typography and typesetting, with an emphasis on how the various imaging systems differ. Separate chapters cover image scanners and modifying line art and halftones.

Solomon, Martin. **The Art of Typography: An Introduction to Typo.icon.ography. Understanding contemporary type design through classic typography**, Watson-Guptill, New York, NY, 1986.

This book reviews and provides a historical perspective on the major typefaces. It's also an excellent text for intermediate and advanced students of typography. Contains numerous projects that will help you learn by doing.

Swann, Alan. **How To Understand and Use Design and Layout**, North Light Publishers, Cincinnati, OH, 1987.

This handsomely illustrated volume does an excellent job of balancing theory and practical example. Numerous rough layouts illustrate various formats and ways of placing type on a page. Four-color photographs of printed publications show these concepts translated into reality.

Tufte, Edward R. **The Visual Display of Quantitative Information**, Graphics Press, Cheshire, CT, 1987.

One of the classics, this book describes various charting and graphing tools, and helps you choose the right type of graphic to get your message across. Describes possible pitfalls and ways of maintaining data integrity.

University of Chicago. **A Manual of Style,** 13th ed., The University of Chicago Press, Chicago, IL, 1982.

This should be kept next to your computer. Its tightly packed 700-plus pages provide the answers to questions asked by the most conscientious editor or writer. It describes the proper way to handle punctuation, illustrations, quotations and abbreviations, as well as design and typography.

Webb, Robert A., ed. **The Washington Post Deskbook on Style**, McGraw-Hill, New York, NY, 1978.

This book provides precise and quick answers to commonly encountered questions concerning abbreviation, capitalization, numerals, punctuation and spelling.

White, Alex. **How to Spec Type**, Watson-Guptill, New York, NY, 1987.

A straightforward and entertaining review of the basics of typography. Contains numerous examples illustrating the major do's and don'ts involved in successfully handling type. Especially strong on copyfitting techniques.

White, Jan V. **Editing by Design: A Guide to Effective Word-and-Picture Communication for Editors and Designers**, R.R. Bowker, New York, NY, 1982.

A classic text, this book underscores the importance of a "form-follows-function" approach to graphic design. A great deal of emphasis is placed on integrating photographs and artwork into a finished publication.

BIBLIOGRAPHY

White, Jan V. **Mastering Graphics: Design and Production Made Easy**, R.R. Bowker, New York, NY, 1983.

Elaborates on the ideas first expressed in **Editing by Design**. Although written in pre-desktop publishing days, it includes numerous "do-it-yourself" applications examples. It's hard not to be excited or motivated by the way the illustrations relate theory to reality.

White, Jan V. **Designing for Magazines: Common Problems, Realistic Solutions**, R.R. Bowker, New York, NY, 1982.

This book uses numerous "before" and "after" examples to illustrate how basic design principles can be applied to the component parts of a magazine: masthead, logo, body copy and illustrations.

White, Jan V. **18 Ready To Use Grids for Standard and 8 1/2" x 11" Pages**, National Composition Service, Arlington, VA.

This short publication, available from the National Composition Service (1730 North Lynn St., Arlington, VA 22209), illustrates the diversity of text and photo placement made possible by utilizing the grid system to its fullest. Following a short introduction, the booklet consists of left-hand pages that show the grid full-size facing right-hand pages that illustrate the different ways the grid can be utilized. Column widths and gutter dimensions are clearly illustrated.

Xerox Corporation. **Xerox Corporate Standards**, Watson-Guptill, New York, NY, 1989.

Designed to help corporations involved in desktop publishing establish and maintain a consistent corporate identity. Addresses both design and human issues.

Publications

Font & Function: The Adobe Type Catalog, Adobe Systems, Inc., Mountain View, CA. Quarterly.

Combines advertising and helpful information in an outstandingly designed package. Frequently updated, it describes the basics of effective typography and contains sample alphabets illustrating the entire Adobe typeface library. Free for the asking. (800)83-FONTS.

How Magazine, F & W Publications, Cincinnati, OH. Bimonthly.

This lavishly illustrated publication provides step-by-step design help for less experienced graphic artists and desktop publishers. Subject areas include layout, grids, color and other basics.

ITC Desktop, International Typographic Corporation, Hammarskjhold Plaza, New York, NY. Bimonthly.

A new publication produced by ITC, which monitors typeface licenses and publishes the famous *U&LC* magazine. It focuses on specific design issues that relate to desktop publishing.

Newsletter Design, Newsletter Clearing House, P.O. Box 301, Rhinebeck, NY. Monthly.

Each issue contains numerous examples of published newsletters and concise comments on the successes and problems of their design. Contributors represent a wide range of disciplines, providing a perspective not available in many books and newsletters.

PC Publishing, Hunter Publications, Des Plains, IL. Monthly.

Produced entirely using desktop publishing techniques, this monthly publication features a great deal of buying information, as well as tips and tricks for the novice.

BIBLIOGRAPHY

Personal Publishing, Renegade Publications, Itasca, IL. Monthly.

Personal Publishing offers a "hands-on" approach to desktop publishing. It provides practical advice and examples of attainable goals for the self-publisher.

Print: America's Graphic Design Magazine, RC Publications, New York, NY. Bi-monthly.

A large-format publication that showcases the latest trends in publication design and production. Emphasis is placed on the careers and design philosophies of practicing designers. Densely illustrated, it's a great idea book that will challenge users to reach new levels of sophistication.

Publish! PCW Communications, San Francisco, CA. Monthly.

A lavish publication featuring the latest hardware and software, as well as profiles of leading desktop publishers around the country. It coined the term "makeover" for desktop publishing; the publication's "how-to" approach is a big help to budding designers and DTP users.

Step-By-Step Electronic Design: The How-To Newsletter for Electronic Designers and Desktop Publishers, Dynamic Graphics, P.O. Box 1901, Peoria, IL 61656-1901. Monthly.

This 16-page monthly newsletter describes both software-specific techniques and design concepts that can be used by any desktop publishing hardware or software.

The Page, Box 14493, Chicago, IL 60614. Monthly.

A 16-page monthly newsletter containing tips, procedures, ideas and examples useful to all Macintosh desktop publishers. It's especially strong in showing how various page layout and illustration programs can be used together.

TypeWorld, Typeworld Publications, Salem, NH. Monthly.

Hardware-oriented, this publication focuses on the technical aspects of electronic publishing and various facets of the interface between personal computers and phototypesetting equipment.

U&LC, International Typographic Publications, Salem, NH. Monthly.

Although it has its basis in traditional phototypesetting, it was among the first to herald the advances made possible by computer-based publishing. Its informal writing style balances its extremely detailed treatment of the latest technical aspects of typography.

Verbum: The Journal of Computer Aesthetics, P.O. Box 15439, San Diego, CA 92115. Quarterly.

Illustrates just how far the state of the art has advanced in this quickly evolving art form. Even if you're not a computer artist, this will inspire you.

Associations, User Groups and Workshops

National Association of Desktop Publishers
P.O. Box 508, Kenmore Station
Boston, MA 02215-9998

Newsletter Association
1401 Wilson Boulevard, Suite 403
Arlington, VA 22209

The Newsletter Clearinghouse
44 West Market Street
Rhinebeck, NY 12572

BIBLIOGRAPHY

Dynamic Graphics & Education Foundation
6000 North Forest Park Drive
P.O. Box 1901
Peoria, IL 61656-1901

Workshops on "Designing for Desktop Publishing," "Basic
Layout and Pasteup," "Typography in Design," "Publication
Design" and more.

Electronic Directions
21 East Fourth Street
New York, NY 10003

Software-specific courses and seminars on "Ventura Publisher," "PC Pagemaker," "Using Ready, Set, Go!," "Using Quark
Xpress," "Using Adobe Illustrator," "PostScript for Designers"
and more.

Performance Seminar Group
204 Strawberry Hill Avenue
Norwalk, CT 06851

Seminars on "Designing Effective Newsletters," "How to Write
and Design Sales Literature" and more.

Promotion Perspectives
1955 Pauline Boulevard, Suite 100A
Ann Arbor, MI 48103

Seminars on "Newsletter Editing, Design and Production"
and "Fundamentals of Design for Desktop Publishing" and
more. Participants receive an unusually complete set of working tools and hand-out materials.

INDEX

INDEX

INDEX

the
Ventana Press

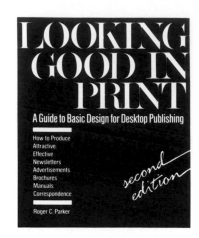

Desktop Design Series

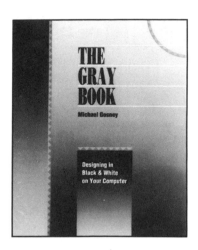

Looking Good in Print, Second Edition
$23.95
410 pages, Illustrated
ISBN: 0-940087-32-4

With over 100,000 in print, **Looking Good in Print** is looking
even better. More makeovers, a new section on designing newsletters and a wealth of new design tips and techniques to
broaden the design skills of the ever-growing number of desktop
publishers.

Newsletters from the Desktop
$23.95
290 pages, Illustrated
ISBN: 0-940087-40-5

Now the millions of desktop publishers who produce newsletters
can learn how to improve the design of their publications.

Inside Xerox Ventura Publisher: The Complete Learning and Reference Guide, Third Edition
$24.95
692 pages, Illustrated
ISBN: 0-940087-61-8

The all-time best-selling Ventura book is now revised and
updated to give desktop publishers access to the full power of
Ventura 3.0 and help them produce better-looking documents
with strategies the pros use.

Type from the Desktop
$23.95
290 pages, Illustrated
ISBN: 0-940087-45-6

Learn the basics of designing with type from a desktop publisher's perspective.

The Gray Book: Designing in Black and White on Your Computer
$22.95
220 pages, Illustrated
ISBN: 0-940087-50-2

This "idea gallery" for desktop publishers offers a lavish variety of
the most interesting black, white and gray graphic effects that
can be achieved with laser printers, scanners and high-resolution
output devices.

The Presentation Design Book
$24.95
280 pages, Illustrated
ISBN: 0-940087-37-5

How to design effective, attractive slides, overheads, graphs, diagrams, handouts and screen shows with your desktop computer.

Desktop Publishing with WordPerfect, Second Edition (For 5.0 and 5.1)
$21.95
350 pages, Illustrated
ISBN: 0-940087-47-2

WordPerfect offers graphics capabilities that can save users thousands of dollars in design and typesetting costs. Includes invaluable information on creating style sheets for consistency and speed.

TO ORDER additional copies of *The Makeover Book* or any of the other books in our desktop design series, please fill out this order form and return it to us for quick shipment.

	Quantity	Price			Total
The Makeover Book	_____	× $17.95	=	$	_____
Looking Good in Print	_____	× $23.95	=	$	_____
Desktop Publishing w/ WordPerfect	_____	× $21.95	=	$	_____
Type from the Desktop	_____	× $23.95	=	$	_____
The Presentation Design Book	_____	× $24.95	=	$	_____
Newsletters from the Desktop	_____	× $23.95	=	$	_____
The Gray Book	_____	× $22.95	=	$	_____

Shipping: Please add $4.10/first book for standard UPS, $1.35/book thereafter; $7.50/book UPS "two-day air," $2.25/book thereafter. For Canada, add $8.10/book.   = $ _____

Send C.O.D. (add $3.75 to shipping charges)   = $ _____

North Carolina residents add 5% sales tax   = $ _____

Total   = $ _____

Name _____

Company _____

Address (No P.O. Box) _____ _____

City _____ State _____ Zip _____

Daytime Phone _____

_____ Payment enclosed (check or money order; no cash please)

_____VISA   _____MC   Acc't # _____ - _____ - _____ - _____

Expiration date _____ Signature _____

Please mail or fax to:

Ventana Press, P.O. Box 2468, Chapel Hill, NC 27515

919/942-0220, FAX: 919/942-1140